Developments in Swedish Social Policy

Developments in Swedish Social Policy

Resisting Dionysus

Arthur Gould
Reader in Swedish Social Policy
Loughborough University
Loughborough
UK

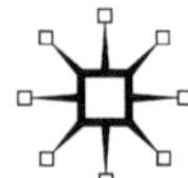

First published 2001 by
PALGRAVE
Houndmills, Basingstoke, Hampshire RG21 6XS and
175 Fifth Avenue, New York, N. Y. 10010
Companies and representatives throughout the world

PALGRAVE is the new global academic imprint of St. Martin's Press LLC Scholarly and Reference Division and Palgrave Publishers Ltd (formerly Macmillan Press Ltd).

ISBN 0–333–77450–7

This book is printed on paper suitable for recycling and made from fully managed and sustained forest sources.

A catalogue record for this book is available from the British Library.

Library of Congress Cataloging-in-Publication Data
Gould, Arthur.
Developments in Swedish social policy : resisting Dionysus / Arthur Gould.
p. cm.
Includes bibliographical references and index.
ISBN 0–333–77450–7
1. Social service—Sweden. 2. Sweden—Social policy. I. Title.

HV338 .G682 2001
361.6'1'09485—dc21

2001016427

10 9 8 7 6 5 4 3 2 1
10 09 08 07 06 05 04 03 02 01

Printed and bound in Great Britain by
Antony Rowe Ltd, Chippenham, Wiltshire

To Andrea: the love of my life

Contents

List of Tables

Preface

On *Valborgsmässoafton*, the Swedish celebration of the end of winter at the end of April 1986, I stood with my newly-found Karlskoga friends round a bonfire. Conny Holmqvist, who sadly died in 1998, looked out towards the sunset and asked me what I thought of the view. "Just another lake!", I replied. Conny took my cynical remark in good faith and thereafter, whenever something truly amazing happened, he would say "Just another masterpiece/mountain/performance!".

Almost without exception, my Swedish friends and acquaintances are passionate lovers of their country's landscape. They hive off to their *stugor* (small, red country cottages) whenever possible. They walk, they yacht, they swim and continue to collect berries and mushrooms in their never-ending forests. That spring in Karlskoga, I also discovered that many Swedes were attached to other traditions. I went to social occasions where everybody knew and sang traditional songs. These were followed by a series of witty speeches by various participants. Swedes know how to enjoy themselves. They appreciate leisure. Unlike the Japanese, another industrious people, the Swedes demand substantial holidays and entitlements to leave of various kinds, in return for their hard work. It always seems to me that when I make contact with people in Sweden they are either on holiday, have just returned from holiday, or are about to embark on one. How civilised!

I mention all this for two reasons. A superficial reading of this book might leave the impression that (a) I see Swedes as strict and joyless and (b) that I lack affection for the society I describe or (c) that I lack sympathy with its culture. None of these could be further from the truth. On the contrary, my own approach to life is very Swedish. I like to think of myself as relatively rational, organised and clean. I abhor excess. I drink in moderation, am never drunk, smoke only the occasional cigarette and I am a drug-free zone. I drive a 1987 Volvo, sleep in an enormous IKEA bed and believe that Mozart's *Magic Flute,* directed by Ingemar Bergman, sounds better and more beautiful in Swedish than German. However, I am also a social scientist and a sceptic. I admire Swedish society, its public transport system and its welfare state but not unreservedly. I do have affection and respect for what this small – in terms of population – Scandinavian country has achieved, but I am not an uncritical Swedophile.

The intention to write this book began in the mid-1990s. I had already written a number of articles and books about Sweden and it was obvious even then that the last decade of the 20th century was going to be a significant period in the development of Swedish social policy. The task of trying to make sense of my knowledge and experience of Swedish people, their culture, institutions and society, has been a very enjoyable one. I would like to think that if Conny had lived to read it, he would not have said, "Just another book!".

Arthur Gould
April 2000

Acknowledgements

My initial thanks must go to the Nuffield Foundation for its continued support. Since 1986 it has enabled me to visit Sweden several times to carry out interviews and collect source material. The Foundation is not only swift in its response but flexible and understanding in its administrative requirements. I must also thank all my Swedish informants who over the years have been very tolerant of my broken Swedish, generous with their time and very helpful with their information and views. The staff at the Swedish embassy have provided me with back copies of *Dagens Nyheter*, an indispensable source of daily news for me but a joyless task for them. Friends and colleagues in Sweden have been very welcoming, helpful and hospitable.

I am particularly grateful to Sten-Åke Stenberg and Elinor Brunnberg for critical comments on early drafts of Chapters 7 and 8. Sten-Åke, who is now a professor in Stockholm University's *Institute for Social Research*, has remained a good friend in spite of the fact that he disagrees with almost everything I have to say about his country. The source of this strange friendship seems to reside in the fact that our mothers were both high class cleaners. His worked in the Riksdag, while mine made sure that Henry Ford's executive office in London was spick and span. Åke Svenson has also been a constant friend. He has tried to keep me on the right path politically but with little success. With Brian Ashley, a British resident of Stockholm, there have been many opportunities to share our impressions of Sweden and the Swedes, while Big Almström, his partner, has come to the defence of her country on more than one occasion.

Thanks must go to my colleagues in the Department of Social Sciences and to Loughbolough University for making my 1999 sabbatical possible. Sabbaticals are essential for in-depth research and part of what makes some universities civilised. Lastly, I would like to thank those anonymous colleagues who, in 1999, consented to my becoming a *Reader in Swedish Social Policy*. It is a title which reflects my abiding research interest and one of which I am very proud.

Glossary

AMS	Arbetsmarknadsstyrelsen, the labour market board
DN	*Dagens Nyheter*, a daily Swedish national newspaper
Ds	Ministerial reports
EMU	European Monetary Union
LO	Landsorganisationen, the trade union federation of manual employees
LSS	Law on support and services for the functionally impaired
LVM	Law on the care of adult misusers
OECD	Organisation for Economic Co-operation and Development
PK	Pensioners' national advisory committee
PRO	National organisation of pensioners
RD	*Riksdag och Departementet*, a fortnightly journal.
RPG	National association for the community of pensioners
SA	means-tested social assistance
SACO	Central organisation for Swedish academics
SAF	Sveriges Arbetsgivares Förening, the Swedish federation of employers
SEK	Swedish krona
SoS	Socialstyrelsen, the administrative board for health and social affairs
SOU	Statens Offentliga Utredningar, the state's official investigations
SPF	Sweden's pensioners' association
SPI	Swedish pensioners' interests party
SPRF	National association of Sweden's pensioners
TCO	Tjänstemännens Central Organisation, the trade union federation of non-manual employees

1
Postmodern World . . .

> At this time Sweden was supposed to be a much freer country. And there I had the experience that certain kinds of freedom may have, not exactly the same effects, but as many restrictive effects as a directly restrictive society.
>
> (Michel Foucault cited in Eribon 1991 p. 74)

Introduction

What has happened to *the* welfare state? As we enter the 21st century, can it even be said that the set of institutions, practices and policies associated with the golden age of Swedish modernism and social democracy has survived the impact of a new era of postmodern capitalism? Alongside major changes in technology, cultural production and economic organisation, the postwar welfare state has, in the last few decades, undergone dramatic change in many countries. During the late 1970s and the 1980s, there was a distinctive shift from the universalist features of state welfare to the more particularist/selective characteristics of welfare pluralism. For some considerable time Sweden resisted this trend. However, from 1989, there were clear signs of change. Economic problems resulted in growing unemployment and pressures to reduce public and social expenditure. Sweden applied to join the EU and to adopt the convergence criteria associated with the emerging single currency of the Euro. Parallel with these developments, the Swedish economy was having to adapt to the globalisation of the world's economies and more intense international competition; information technology was having a major impact; cultural boundaries were being challenged.

This study is about the cumulative impact of these changes upon the Swedish welfare state and will assess the extent to which its distinctive characteristics have been challenged in the last decade and are likely to be challenged in the years to come. It is also about how and why these changes have been resisted. It will be argued that in Sweden, the aims and values of the welfare state were much more deeply embedded in cultural values and institutional practices than elsewhere; Sweden's reputation as a welfare leader was more closely associated with a national identity based on rational modernism; and that popular expectations of high value benefits and good quality services made attempts by two governments in particular (the Bourgeois coalition 1991–94 and the Social Democratic, 1994–98) to change the welfare state very difficult.

To provide a context for the changes that have occurred in Sweden in the 1990s, this introductory chapter will outline the fate of the welfare state under conditions of postmodernity. It will be followed by an account of the approach adopted in this study of Swedish social policy.

Postmodernity and welfare

Sociologists have used a variety of terminologies to distinguish between the decades following the Second World War and the period since the mid-1970s. Neo-Marxists have stressed the structural, economic changes and capitalism's new mode of regulation – contrasting Fordism with post-Fordism (Murray 1989). Lash and Urry preferred the terms *organised* and *disorganised* capitalism (Lash and Urry 1987). Beck and Giddens have opted for *modernity* and *late modernity* (Beck *et al.* 1994). Finally there are the terms *modernism/postmodernism* and *modernity/ postmodernity*, where the former refers to the analysis of cultural aspects of social change and the latter to the wider social transformation.

To labour at each of the distinctions between the terms above would be of dubious value and rather confusing. The term most suited to my purposes – to explore the ways in which Sweden, the exemplar of modernity, has adapted to the major changes of our time – is *postmodernity*. This will be used, as Harvey used it in his *The condition of postmodernity*, to refer to, "a sea-change in cultural as well as political–economic practices since around 1972" (Harvey 1989 p. vii). Postmodernity has the advantage of covering both the structural changes referred to by the *post-Fordists* and the more cultural concerns of the *postmodernists*. To contrast modernity and postmodernity, Harvey cited a definition of the former in an architectural journal.

> "Generally perceived as positivistic, technocentric and rationalistic, universal modernism has been identified with the belief in linear

> progress, absolute truths, the rational planning of ideal social orders, and the standardisation of knowledge and production." Postmodernism, by way of contrast, privileges "heterogeneity and difference as liberative forces in the redefinition of cultural discourse." Fragmentation, indeterminacy, and intense distrust of all universal or "totalising" discourses ... are the hallmark of postmodern thought (Harvey 1989 p. 9).

Far from seeing modernity as rational and progressive, postmodern thinkers highlighted its irrational and regressive consequences. Lyotard, according to Leonard, argued that:

> Against the progress that has been supposedly achieved ... the crimes against humanity must be weighed. Other names signifying recent history – Dresden, Hiroshima, the Gulag, Cambodia – all refer to crimes, like Auschwitz, justified in the name of ideologies committed to the pursuit of progress and order ... (Leonard 1997 p. 8)

Any contemporary analysis of Sweden cannot approach its past without bearing in mind the possibility that modernity in Sweden might be subject to similar criticisms. As will become clear, the humane and progressive aspects of Swedish society and welfare have often been clouded by repressive, disciplinary and authoritarian overtones.[1]

Structural change and the decline of the welfare state

The Western welfare state enjoyed a period of growth and expansion from the end of the Second World War until the mid-1970s. It was part of a set of institutions designed to stabilise the extreme fluctuations of unfettered capitalism. Alongside Keynesian policies to maintain full employment it was associated with a period of unprecedented economic prosperity, security and opportunity. The welfare state was part of a political consensus in which governments of the left and the right sought to plan economic and social life through the corporatist involvement of business and trade union representatives. As economic growth faltered and both unemployment and inflation rose disillusion with the Keynesian settlement set in.

A neo-liberal hegemony emerged, particularly in the USA and Britain, which was critical of state intervention in general and of the welfare state in particular. Social security benefits were said to be too high and destroyed incentives to work; taxation was destroying the willingness to invest; state monopolies in health, social services and education were inefficient. Welfare bureaucrats and professionals were more interested in advancing their own self-interest than they were in satisfying the public's needs and solving society's problems. The disillusion of those on the right was matched by those on the left. Libertarians of the left criticised teachers and doctors for increasing the demands for their own services. Neo-Marxists complained that the welfare state functioned in the interests of capital more than it did of labour. Social democrats complained that social inequalities were widening.

Western countries were forced to consider reforms which would enable them to compete with Japan and the emerging economies of East Asia (Gould 1993a). Mass production of standardised products was replaced by the flexible production of customised products. Management decisions and plant bargaining became decentralised. Employees who were once treated as a homogeneous mass were subdivided into core and peripheral work forces. Tripartite corporatism in which government involved trade union and business federations in the policymaking process was replaced by a more cosy relationship with business which excluded the workers. The power of the labour movement was weakened through unemployment and insecure employment. All of this was underpinned by the revolution in information technology that has transformed our working and social lives.

The deregulation of financial markets and information technology ushered in a process of globalisation in which the autonomy of national governments was weakened. For many Western countries, the 1980s was a traumatic period in which they tried to adapt to the new competitive and globalised environment. In Britain, Conservative governments allowed unemployment to rise; anti-trade union legislation was introduced; employment rights were weakened; nationalised industries and parts of the welfare state were privatised; power was removed from local authorities; and government refused to consult with welfare bureaucrats and professionals. Consensus politics were abandoned and the Keynesian welfare state was eroded in favour of a right wing version of welfare pluralism.

While the changes in Britain were not identical to those occurring in other European countries, studies of welfare towards the end of the 1980s suggested the emergence of a common pattern (Johnson 1987; Morris 1988). The welfare state had been so-named because the state had taken upon itself the responsibility of providing care and security for the whole population. Now, under the pressure of low growth, the ageing of the population and mass unemployment, the state was seeking to divest itself of those responsibilities. Private and occupational welfare were encouraged and more reliance placed upon the voluntary and informal sectors. Cerny argued that what had been the welfare state had in fact become the *competition state* (Cerny 1990). "Competition" had been a dirty word in the old welfare state. It had belonged to the private sector but rapidly became a basic principle for the running of schools, hospitals and social services.

Many of these changes were initially greeted with suspicion by social scientists and those on the left. The passing of the "golden age of welfare" was mourned. Growing class inequalities, less power for organised labour and poorer welfare services and benefits were deplored. The welfare state had been seen by many on the left as progressive and humane and, by some, as having the potential to lead to democratic socialism. As the 1980s developed however, others began to see the decline of the welfare state more dispassionately, to criticise it for its shortcomings and subsequently to embrace a radical form of welfare pluralism as an opportunity.

The cultural turn

The work of Michel Foucault, which had questioned the liberal and humane claims of the enlightenment, was influential among a new generation of social policy analysts in raising doubts about the beneficial effects of welfare policies and institutions. Instead of stressing the benefits of welfare policies, the totalitarian effects of welfare discourses were emphasized (Hewitt 1992; Squires 1990). People were not liberated by the power of welfare professionals and administrators; they were controlled and manipulated through professional knowledge and discursive practices. It is interesting in this respect to wonder whether Foucault's years in Sweden as a young man[2] influenced his growing cynicism[3] about progress. It was Foucault's work that led to such a strong emphasis in postmodern thinking on heterogeneity, difference and identity. Whereas modernity's welfare state had been concerned largely with issues of class and *redistribution*, postmodern welfare was more concerned to afford issues of race, gender and disability the *recognition* they deserved (Fraser 1995). It was said that the false egalitarianism of state welfare had, in reality, privileged working class men to the neglect of the needs of other social groups. For Penna and O'Brien, cultural oppression had to be seen as just as important as economic hardship. The modernist welfare state had excluded and ignored many social groups as unworthy or deviant. The labour movement had been dominated by the class politics of white males. Welfare arrangements had often exacerbated problems of poverty rather than alleviated them.

> Traditional social democratic and liberal politics have been unable to value positively the broader range of rights implied by a politics of difference. (Penna and O'Brien 1996 p. 57)

A similar analysis by Hillyard and Watson (1996) condemned the welfare state for its surveillance and monitoring activities and for its restrictive definitions of what is "normal". Welfare had been about regulation and control. It had created more casualties than it had beneficiaries.

Those regarded as insignificant and even deviant during modernity were now recognised as having legitimate claims to social policy provision. Homosexuality was an issue that social policy in the past had either neglected or frowned upon. In a postmodern age it was thought right that gay men and women should be given the legal protection and social policy rights which heterosexuals took for granted. People with disabilities in modernity were provided for, but paternalistically, and in a way that prevented their participation in mainstream society. Under conditions of postmodernity they felt able to demand liberation. Similarly, the view of the demonised and stereotyped drug addict had changed. Not only was non-problematic use a basic assumption behind British and Dutch policies of harm reduction and decriminalisation,[4] but those with drug problems were not seen as totally out of control. In varying degrees they were now seen as rational beings who in many respects were no different from the rest of the population (ACMD 1982).

> The concept of addiction has largely been abandoned and supplemented by more flexible identities. (Bunton 1998 p. 214)

As will be seen in Chapter 9, this is an aspect of postmodernity that has had little influence in Sweden.

The tendency in postmodern thinking to associate the welfare state with power, cultural oppression and the terrorism of grand narratives, was criticised by Taylor-Gooby for providing the New Right with hostages to fortune (Taylor-Gooby 1994). He argued that the weakening of ideological support for the welfare state on the left simply played into the hands of those on the right. In Taylor-Gooby's view, it was nonsensical to talk about the death of grand narratives when neo-liberalism had itself become the global grand narrative. Without concepts of solidarity, universalism and social justice, he suggested, any hope of combating poverty and inequality were vain. More recently, Taylor-Gooby has argued that "while trends to diversity, fragmentation and globalisation exist, structures of inequality, the power of capital and state welfare policies matter" (Taylor-Gooby 1997 p. 188). He questioned the argument that globalisation severely limited national autonomy in welfare matters. He suggested that different countries had responded differently to the same circumstances – something to be borne in mind in the reading of this book.

But the renewed interest in the cultural correlates of welfare has not emerged simply to emphasize issues of repression and identity; it has arisen as a necessary complement to analyses which have focused upon political economy. The neglect of cultural explanations can be attributed to the 1960s critique of the functionalist preference for seeing society in terms of consensus rather than conflict. The Parsonian *central value system* had little relevance for a generation of sociologists concerned with class exploitation. What had been regarded as "culture" by some became "ideological repression" to others. Nor did the use of culture endear itself to political economists when it was used as an explanation for poverty or the inequalities experienced by ethnic minorities. Now – under conditions of postmodernity – it is possible to talk about culture again and its value in the analysis of social policy is being resurrected. Culture is seen to fill "the gaps in the structuralist–individualist debates and the gaps in the structure–agency formulations" (Clarke 1998 p. 10). It deals with social meanings and symbols. Clarke suggests that there are:

> good reasons to push the exploration of meaning beyond the social construction of specific social problems, client groups and expert knowledge into studies of how the meanings of "the people", "the nation" and "the welfare state" have been constructed, contested and remade. (ibid. p. 11)

A recent collection of papers has explored this relationship between welfare and culture in a number of European countries (Chamberlayne *et al.* 1999). In the introduction it is suggested that "the lived in experience of welfare appeared to be embedded in a complex network of relationships and shared assumptions" (ibid. p. 7). Two of the editors claim that cultural norms have always been an implicit aspect of social policy analysis but that the recent interest in comparative studies has "made for a new problematisation of the relationship between welfare and culture" (ibid. p. 11). While it is the intention of this study of Swedish welfare to use the concept of culture to explain the reaction of modernist Sweden to a postmodern world, this is not because it is felt that political and economic factors have no importance. The emphasis here has been on the interplay of a wide range of factors including the cultural – not to elevate culture above all other factors but to restore it to its rightful place alongside them. As Ellingsaeter says in her critique of the way in which "regime typologies simplify the complex operation of policy mechanisms":

> Both the formation of policies and the actual outcomes are conditioned by ... the economic, institutional and cultural settings in which they are embedded (Ellingsaeter 1998 p. 60).

The approach adopted in this study

The use of the terms modernity and postmodernity have been justified because they embrace both the structural and the cultural. This has been useful in reconciling the two aspects of my work on Sweden to date. During the early 1990s I wrote a number of pieces on the development of the Swedish welfare state (Gould 1993a, 1993c, 1995, 1996a). Much of the analysis concentrated on the political and economic aspects of change. The Swedish economy experienced a range of problems in the 1990s which successive governments tried to tackle. The consequences for the rest of society, however, were not so drastic as those experienced in Britain between 1979 and 1996. The degree of privatisation was less, local authorities retained much of their autonomy and the trade unions remained a powerful and significant part of society. As a social democrat, I was concerned that this once famous model was being eroded, yet full of admiration for the way in which the Swedish welfare state resisted change. Having lived through the Thatcher years, I was always expecting history to repeat itself and was pleasantly surprised when it didn't.

Over a slightly longer period of time, from 1986, I was also preoccupied by a more esoteric aspect of Swedish social policy. This interest arose from work carried out on debates about social control in the early 1980s in which I concluded that there was a clear authoritarian element in Swedish society which could not be reduced to terms like "left" and "right" (Gould 1988). It pervaded Swedish society. This thesis was subsequently confirmed by a range of studies of Swedish drug policy which sought to explain the pursuit of a drug-free society in terms of moral panic and cultural traditions (Gould 1989, 1990, 1993b, 1994a, 1994b, 1996b, 1999b). The more I began to understand the nature of drugs and their effects, the rationales of harm reduction, decriminalisation and legalisation, the more critical I became of what the Swedes call *the restrictive line*. The analysis here tended to be in institutional and cultural terms.

Initially, the two interests ran on parallel but separate lines, but as time went on there was a need to reconcile these two preoccupations – to demonstrate their mutual relevance. I did not see the cultural aspects of drug policy as somehow detached from and irrelevant to the rest of social policy. On the contrary it seemed to me that this was an example of what Richard Titmuss once referred to as a "small sector of human affairs" that could tell us a lot more about wider social relationships (Titmuss 1970 p. 14). Moreover, the changes taking place in both social policy generally and drug policy in particular had to be seen in the wider context of domestic and international economic developments. The problem was partly solved by seeing Swedish modernity in conflict with international forces of postmodernity and partly by employing a sociological distinction derived from Benedict (1961), Nietzsche (1993) and others – that of *Apollonian* and *Dionysian* values and cultures (see also Chapter 10). Mishra was the first social policy writer to make this connection:

> If there is one major implication of postmodernity for welfare it is that the Dionysian spirit of innovation, change and material progress embodied in the market economy has emerged as pre-eminent ... The Apollonian spirit embodied in social welfare, *no matter how expansive* (my italics), seems destined to remain a subsidiary element, one which in the broadest sense must harmonise with the imperatives of the economy (Mishra 1993 p. 35).

This Apollonian spirit is confirmed – as will be seen in Chapter 2 – by Daun's depiction of Swedish culture as characterised by values of rationality, order, self-control and sobriety (Daun 1996). The Swedish welfare state was an attempt to create an orderly society in which the fluctuations of a capitalist economy were tempered in the interests of security, social justice and equality (Tilton 1979). Policies and programmes were planned and organised in the light of social scientific research. It is hardly surprising that such principles and values should also find themselves in conflict with the behaviour of those who used alcohol excessively. The "alcoholic" represented the antithesis of rationality and order. What we had here was a fundamental reflection of the dichotomy of the *Apollonian* and the *Dionysian* where the former represented *order, sobriety and moderation*, and the latter, *disorder, drunkenness and excess*. This distinction can be applied to the dilemmas facing Sweden in the 1990s when the Apollonian values of Swedish culture were seen as being under threat both from without (the forces of globalisation, privatisation and deregulation which reduce the ability of national governments to pursue national goals; the more liberal policies of EU countries towards drugs, alcohol and prostitution) and from within (those who use alcohol and drugs to excess, the drug dealer, drug liberals, prostitutes and their clients). Sweden's restrictive line on alcohol and drugs could be seen as a defence against the Dionysian forces of excess and intoxication, while the welfare state was a symbol of order which prevented a capitalist society descending into free-market chaos.

This should not be taken to imply a simplistic, reified view of culture. I hope that the detailed accounts of the debates and conflicts in these chapters, are proof enough that I see culture as much of a contested terrain as the structures of welfare organisations or distributive policies. Swedish *culture* cannot easily be defined. It is constantly being influenced by external cultural forces through travel, global communication and international styles and fashions. Moreover, not only has Sweden become a multicultural society through the arrival of immigrants and refugees from Southern Europe, the Middle East and Africa, but even among *Nordic* Swedes, what constitute Swedish values and traditions is a matter for debate. Clarke has expressed the difficulty of writing about culture by saying that we need to grasp both its "fluidity and solidification" (Clarke 1998 p. 11). If I have erred on the side of the latter it has been for the sake of simplicity, it is not because I am unaware of the former. There is a *Swedish way*, however difficult it may be to pin down, which is embodied in a set of institutions and values. The advocacy of the restrictive line and the defence of the Swedish welfare state are two of the ways in which this has been expressed by people who see themselves as under threat.

The role of the labour movement

One thing I have tried to avoid is an over concentration on Swedish social democracy and the labour movement. This is not because I do not appreciate the contribution it has made to the development of

Swedish society in the twentieth century, nor because I have failed to see how embedded social democratic values are in Swedish institutions. Rather it is because others have already stressed social democracy to the exclusion of other forces, influences and traditions (Esping-Andersen 1985 and 1990; Korpi 1983 and 1989). They or their successors will write about Swedish welfare in the 1990s and perhaps focus more strongly on the labour movement.[5] However, as Ginsburg has argued, other analysts of Swedish welfare have focused upon more pluralistic influences such as interest groups and movements and the role of the middle class (Ginsburg 1993 and 2000).[6] While such approaches have much in common with the one adopted here, they tend to focus upon interests rather than values.[7] Social policy changes in this study are seen in terms of a range of competing forces operating within a set of political, institutional and cultural constraints. Certainly there will be other interpretations of this period. Social science proceeds by adopting a wide range of theories, methodologies and interpretations. I offer this interpretation in the hope that it makes a valuable contribution to the total picture, not in the belief that it provides a definitive account.

Sources

Although I have never lived in Sweden for more than two months at a time, I have been fortunate enough to visit almost every year since 1982. This has helped to maintain a watching brief over events, in keeping in touch with friends and colleagues, and in visiting libraries and bookshops. In addition to public and university libraries it has been extremely useful to be able to use the libraries of administrative boards and voluntary organisations. Over time, interviews have been carried out with a wide range of policy actors: politicians, academics, journalists, administrators, civil servants, and representatives of trade unions and pressure groups. I had already interviewed people for projects on long-term unemployment, the EU and drugs prior to commencing this book. To complement this material, I undertook a further visit in September 1999, to discuss a range of matters arising from my first draft, particularly in relation to the chapters on the elderly and women – two topics I had not written about previously. Such interviews, past and present, have proved invaluable not only for the additional material which they provide but also as a way of checking questions of fact and interpretation about which I was unsure. They have also often revealed insights about policy actors, relationships or events about which I knew little. Invariably the interviewee has also been able to provide additional publications or references which have been of immense help.

Back in Britain, it has been increasingly possible to keep in touch with events in Sweden via the Internet. Many Swedish organisations have a home page with references to recent publications, responses to government initiatives, their own research and so on. Two other sources of information have been indispensable. *Dagens Nyheter* (*DN*) is a daily broadsheet, quality newspaper which claims to be "independent liberal" in its editorial stance. It is certainly neither Social Democratic nor Conservative. It features a wide range of articles on social policy on a daily basis. While editorials and some feature articles may be heavily influenced by the paper's own agenda, there is a wealth of relatively objective reporting on local and central government initiatives, interest group activities and current research findings. Although it is critical of many aspects of the Swedish labour movement it has publicised sympathetically the difficulties faced by individuals, groups and local authorities trying to cope with government cutbacks in the 1990s.

An important feature of the newspaper for a researcher is the daily *debate* article in which leading figures in politics (all parties), academia, the economy, trade unions, pressure groups express their views at length on an issue of current importance. Press cuttings – covering a wide range of social policies and issues – were selected, photocopied and filed on a monthly basis from September 1991 to September 1998. *Riksdag och Departement* (*RD* – Parliament and Ministry) is an excellent fortnightly journal which summarises almost every parliamentary and governmental document of any significance – commission reports, government directives and proposals, parliamentary debates and decisions. Both these sources enabled me to follow the dynamics of social policy debates and the whole policy process. They not only provided a broad picture of developments, but also alerted me to the original sources which on occasion needed to be consulted.

The scope and structure of this study

Most studies of welfare states have to be selective as it is impossible to cover everything that the term can be said to include. However, any study that claims to be about a welfare state should attempt to do much more than dwell on one or two services, programmes or issues. This study certainly does that but important areas have been omitted. There is nothing on education or housing for example. I could have devoted a whole chapter to ethnic minority issues but for various reasons chose not to do so. What I have to say about the Swedish welfare state should, therefore, be read with the proviso that it is based solely on the material presented here.

The next chapter will elaborate on the theme of Sweden as the supreme example of modernity and Chapter 3 will outline the development of the welfare state, its structure and achievements from early in the twentieth century until 1991. The rest of the book will be primarily concerned with the two governments which presided during the 1990s. Unless stated otherwise, the terms Centre-Right or Bourgeois government will refer to the period 1991–94 while Social Democratic government will refer to the period 1994–98. Chapter 4 will describe the economic and political changes in the 1990s that had most relevance for the changing nature of welfare including Sweden's application and subsequent decision to join the EU. Chapter 5 will cover developments in a range of welfare benefits and services – social security, social services, social assistance and health care – and the extent to which social inequalities have become more narrow or wider. Subsequent chapters take client groups and issues as their main focus. Chapter 6 will look at how the elderly, have fared; Chapter 7 will deal with women. Chapter 8 will explore social issues around employment. Chapter 9 examines two areas which have touched on Swedish national sensitivities, particularly in relation to the EU, alcohol and drug policies.

This selection of specialist areas partly can be justified in order to get away from too narrow a focus on service provision and partly because each topic has been regarded by Swedes themselves and, to a certain extent, outsiders as policy *models* for others to follow. Sweden was regarded as having developed *the* welfare state; the elderly were seen to be better cared for in Sweden than elsewhere; Sweden was regarded as a world leader in gender equality; full employment, an active labour market policy and employment rights were seen as the foundation of a generous welfare state; lastly – and this may seem idiosyncratic at first sight – Sweden's restrictive alcohol and drug policies were important aspects of public health policy. All of them represented important aspects of social democratic ideals but – and just as significantly – also of a rational and modern society. The EU is referred to in a number of these chapters as the concrete embodiment of anonymous international forces and as a source of liberal ideas, which have been seen by many Swedes as a dangerous threat to their welfare state. The argument will conclude with an analysis of change and the political, institutional and cultural resistance to change. It will be suggested that

Sweden's very reputation as an exemplar of Apollonian modernity made it difficult to adapt to the condition of Dionysian postmodernity.

Conclusion

In the late 1970s and early 1980s, a range of socioeconomic forces led to the decline of the modernist welfare state. While some regretted its loss, others have come to see its passing as an opportunity to establish a new welfare system based upon postmodern values of pluralism, difference and diversity.

One of the principal aims of this book is to look at how, in the 1990s, a society regarded as an exemplar of modernity has adjusted, or not, to the circumstances of a postmodern world. More specifically, to what extent has the "People's Home" founded upon principles of rational planning, social justice and sobriety become postmodern? This will be operationalised in three ways. We need to find out whether the Swedish welfare state has become more pluralist. Is there evidence not only of cutbacks in state benefits and services but of alternative provision in the form of private, occupational and voluntary welfare? Next we need to ask whether the labourist politics of the modernist welfare state have given way to a welfare politics which accommodates other social identities and movements. And to the extent that Sweden remains true to its modernist traditions, one will also be obliged to ask whether, alongside its more humane and solidaristic aims, it continues to harbour particular forms of repression or discipline.

The next chapter will examine Sweden's modernist tradition.

2
. . . Modern Society

> The large process of socialisation which transformed "peasants into Swedes" ... implied that national identity was wed to modernity. Modernity was nationalised and became Swedishness. (Frykman 1996 p. 63)

> Eugenics, order, rationality and conscientiousness have been shown to have left their mark on the institutional social policy of the social democratic People's Home. (Holgersson 1994 p. 119)

Introduction

The task of this chapter is to suggest that a number of interrelated elements in the early twentieth century contributed to Swedish modernity: the modernist belief in science, progress and rationality, linked with more traditional notions of order and discipline, a functionalist aesthetic in art and architecture and a social engineering approach to social problems. The politics of social democracy – which aimed to bring a degree of state control to a capitalist economy and to promote social planning – complemented and was complemented by these. Sweden's subsequent economic and social success contributed to a sense of national pride and superiority. Sweden was considered, by itself and other countries, to be a model of progress and modernity.

Sweden: the "prototype" of a modern society

The composite and reified representation of "modernity" advanced by postmodern theorists is often far too neat, but if one country conformed to most of the criteria, it was Sweden. To use the definitions cited in Chapter 1, modern Sweden was "positivistic, technocratic and rationalistic"; it did believe in the "rational planning" of an ideal social order. "Economic and social life" were regulated "through the corporatist involvement of business and trade union representatives". Around 1970, there was enormous interest shown in Swedish modernity by other Western countries.

The very titles of books written are evidence of the kind of esteem in which the country was held. *Sweden: the prototype of a modern society* (Tomasson 1970) describes a society in which rational scientific knowledge was highly valued, in which traditional ways and institutions were changed if no rational justification could be found for them. A similar claim was made by Jenkins in the his *Sweden: the progress machine* (1968). Jenkins described a highly organised society in which technological change was embraced and valued and in which the old was expected to give way to what was rational and practical. His view was that Sweden was "thing-oriented" rather than "people-oriented" arguing that the advanced state of the cooking facilities in a restaurant was more important than the quality of the service or the food. Roland Huntford turned much of this on its head when he described Swedes as the *new totalitarians* (1971). In his view Swedes were conformists inhabiting a highly controlled and centralised society committed to "technological perfection" (ibid. p. 348). He suggested that the Swedish desire for a "benevolent and authoritarian state" resembled the German experience which resulted in Nazi domination (ibid. p. 63). Interestingly – given what I have to say later about temperance, sobriety and rationality – Huntford also implied that heavy drinking in Sweden was a "way of escaping a repressive society" (ibid. p. 344)

Functionalism, the Stockholm Exhibition and national identity

The view of Sweden as rational and modern however did not originate in the 1960s. Even in the 1930s and 1940s Childs and others described Sweden as a model society. Childs is remembered for saying that the Swedes had found a "middle way" between capitalism and communism (Childs 1936). Although Childs referred to housing conditions and pensions, he was concerned principally to show that Sweden had avoided the excesses of capitalism through the control of monopolies. This was achieved by a powerful co-operative movement, state industries and state regulation. With regard to the latter it is interesting to note that Childs himself thought it important to devote a whole chapter of his book to "liquor control". In describing how Swedes had achieved economic recovery from the 1930s depression so much more quickly than other Western countries and how society had achieved a high degree of prosperity for the mass of the population, Childs, time and again, referred to qualities of "reasonableness", "moderation", the willingness to "compromise", the "pragmatic" approach to problems of all kinds. Swedish society was not "utopian" but it came close with a "certain wholeness, a certain health" and fundamental distinctiveness "of order, of stability, of sanity" (ibid. p. xiv).

Sweden was advanced technologically.

> It is a machine civilisation; there are proportionately more telephones, more electrical devices, more automobiles in Stockholm than in any other European city; the rural areas are more completely electrified than anywhere else in the world (ibid. p. xiv).

Collective housing was very functional, particularly for the growing numbers of married women in Stockholm who were professional workers. There were communal meals of high quality; communal nurseries for the children; kitchens equipped with domestic appliances; sun-bathing facilities with a shower room were provided on flat roofs; interiors were in "the modern style" (ibid. p. 58). In discussing the influence of the Swedish Arts and Crafts Society, Childs said that

> it had done much to sweep away the heritage of nineteenth-century stuffiness and the atrocities of *l'art nouveau*. This does not mean that every workman's flat is a mean between Corbusier and Elsie de Wolff. But light, space, simplicity and bright colour have replaced to a surprising extent the heavy, crowded, dark flats of two or three decades ago ... Functionalism, the international style, has made headway amongst the younger architects (ibid. p. 131).

Although he added that he did not think such a style would take a deep hold, that is exactly what it did.[1]

There can be little doubt that the Swedish authorities sought to become known for their modernity. The Stockholm Exhibition of 1930 – two years prior to the beginning of the Social Democrats' 44-year long reign – was a celebration of the rational, the technical and the functional (Pred 1995). It was a gigantic display of invention, production, consumption and propaganda similar to many others which had been mounted throughout Europe since the Great Exhibition of 1851 held in the Crystal Palace. It was a conscious attempt to give Swedes a new sense of national identity. Ruth described the Exhibition as providing:

> a springboard of functionalism in all of Scandinavia ... Its proponents marched forward exuding enormous self-confidence; they possessed a world view and a view of humanity which held that life and society can be broken down into a number of basic functions, and that these can then serve as the foundation for planned action (Ruth 1984 p. 77).

Ruth suggested that the origin of this great project actually began with the Conservatives who had begun to look for national symbols other than the traditional ones of Sweden's past to challenge the success of Social Democrats in winning the support of working people on the one hand and to stem the flow of emigrants to the USA on the other. The right rejected a romantic anti-industrialism, applauded the need for industrial skill and "stood out ... as a champion of rationality" (ibid. p. 81). "Greatness, it appeared, could be achieved in a different way – through a policy of rational co-operation between government and industry (ibid. p. 83)". Ruth cites what he thought was the first reference to Sweden as a model for others to follow by a conservative visionary, Ludwig Nordström. In a book published in 1919 he asked:

> Why could not Sweden become a model country for the rest of the world? It has everything necessary with its excellent race, its developed institutions, its talents, its instinct for sport, and its ethical prospects? (Ibid. p. 83).

Ruth went on to argue that Nordström's "dream of Sweden as a forerunner of a scientific world order was taken over by a new generation of architects, scientists, and social engineers in the wake of the Stockholm Exhibition." (ibid. p. 84) Nordström subsequently initiated the campaign against urban squalor in the name of scientific planning.

The conservatives may have initiated the idea of linking national identity with rationality and scientific progress but it fell to the Social Democrats to complete the project.

Social democracy, discipline and social engineering

Sweden's powerful labour movement developed towards the end of the nineteenth century as a reaction to the squalor and poverty engendered by early capitalism. Poor farm workers who emigrated to industrial towns and cities found themselves subjected to a new regime of discipline by their employers. Factory life demanded an increase in the pace, intensity and efficiency of work and emphasized the need for punctuality and attendance. But as Horgby pointed out, discipline "led to a changing cultural pattern among the working class" (Horgby 1986 p. 253). This is illustrated by Ambjörnsson in his study of a Northern coastal community in the late nineteenth and early twentieth centuries. He described how the labour movement in Sweden was built by disciplined workers who organised themselves and advanced their class interests by being *skötsam* – orderly and conscientious (Ambjörnsson 1989). It was true that paternalistic employers had demanded orderly behaviour by their workers in and out of work in return for homes, fuel, medical care and other benefits, but in time workers used these very qualities to improve their mutual lot – forming temperance lodges, educational associations and trade unions.

> The workers were to evidence self-discipline, observe punctuality, not cause public disturbances and, naturally, remain sober. The unions often discussed whether alcohol should be banned altogether, and they appointed committees to deal with those members who failed to meet their job obligations: doing a good job became a point of honour. But it was also a point of honour not to cowtow to an employer. (ibid. p. 63)

The moral aspects of Swedish social policy have tended to be overlooked by those who have emphasized either the Social Democratic ideology or the country's rational approach to social issues. It was stated above that Swedish society was regarded by various writers as pragmatic rather than moralistic. Sexual advice and education was often used as an example. Furniss and Tilton did however point to "paternalist" and "Christian" traditions which had influenced the welfare state (Furniss and Tilton 1977 p. 123). Another example came from Holgersson, who in writing about the development of Swedish social services in the twentieth century, argued that whereas the solidaristic tradition of the Social Democrats had influenced most aspects of social policy, social services continued to display characteristics of paternalism, charity, the work ethic, individualism, repression and Puritanism (Holgersson 1981 p. 74). Discipline, self-control, sobriety and orderliness were all aspects of rational behaviour demanded by both employers and the labour movement, and an important aspect of the rational society that Sweden aspired to become.

Among those Social Democrats who were influential in the establishment of the Swedish welfare state, it is possible to discern many links with the project of rational planning in their approaches to social policy. While they all shared values of social justice and equality, there were also elements of technocratic, nationalistic and moralistic thinking. Wigforss was credited with being not only an able Finance Minister but Swedish social democracy's most original and perspicacious thinker. Olsson describes him as one of "the main architects of Swedish social and economic planning" along with Gustav Möller and the two Myrdals, Alva and Gunnar (Olsson 1990 p. 113). Sweden's way out of the Great Depression was in no small part due to Wigforss' economic imagination which anticipated what was later accepted as Keynesianism. The six principles he set out in his writings – equality, freedom, democracy, security, conscious control of the economy, solidarity – were resonating in the party's programme long after his death (Tilton 1979).

This coherent set of principles led to the formulation of the idea of three stages in the achievement of socialism by parliamentary means. The first stage was the struggle for *political democracy*; the second was *social democracy*, which was accomplished by 1960 with the main programmes of state welfare in place. The final stage referred *to economic democracy* which was supposed to be achieved with the Co-determination law of 1976 (which gave the right to participate in management decisions to trade union representatives) and the establishment of the wage-earner funds in 1983 (which gave trade unions a control over a share of the profits of private companies). In social democratic ideology the welfare state was a step on the road towards a socialist society.

Gustav Möller, Minister for Social Affairs for 20 years, was another influential figure in the creation of the Swedish welfare state. According to Rothstein he closed down or by-passed the traditional bureaucracies and created "new forms of central, regional and local public organisations" (Rothstein 1985 p. 159). Möller was well aware that civil servants – whose background tended to be upper class – could easily frustrate democratic decision-making if they so chose. Möller's agencies – particularly the Labour Market Board and the National

Housing Board, both established in 1948 – were created to prevent this from happening. The running of administrative boards became the responsibility of representatives of those organisations significantly affected by the decisions. Thus teachers would be represented on the schools board, doctors on the medical board and trade unionists on the labour market board. Agencies were formed to further the interests of the people's welfare, not to frustrate them.

While Alva and Gunnar Myrdal were social democrats, they are identified more with "the rationalist conception of preventative social policy" (Furniss and Tilton 1977 p. 123). They had travelled extensively in the USA and Europe before they resettled in Stockholm in the 1930s. There they had regular meetings with other social scientists to discuss practice rather than theory. Carlson claimed that their most important meetings were with "radical architects and industrial designers" of the functionalist school (Carlson 1978 p. 147). Carlson also suggested that "the Myrdals drew together the two developing intellectual strands" of population control and social democracy (ibid. p. 121). "Their population programme represented a blueprint and justification for a significant portion of the Swedish welfare state" (ibid. p. 121). Welfare provision was advocated as a way of preventing social pathologies from arising in the first place. Its justification was more in terms of efficiency and economy than ideology. According to Holgersson:

> Emphasis was placed on utilising resources efficiently and arranging people's lives as sensibly as possible, at home as well as in society. (Holgersson 1994 p. 118)

Holgersson's phrase "arranging people's lives" is similar to Hirdman's "putting people's lives in order" (Hirdman 1989).[2] These phrases, coined to describe the social engineering approach, are still used today by Swedes critical of the state's eagerness to intervene in people's lives. In the course of this book they will appear on a number of occasions.

In her 1941 study of family and demographic policy based upon the joint work of Alva and Gunnar, Alva stated that:

> The author believes that social planning should be a rational procedure based on factual knowledge and pursued by means of logical analysis. She insists moreover that the immensity and intensity of today's social problems and the vast scope of today's' social actions are challenges to social science to proceed more courageously – to

> advance from merely recording facts to constructing rational plans for purposive changes. (Myrdal 1968 p. 1)

Two paragraphs later she referred to this as "constructive social engineering", which in her view could only be effective if it was built upon clearly-formulated value premises. These were supplied by socialism. For her, socialism was modernity. It was the most rational way of dealing with human needs and social problems.

In a later work, Alva criticised the International Labour Organisation for lagging behind the social policy "progress" achieved by "our country and other leading countries" (Myrdal, 1944 p. 447). It was important that "the most modern and the most socialist" proposals should be considered by ILO (Ibid. p. 458). Alva Myrdal's criticism of the ILO also expressed her belief that the social policies developed in the Nordic countries and especially Sweden contained important lessons from which the rest of the world could benefit.

> We in Scandinavia can, without arrogance, demand great respect for our reforms and guidelines in social policy circles. On us is the burden of ensuring that after the war this organisation should be developed to become a really stimulating, investigative and advisory organ of international social policy. (ibid.)

This pride in what was being created is also expressed by the term *Folkhemmet* – the People's Home. The concept was coined by the first Social Democratic prime minister, Per Albin Hansson in 1928 in a parliamentary debate.

> The home's foundation is community and concern. The good home does not know privilege or the feeling of being slighted ... In the good home, equality, considerateness, co-operation and helpfulness hold sway. Applied to the great people's and citizens' home this should mean the demolition of all social and economic ranks which now divide citizens into privileged and slighted, into rich and poor, propertied and impoverished, exploiters and exploited (cited in Carlson 1978 p. 119).

The use of the term *home* to describe the nation is, I would suggest, an important symbol for the Swedes. Hansson was anxious to stress the egalitarian nature of the home but Swedish homes are also clean and orderly. It is not enough that individual homes are in good order, it is important that the nation's house is also clean and tidy. When in the 1980s, Ingvar Carlsson wanted to express his country's hostility towards illegal substances, he said he wanted a "house clean of drugs".

The word *folk* is important here too. Like the German *volk* it also has the connotation of "nation" and even "race". While it also means "people" it does not mean *any* people. Zaremba suggests that when Hansson spoke of the folk he meant "conscientious Swedes" (Zaremba 1999 p. 301). Certainly it would seem that Hansson deliberately appropriated nationalist symbols. In his view, it had been a mistake for the German left in the 1930s to allow the enemies of democracy to have a monopoly on nationalistic sentiments. (ibid. p. 296). Zaremba quotes the historian Alf W. Johansson as saying that Hansson was able to "integrate the central nazi concept of a *folk* community with social democratic, egalitarian rhetoric" (ibid. p. 295).

Pride in the achievements of one's country is understandable and even commendable. After all, it must be less threatening that a country boasts of its social welfare rather than its armaments, its economic power or even its technological superiority. What is important from the point of view of this study is that we recognise that what has happened to Swedish social policy in the last ten years is made more comprehensible by being aware of the national, symbolic and cultural significance of the Swedish welfare state.

Heclo and Masden once wrote that the "Social democratic project had become the nation's project" (Heclo and Masden 1986). It may be that they got it the wrong way round. The nation's project had become the Social Democratic project. The Social Democrats had shown themselves to be the political party most closely identified with the deeper aims and aspirations of the mass of the population. Social Democratic values and policies may be important to understanding the nature of the Swedish welfare state but they are part of a much wider social context to which the contribution of other traditions has been devalued.

Compulsory sterilisation

Modernity in the early twentieth century included a range of ideas about science, technology and progress which were exemplified by a concern with eugenics. Eugenicists were concerned about a number of demographic issues but one in particular has received considerable publicity in Sweden – compulsory sterilisation. While it as important not to exaggerate its significance, it does form a useful illustration of an aspect of modernity once thought progressive, which is now considered repulsive and inhuman. It is also an example of an aspect of social policy which, it is alleged, Sweden took further than other democratic countries. Many chroniclers of the welfare state have concealed the details and their recent revelation has encouraged the government to set up a Commission to inquire into the matter and to propose principles for making compensation to the surviving victims of the policy (*RD* 1997 No. 25 p. 3).[3]

The facts are simply that eugenic laws were passed in 1935 and 1941 which resulted in 60 000 compulsory sterilisations (90 per cent women) taking place in Sweden before they were stopped in 1976 (Zaremba 1997a). The reasons advanced at the time were "to prevent the birth of individuals who, most likely, must become a burden to themselves and others" (Smith and Zaremba 1997).

> The "degeneration danger" became one of the most potent images of social threat in Scandinavia. Most things were considered hereditary: crime, a propensity to commit rape, mental handicap, but even the inability to be thrifty, masturbation and vagabondism. (Zaremba 1997a)

Alcoholic parents were another category. (Tännsjö 1997)

What seemed to shock many commentators was the scale of the policy, the fact that it continued until well into the 1970s (albeit on a much smaller scale) and with the complicity of Social Democrats. However, if the social engineering implied by the *science* of eugenics was not peculiar to the Nazis, neither was it peculiar to the Swedes. The Danes and the Austrians seem to have been similarly involved, and Anglo-Saxon countries also adopted such policies to an extent. Nonetheless, it can perhaps be suggested that the grand nature of the Swedish modernist project – the pursuit of the *good* society – gave such policies a stronger rationale. It would however seem hypocritical of Swedish conservatives to suggest that such policies were social democratic in nature. Conservatives like Linders felt that "asocial individuals at the bottom level ... could be sterilised ... to help ensure the qualitative bettering of the population material." (Carlson 1978 p. 99) The policy also had support among prominent women of the time (Zaremba 1997b), the media (Boethius 1997) and the church (Vinterhead 1997). Nonetheless, Social Democratic governments certainly endorsed the policy. In a review of Social Democratic policies in the 1940s by senior figures in the labour movement (such as Ernst Wigforss, Per Albin Hansson, Tage Erlander as well as Alva Myrdal).

J. Axel Höjer, declared one of the principal aims of public health policy to be that "no-one shall be ill because of inferior genes" (Höjer 1944 p. 346). He went on to say:

> ... if those in every age group defined as mentally deficient – with a mental age of 12 or under – became sterilised, within two generations we would have reduced the numbers ... by 25% and within ten generations by 75%. This is practical genetic hygiene ... That certain inheritance combinations or deficiencies are *incompatible with an ordered society* [my italics] of complete physical and mental health, is obvious. (Höjer 1944 p. 346)

Alva Myrdal, while recognising the dangers of taking compulsory sterilisation too far, wrote the following in her 1941 study of family and population policy:

> In some instances ... an offspring is so undesirable that even a democratic state will want to enforce limitations of parenthood. Negative eugenics has its place as a means for population policy. The necessity of enforcing a radical elimination of extremely unfit and worthless individuals through sterilisation is generally recognised. Even if their low quality should not be of hereditary character, they would as parents create too undesirable an environment for children (Myrdal 1968 pp. 115–6).

A rational, ordered society not only required a comprehensive welfare state but policies which aimed to rid society of its social and genetic imperfections.

National superiority

It would be unsurprising if a nation which has achieved so much social and economic success in the past did not produce the occasional expression of smugness. Criticisms of Swedes' nationalistic belief in the superiority of their society, have been made by Per Ohlsson, editor of *Sydsvenska Dagbladet*. In *The island of the gods: the extremely Swedish*, he claimed that the sense of being the cleanest, the healthiest and the most free of nations went back 500 years (Ohlsson 1993). He also claimed that Sweden's protective state was the modern equivalent of a long, patriarchal tradition. In his view, Swedish nationalism was the more extreme for becoming wedded with ideas of welfare and solidarity.

Where nationalism in other countries may have become the prerogative of the right in opposition to socialist internationalism, in Sweden, nationalism became a celebration of national welfare superiority. Comprehensive welfare was a protection against the threat of irrational economic forces. In this context, according to Ohlsson, it was easy to see why those who argued for Sweden to join the EU should be seen by opponents of entry as betraying the country's values and traditions.

Billig has pointed out how social scientists have tended to be preoccupied with the worst excesses of nationalism in other countries while ignoring the forms it takes in their own back yards (Billig 1995). Sweden is no exception to this rule. The reputation that Sweden has had for promoting internationalism has, in the past, disguised its own brand of nationalism. Alongside a simple affection for one's country exists the common practice of ritualistically raising the national flag outside one's home,[4] a distinct sense of national superiority and the displays of neo-nazism in the 1990s. When does an innocent love of one's country become an exaggerated attachment to forms and symbols? Nationalism can take many forms from the banal to the bigoted. What is being suggested here is that nationalist pride in Sweden is expressed in terms of order and discipline, the welfare state and the control of drug-induced behaviour; in short, a discourse of sober rationality which found expression in institutions of modernity.

Conclusion

Sweden was the exemplar of modernity. Its economic and social success in the central decades of the last century encouraged outsiders to see it as a model for the rest of the world. The commitment to a modern, ordered, rational society became a source of national pride and identity. Sweden was in the forefront of technological and science developments and its art and urban planning were influenced by functionalist ideals. Its labour movement was disciplined and based on values of sobriety and solidarity. All of this gave rise to an understandable sense of national superiority. Swedish welfare was regarded as a model for others to follow. This leadership role was not only attributed to Sweden by its outside admirers, it was proclaimed by Swedes proud of what their country had achieved. The desire to be "best in the class", a world leader, was expressed by the conservative Nordström in 1919 and by Alva Myrdal in 1944. It still finds its expression today in the goal of a drug-free society; the claim to lead the world in gender equality;

and being the first country to criminalise those who purchase the services of prostitutes. Swedes in the twentieth century sought to create an ideal social order and were believed by many commentators to have succeeded. It is hardly surprising that under conditions of postmodernity, Swedes should have been reluctant to abandon the values and institutions they had taken so long to create.

3
The "People's Home"

> Sweden's welfare state policies can be depicted as visionary modernist, supported by social democratic political and social hegemony.
>
> (Ellingsaeter 1998 p. 71)

> ... eugenics, order, rationality and conscientiousness have been shown to have left their mark on the institutional social policy of the social democratic People's Home
>
> (Holgersson 1994 p. 119)

Introduction

This chapter will present a brief outline of the development of the Swedish welfare state prior to 1991.[1] It begins with the emergence of the "People's Home", moves on to its growth and consolidation in the years following the Second World War, and the increasing problems facing the economy at the end of the 1980s. While the long reign of the Social Democratic party and the strength of the trade union movement can take much of the credit for Sweden's social achievements, it should not be forgotten that other organisations and institutions also played an important role.

The People's Home

Sweden's industrialisation may have occurred much later than that of Britain but political and social change occurred in parallel. What is also striking is that as the foundations for a modern welfare state in Britain were laid in an era of reformist liberalism (1906–14) so the early measures in Swedish welfare took place between 1900 and 1920. Verney claimed that there was a marked shift from defence expenditure to expenditure on social welfare and education during this period (Verney 1972). His argument was that the Social Democrats subsequently "extended very considerably" the social reforms begun by the Liberals. This makes sense if one looks at different accounts of the development of Swedish welfare. All of them mention the introduction of old age pensions in 1913. Others describe the reform of the poor law in 1918 which remained relatively unchanged until 1956 (Holgersson 1981).

Verney's argument makes sense too if one considers that, even in the 1930s, Sweden was regarded abroad as a model of welfare in which "there were no slums" (Verney 1972 p. 47). This could not have been achieved in just a few years of social democratic rule. The 1930s were however, a period of social innovation. Two areas received significant attention – employment policy (largely because of the unemployment created during the depression) and family policy (due to a major worry about the declining birth rate). Olsson has summarised the principle measures as follows (Olsson 1990 p. 110):

- new state employment creation programmes
- state subsidies to voluntary (trade union) unemployment benefit societies
- a housing programme for families with many children including subsidies and interest-subsidised construction loans
- the indexation of pensions to regional differences in the cost of living
- maternity benefits to around 90 per cent of all mothers
- free maternity and childbirth services
- state loans to newly married couples
- the introduction of two weeks holiday for all for all public and private employees

The pro-natal programmes owed as much to the influence of the Myrdals' social engineering as to social democratic ideology.

The 1930s saw the emergence of what are often referred to as *historical compromises* which had important implications for the development of the welfare state. The *first* was between the Social Democratic party and the Agrarian (later Centre) party. In contrast to many other countries where the landed interest has been identified with parties of the right, Sweden's farmers lent their support to the aspirations of the labour movement. This alliance was an important explanation for the electoral weakness of Swedish conservatives. The *second* historical compromise was reached by LO (the federation of manual trade unions) and SAF (the federation of Swedish employers) in 1938. These two formidable labour market organisations agreed to negotiate an annual pay award which would set national guidelines for their members. It was this relationship which provided a successful basis for postwar corporatism in Sweden.

Although Sweden remained neutral throughout the Second World War, it was none the less affected by it. The economy itself benefited from the demand for Swedish steel and manufactured goods. Moreover, a degree of mobilisation was necessary due to the threat of the war and the resulting increase in taxation was put to more social uses after 1945. The lack of devastation gave Sweden a head start in the postwar years and rates of economic growth were high. Like Britain and many other countries, it set about the task of reconstruction, and social reform continued apace. The flat-rate old age pension system was "expanded, protected from inflation and made almost independent of need" (Jenkins 1968 p. 53). Compulsory health insurance with earnings-related sickness benefits was introduced in 1955. By the 1950s, Fleisher was able to reaffirm that Sweden was "known as the welfare state" and that it was considered to be "far advanced in welfare and provided a model for us all" (Fleisher 1956 p. 11).

Swedes had elected Social Democratic governments from 1932 and continued to do so until 1976 – an unbroken period of 44 years. The proportion of the electorate voting for the Social Democrats was often above 45 per cent. A high percentage of manual workers voted for them and the British phenomenon of the "working-class conservative" hardly existed. Eighty per cent of manual workers were also members of unions affiliated to LO, a figure that was to increase still further. The close collaboration of the two halves of the labour movement ensured considerable support for the expansion of welfare provision. Support was also forthcoming from the Centre (the old Agrarian) party and the Liberal party. These two parties had a combined electoral support of 30 per cent for much of the post-war period while the Conservative party could only muster around 14 per cent (Ersson 1991 p. 198). During this time it was never in a position to form or dominate a government.

Towards socialism

By the end of the 1950s, the controversial state earnings-related pension scheme was introduced to give manual and non-manual employees alike about two-thirds of their best period of earnings on retirement. This important development is sometimes described as the *third historical compromise* since it bound together a joint interest in the welfare state between the working and middle classes. In the 1960s the comprehensivisation of primary and secondary education also took place. The foundations of the welfare state were now well in place. Over the next two decades, public services were expanded, benefits were improved and eligibility to them widened (Olsson 1990 p. 116).

Foreign commentators, usually American, came to test whether the welfare state was improving the lot of the people or destroying individual incentives and creating moral malaise. Had the state gone too far with its "experiment" or was there still scope for further intervention, asked Fleisher in the 1950s (Fleisher 1956). His answer was to recognise that there was little destitution, no slums and no beggars on the streets. Everybody (that is all males at that time) had a job and everyone had access to a high standard of medical care. He wondered whether there was too much security and complacency. But on balance, he was impressed with what a comprehensive welfare system had achieved and admitted that the Swedes could bring the experiment to an end at any time simply by voting for the parties of the right. Rosenthal in the 1960s asked similar questions and came to similar conclusions – no decline in moral standards because of the welfare state, no loss of incentives, no lack of free enterprise (Rosenthal 1967 p. 172). He even went so far as to suggest that the USA had something to learn from the "Swedish social laboratory" in terms of public participation in and support for public programmes. Jenkins, another American visitor, praised the high degree of security achieved by the Swedish system and felt that even the resulting queues for free and subsidised services testified to the success of the system (Jenkins 1968).

The *Active Labour Market Policy* devised by two LO economists in the early 1960s proved to be a very effective way of dealing with unemployment on a selective basis so that the inflationary effects were minimal. LO began to pursue a policy of wage solidarity which aimed to reduce inequalities in pay. It also had the effect of driving uncompetitive firms out of business while providing benefits for large companies. The economy was dominated by large companies such as Volvo, Saab, Ericsson and Electrolux which were very successful internationally. Sweden combined economic growth and social security in a way which encouraged both envy and emulation. It was a world leader in social expenditure and ranked high among rich countries in terms of GDP per capita (Ersson 1991 p. 202).[2]

Into the 1970s, the pattern was repeated. Furniss and Tilton compared the USA, Britain and Sweden and concluded that America should strive for the same social policy goals as the Swedes, thereby reducing inequalities, encouraging citizen participation, improving the efficiency of labour markets and free enterprise generally (Furniss and Tilton 1977 p. 203–4). They rejected conservative and radical left criticisms which claimed either that state welfare destroyed the incentive to work and invest, or that it was an institution which furthered the interests of capitalism.

In Sweden, however, socialist discontent with welfare achievements were gaining ground. Research indicated that the welfare state still had many problems to solve (Inghe and Inghe 1970). Inequalities, particularly of wealth and economic power remained stark (Larsson and Sjöström 1979). Social services continued to manifest characteristics of the old poor law (Holgersson 1981). Trade unions in particular saw the results of their solidaristic wage policy as improving the profits of large Swedish companies. These critiques led to further demands for improved benefits and services, greater social equality, higher taxation and public expenditure. Doctors became members of a salaried profession in what was already a largely publicly-provided service. Parental leave was introduced for both parents and the right to educational leave was granted to all employees in 1974. By 1975 public sector employment had risen to 25 per cent of the workforce. Trade unionists were a given a right to representation on management boards in 1976. Trade union pressure on the Social Democratic government led to an acceptance of proposals for acquiring a share of company profits for their members.

Not only were greater domestic demands being made upon the welfare state, but the external environment in which the Swedish economy participated was facing major problems. The Middle East war, the oil crisis, rising inflation and unemployment were leading to difficulties which challenged the validity of postwar Keynesian economic policies. At a time when Wilensky coined the phrase "welfare backlash", it seemed as if Sweden was one of the first countries to revolt (Wilensky 1975). In 1976, a Centre-right coalition was elected consisting of the Centre, Liberal and Conservative parties with a majority over the Socialist parties of 11 seats. Although the Social Democrats remained the largest party in the Riksdag, they had suffered a significant defeat, which was to be repeated three years later.

The backlash however failed to occur. Faced with severe economic difficulties the Bourgeois parties found themselves giving state aid to failing industries. Little was done to curb public or social expenditure, and they were finally rejected by the electorate for, among other things, attempting to reduce sickness benefits.

Consolidation

When the Social Democrats were returned in 1982, a 14 per cent devaluation of the Swedish krona seemed to restore the country's economic fortunes. While Britain and the USA were in the throws of a neo-liberal revolution full employment remained a priority as did the improvement of social provision and the expansion of the public sector. However, as Ginsburg has pointed out, even in the early 1980s there was a:

> distinct shift in the economic and social policy discourse within governing and industrial circles towards what was dubbed a "third way" ... neither traditionally Keynesian nor overtly liberal (Ginsburg 2001).

More positively, the Social Democrats were at last able to introduce the controversial Wage Earner Funds. Even in its diluted form, the measure angered SAF, commerce and the opposition parties. Every October until they were finally abolished, business people would march in protest against them in Stockholm. Moreover, SAF was becoming increasingly disillusioned with its corporatist relations with the government and LO.

It was, however, still possible at the beginning of the 1980s to imagine that Sweden might achieve socialism by democratic means (Korpi 1983; Stephens 1979). As the decade wore on, the possibility became increasingly unlikely. International trends were in the opposite direction. The deregulation of financial markets, the privatisation of national assets, the intensification of competition and the decline in the autonomy of national governments, were making it difficult for countries to maintain full employment and comprehensive systems of state welfare.

Yet, by the end of the decade, supporters of the Swedish welfare state remained optimistic. Olsson wrote a number of papers during a period when neo-liberal politics were clearly affecting other welfare systems. He concluded that:

> Despite a slowdown in the growth of social programmes and of social expenditure, both during the bourgeois years of the late 1970s and early 1980s but in particular during the economically more prosperous years of Social Democratic rule during the rest of the

> 1980s, Swedish social policy has not been substantially affected by the crisis of the welfare state (Olsson 1990 p. 33).

Similarly Esping-Andersen's *The three worlds of welfare capitalism* used the concept of *decommodification* to argue that the social democratic model remained distinctive (Esping-Andersen 1990). In many capitalist countries, he argued, people were dependent upon the market to provide for their needs. They were commodified. The more developed the welfare system, the less their dependency upon the market. In the Scandinavian welfare states in general and in Sweden most of all, decommodification had become a reality for many. Pierson in another review of welfare statism generally, devoted a significant amount of space in his penultimate chapter to Swedish social democracy and the wage earner funds (Pierson 1991 chapter 6). He too remained optimistic about the former if not the latter. However, in the same chapter in a revised edition published seven years later, neither Sweden nor the funds received a mention (Pierson 1998 chapter 6).

Gathering clouds

There was little around the time of the general election of 1988 to suggest trouble was brewing for the Swedish economy, but for the next few years the country lurched from one crisis to another.

By the end of the 1980s, the Swedish public sector had grown to employ over one third of the workforce. Public expenditure (including transfer expenditure) had risen to two-thirds of GDP and social expenditure to over one-third. Sweden had for many years experienced the highest tax rates in the world. The income replacement level for sickness benefit, parental benefit and unemployment benefit was 90 per cent. Six per cent of the population were in receipt of social assistance (compared with 4.1 per cent in 1980) (Statistical abstract of Sweden 1985, Statistical yearbook of Sweden 1994). A further 6.8 per cent of the labour force was in receipt of disability pensions (4.9 per cent in 1980) (ibid.).

The economy however was not in good shape. According to Pontusson, investment by Swedish companies abroad accelerated throughout the 1980s. It had amounted to around SEK 5 billion in 1980 and reached SEK 45 billion in 1990. Investment by foreign companies in Sweden however rose from a mere SEK 2 billion in 1980 to SEK 5 billion in 1990. The balance of payments deficit was also worse in 1989 than it had been in 1982 (Pontusson 1992 pp. 307 and 322). Partly as a consequence of unemployment being so low – it was only 1.5 per cent in 1989 – inflation had averaged 9 per cent from 1984 to

1991 (Lindbeck 1997 p. 64). Economic growth was low compared with Sweden's competitors. While Sweden had been fourth in the international league table for GDP per capita, it was ninth by 1990 (ibid. p. 33). In an attempt to redress the situation, the government tried, with the agreement of LOs leadership, to introduce a wage freeze and a prohibition on strikes in February 1990. Opposition to the latter measure was so great among grass roots trade unionists that it had to be abandoned and without the support of the Communist party for its remaining package of measures, the government fell.

Within a short time, Ingvar Carlsson – who had become Prime Minister after the assassination of Olof Palme in 1985 – formed another government, this time after coming to an agreement with the Liberal party. As a result, four important decisions were made before the General Election of 1991. Low inflation became the principal target for economic policy rather than low unemployment; an application was made to join the European Community (EC); the krona was tied to the ECU; and the tax system was reformed. The latter was an attempt to simplify the system and to reduce the marginal tax rate which had risen to over 70 per cent (Södersten 1990 p. 2). Under the reformed system, no income tax would be paid to central government on incomes below SEK 170 000.[3] Local income tax would be standardised at 30 per cent on such incomes. For incomes above SEK 170 000, there would be a national rate of 20 per cent and again a local rate of 30 per cent. Many tax deductions were reduced or eliminated (ibid. p. 4). The marginal rate for many low income earners was therefore 30 per cent and for high income earners 50 per cent.

If the Social Democrats seemed to have lost their way, the Bourgeois parties seemed to have found theirs. The Conservative party and the Liberal party produced a joint manifesto for the 1991 election with a clear neo-liberal message. But before they could begin their task they needed a healthy mandate from the electorate to implement what they called a *system shift*. Unfortunately for them, they did not get the former and they overestimated their ability to bring about the latter. The strength of the system they were trying to change was made up of more elements than social democratic ideology and was to prove difficult to shift.

Compromise and consensus

Throughout much of the period depicted above, reference has already been made to the role of a wide range of interests in the development of the Swedish welfare state. It is important that these should be made more explicit before we move on to examine the events of the 1990s. The degree to which Swedish institutions encourage and embody values of compromise and consensus can be exaggerated and simplified. Swedish history in the twentieth century has certainly been marked by some severe examples of conflict and confrontation. But the sense of accommodation reveals itself in a variety of ways not least in the behaviour of local councillors and members of the Riksdag. Contributions to debates are listened to in relative silence, in contrast to the rowdy behaviour which characterises foreign assemblies. There is an ease and casualness about Swedish politics which enables opponents to speak to each other at a variety of levels.

Sweden's electoral system is one based upon proportional representation. No government since 1932 has had an absolute majority over all other political parties. The Social Democrats have had to seek support from all of the other parties at different times. When the Bourgeois parties form their centre-right coalitions (as they did 1976–79, 1979–82, 1991–94) three and sometimes four parties have had to co-operate with each other. When Commissions are appointed by government to investigate major policy issues, their membership is politically broadly-based. While their recommendations are not accepted unconditionally, their work is a significant part of the policy process. When a major policy initiative is being made, the proposals are sent out "on remiss" to a wide range of organisations for their views and comments. Another traditional feature of Swedish politics has been the way in which the composition of administrative boards reflects a range of organisational interests. Often this would take the form of tripartite corporatism where business and trade union or professional representatives sat with government administrators to implement the policy decisions of government and parliament.

Inevitably this has meant that even when a policy initiative has originated with the Social Democratic party, and has been accepted by a Social Democratic government and Social Democratic Riksdag members, there has been an input from a wide variety of interests – political, commercial and professional – influencing its formation and implementation. Sweden is and always has been a pluralist society in which a multiplicity of organisations play a part in the policymaking process. It would therefore be odd to regard all welfare policies as purely or even principally, social democratic.

Conclusions

Although Swedish welfare has been heavily influenced by social democratic values and practice, the last two chapters have shown that it was also the product of a process of institutional compromise and consensus which drew heavily on other parts of the culture – other political ideologies; the rational, social engineering approach of the Myrdals; a moral tradition of sobriety; and a sense of national pride and identity. For these reasons it was unlikely that the electoral defeat of the Social Democrats in 1991 would be sufficient to bring about a system shift. In the remainder of this book, many of the political, institutional and cultural themes and values mentioned so far will, from time to time, recur.

4
Political and Economic Change

> Each of Europe's welfare regimes also corresponds to a particular industrial – economic configuration ... which sets the parameters for adjustment. Preserving welfare states will depend not only on the capacity of regimes to modify their respective institutions and programmes, but on the broader adaptability of their economies to international competition and global constraints.
>
> (Rhodes 1996 p. 305)

Introduction

If the Swedish people had wanted a neo-liberal *system shift*, they had the opportunity in 1991. The economy was in trouble and unemployment was rising. Neo-liberal ideas were being widely promoted and there were plenty of illustrations of neo-liberal experimentation in Europe and the USA. There was disillusion with the Social Democrats and they had clearly lost their sense of direction. The Conservative and Liberal parties had a clear platform and both were committed to membership of the EU. The scene was set for a right wing victory. In the end, an ambiguous result gave a confused mandate to the new government. Four years later, the Social Democrats were returned to office. The fruits of neo-liberalism were not to Swedish tastes.

This chapter will briefly describe the two periods of government 1991–94 and 1994–98 and the economic and political events which characterised them. Sweden's relationship with the EU and changes in public and social expenditure will also be examined. Mention will be made of the 1998 election which resulted in a further period of Social

Democratic rule. The chapter will conclude with commentaries by various Swedish experts upon this difficult time in Swedish history.

The Bourgeois government 1991–94

The 1991 election results

Months prior to the election, opinion polls had indicated similar support for the Conservatives (29 per cent) and Social Democrats (30 per cent). Another survey of public opinion claimed that 86 per cent of the population wanted a system shift (Sillén 1990). By the time of the election, the Social Democrats had recovered sufficiently to achieve nearly 38 per cent of the vote, remaining the largest party by far (see Table 4.1). It was not enough however to form a government. Unfortunately for the four Bourgeois parties, they failed to achieve an overall majority and were left in the parlous position of having to rely on a maverick newcomer – the anti-immigration, anti-taxation party New Democracy. The coalition might have been extended to the new party had the Liberal and Centre parties not made it clear that there was no way they would co-operate with the racism New Democracy represented. The only consolation for the Bourgeois bloc was that first time voters were overwhelmingly on their side. Under the country's system of proportional representation, whereby seats in the Riksdag were dependent upon gaining the support of at least 4 per cent of the electorate, the Left party just scraped in but the Environment party failed to do so.

Table 4.1: The Election of 1991

	% votes	No. of seats
Bourgeois parties		
Conservative	21.9	80
Liberal	9.1	33
Centre	8.5	31
Christian Democrat	7.1	26
Total	46.6	170
New Democracy	6.7	25
Socialist parties		
Social Democrat	37.6	138
Left (former Communist)	4.5	16
Total	42.1	154

Source: K. Brunnberg, (1991)

While there were fewer women in the Riksdag than previously, the gender balance in both parliament and government (two thirds men, one third women) remained impressive. The Conservative leader, Carl Bildt, became Prime Minister and his ministers for Finance, Justice and Foreign Affairs were all women. The Minister for Health and Social Affairs and Minister for Equality was the Liberal leader, Bengt Westerberg. This was to prove an interesting appointment. While Westerberg did his best to honour his neo-liberal commitment, he found it very difficult to make cuts in social expenditure. During his three year tenure, social expenditure remained at around 37 per cent of GDP. He even introduced a major reform to boost the help given to people with disabilities. Westerberg also set up two major commissions to investigate gender issues.

The government was to find that on many issues it lacked clear cut support within its own ranks. If one of the parties was unhappy about a particular policy initiative, support would have to be forthcoming from New Democracy or even the Social Democrats. Alternatively, it could be diluted or be dropped. The neo-liberal mandate was doomed from the start.

Economic fortunes

The government was determined to reduce public expenditure and taxation, to improve opportunities for small and medium-sized businesses, privatise state companies and reduce the amount of state welfare provision. In particular it intended to reduce the payroll taxes on employers which, from the mid-1970s, had financed the greater part of the social security system. These measures combined were intended to revive the country's economy. Unfortunately, during it's period of office, the Bourgeois government soon found itself having to cope with a major economic crisis. It presided over "the deepest recession" Sweden had experienced since the 1930s with a fall in GDP of 5 per cent between 1991 and 1993 (Lindbeck 1997 p. 65). Unemployment rose, the public sector deficit grew, and there was also a deficit on the balance of trade. Speculation in the weaker currencies tied to the ECU (the European Currency Unit) accelerated in September 1992. While the British government gave up the defence of sterling, withdrew from the Exchange Rate Mechanism and allowed the pound to float, the Swedish government tried another approach (*DN* 1/11/96). Interest rates were raised dramatically in a bid to stop selling of the krona. The National Bank spent SEK 250 billion buying up Swedish currency. Property and asset prices fell and the government had to bail out major banks "by an amount equivalent to 4 per cent of one year's GNP" (Lindbeck 1997 p. 67). Only after two months was the link with the ECU dropped. The consequence was, in effect, a devaluation of 20 per cent. While this gave an understandable boost to industrial production from 1993 onwards, the cost to the government of trying to preserve the value of the krona had been SEK 25 billion. As Britain's Conservative government was damaged by the currency crisis so was Sweden's Bourgeois coalition. Its claim to be able to manage the economy better than the Social Democrats had been severely damaged. Although the economy slowly began to recover, Swedish living standards had fallen considerably in the early 1990s. By 1994 GDP per capita showed Swedes in seventeenth place among OECD countries (OECD 1997).

Political events

During Britain's neo-liberal period, it was assumed that corporatist bargaining and the corporatist institutions which had developed during the 1960s and 1970s were part of the public sector problem. Not only did Margaret Thatcher shut trade unions and professional associations out of the decision making process, but severe controls on industrial action were introduced. There is little evidence that the Bourgeois government seriously considered disempowering or weakening those organisations which championed the public sector. SAF, the employers' federation, however – which for some time had been showing increasing dissatisfaction with the Social Democrats and what were seen as social democratic institutions – disengaged from all national corporatist bodies at the end of 1992.

In line with SAF proposals, the government did make some attempt to reduce employment rights and the power of trade unions (*RD* 1993 No. 31 p. 4). It became easier to sack badly-behaved employees, to provide temporary employment and certain exceptions were made to the "last in first out" principle. The trade union veto on co-determination boards was abolished and strikers could not blockade the premises of small firms. These changes, however, were quite minor compared with what some on the right had been hoping for. More significantly, one of the first acts of the new government was to abolish the wage earner funds.

There were signs that union membership was beginning to decline, with adverse consequences for the financing of individual unions and LO – but not as a result of any deliberate act of government.

Social Democratic newspapers and the labour movement's insurance company Folksam experienced financial difficulties which led to increased costs for the party. It was possible to interpret these events at the time as a sign that the social democratic model was in serious decline (Gould 1993a pp. 174–5).

When the government became embroiled in the currency crisis in 1992, Prime Minister Bildt became so frustrated by the unwillingness of New Democracy to make up its mind about the package of austerity measures his government wanted to introduce that he turned to the Social Democrats, who agreed to help. From this point on the fortunes of the Social Democratic party began to improve. It had demonstrated that even in opposition it was indispensable to the running of the country; in a national emergency, the Social Democrats were seen to rally to the country's defence. Subsequent attempts by the government to gain the support of the Social Democrats failed however. Attempts to control public expenditure were not successful and even plans for the privatisation of post, telephone, airline and rail services, announced in 1992, came to nothing.[1]

EU

One area in which the Bildt government can be said to have succeeded was in its negotiations with the European Union. Conservatives and business interests hoped that membership of the EU would mean a more competitive, less regulated, economy. Social Democrats who supported entry, felt a strong economy would be the best way of preserving the welfare state. Pro-EU trade unionists looked forward to the emergence of a "Red Europe" (Edin 1995; Randqvist 1995). But fears of membership remained high for many. Opposition to the EU in the past had arisen because it was felt that Sweden's neutrality would be compromised. The application to negotiate entry was, therefore, partly justified by the collapse of the Soviet Union's Eastern European bloc. Neutrality was no longer considered such an important issue. But there were other fears concerning EU membership. Swedish governments in the past had been committed to a high degree of openness. Public documents and information were more freely available than in many other countries. What would happen to the *offentlighetsprincip* if Sweden became part of the much more secretive EU? There were also fears about harmonisation, convergence and national autonomy. If social policy, tax rates and public expenditure were harmonised, it was felt, high Swedish standards would suffer. The convergence criteria required by European Monetary

Union (EMU) would have a similar effect. The European Bank, it was suggested, would decide Swedish economic policy and would be unaccountable for its actions. The Swedish government would no longer have the autonomy to make major economic decisions.

Many Swedes felt that other European countries had given up on unemployment, alcohol and drug misuse problems while they themselves considered these were important areas in which government should act. Moreover, Sweden was a leader in gender equality which itself was linked with the existence of a strong public sector and many women felt that their social and political achievements were at stake. Although the Commission, set up to examine the implications for women and the welfare state, came to positive conclusions, two of its female members wrote dissenting reservations claiming that the public sector generally, and women and the disabled in particular, would suffer (SOU 1993:117 pp. 233–40).

Many of these doubts continued to prevent a large section of the Swedish population from giving the EU its support, but the terms negotiated by the government were sufficiently encouraging for its Social Democratic successor to campaign for a yes vote in the 1994 referendum.

Public and social expenditure (including taxation)

By the end of the 1980s, taxes and social security contributions in Sweden amounted to 56 per cent of its GDP while government final consumption came to 26 per cent (Eurostat 1997 pp. 235 and 238). Most other EU countries had percentages ranging from 35 to 45 and 13 to 20 respectively. Soon after coming to power, the Bourgeois government announced its intention to cut public expenditure by SEK 10 billion each year of the three it would be in office. Each budget made the claim that cuts would be made but the end result never seemed to show much of an impact. When the Conservatives wanted to cut adult education, the Liberals, Centre party and the Christian Democrats did not. When the four Bourgeois parties agreed to abolish the partial pension, New Democracy sided with the parties of the left. This pattern continued throughout the government's period in office.

By 1994, public sector employment was down a few percentage points compared with the first year of the Bourgeois government's period of office; public and social expenditure were little changed; while the public sector deficit and national debt were quite a bit worse. The latter were a long way from meeting the convergence criteria for EMU (3 per cent and 60 per cent respectively) and represented a serious

Table 4.2: Public sector indicators (1992–94)

	1992	1993	1994
Public expenditure as % GDP*	69.4	72.8	70.0
Social expenditure as % GDP**	40.0	38.2	37.2
Public employment as % total labour force***	33.5	32.3	30.5
Public sector deficit as % GDP*	–7.8	–12.3	–10.3
National debt as % GDP*	67.1	76.0	79.3

Sources: The Swedish budget 1998*; Välfärdsfakta social 1997**; Statistical yearbook of Sweden 1995 and 1998***.

problem of indebtedness. The public sector was in surplus in the late 1980s but this had begun to decline from 1989. It had been aggravated partly by the 1990 tax reform which had failed to bring in as much revenue as the old system and partly by the rapid increase in unemployment. While there was some incompetence within the Bourgeois government, its sad performance was also due to international events and the lack of parliamentary power granted to it by the electorate. By 1994 taxes and social security contributions still represented 50 per cent of GDP and final consumption was 27 per cent of GDP (Eurostat Yearbook 1997 pp. 235 and 236). Most EU countries (with the exception of Denmark) remained some way below these figures.

Recognising this, the government had in fact set up a Commission, to examine reasons why it was difficult to change the Swedish system and to come up with recommendations as to how matters might be improved. Assar Lindbeck, the eminent economist, chaired the Commission and came to some interesting conclusions (SOU 1993:16). It recommended further cuts to public expenditure; a reduction in social insurance income replacement rates from 80–90 per cent to 70 per cent; more pluralism and competition in the provision of what were currently public services; a more disciplined budgetary process; four year parliaments; a halving of the number of MPs; the abolition of County Councils (Län) and a curtailment of state grants to a vast range of interest groups. The latter, it was suggested, often impeded the implementation of policies in the national interest through sectional mobilisation made possible by state funding.

Action was taken to lengthen the life of future parliaments and on the tightening up of the budgetary process, both of which enabled the next Social Democratic government to function more effectively. However, few other recommendations were acted on.

The Social Democratic government 1994–98

The 1994 election results

Having flirted with a version of neo-liberalism, 45 per cent of the electorate gave their support to the Social Democrats in the 1994 election (see Table 4.3). The four Bourgeois parties together totalled just over 41 per cent of the vote. Although the Social Democrats had a clear majority over the Centre-right opposition, they did not have an overall majority in the Riksdag. The Left party gained 6 per cent of the vote and the Environment party returned with 5 per cent. New Democracy received just over 1 per cent and was, therefore, ineligible for parliamentary seats. If the previous Centre-right regime had little room for manoeuvre, the new government was spoilt for choice. In theory it needed the support of one other party only to achieve a majority in the Riksdag.

The Conservatives must have been disappointed with their 22 per cent. Mid-term opinion polls often showed them as having the support of nearly 30 per cent of the electorate, but when an election came, they remained stuck at around 20 per cent. As for the Liberal and Centre parties, it seemed that they were in terminal decline. It was difficult to believe that in 1976, when the 44-year period of Social Democratic rule came to an end, the largest of the three Bourgeois parties was Centre with 24 per cent of the vote, followed by the Conservatives with nearly 16 per cent, and the Liberals with 11 per cent.

Table 4.3: The Election of 1994

	% vote	No. of seats
Bourgeois parties		
Conservative	22.3	80
Centre	7.7	27
Liberals	7.2	26
Christian Democrat	4.1	14
	41.3	147
Socialist parties		
Social Democrat	45.4	162
Left	6.2	22
	51.6	184
Environment	5.0	18
Total	97.9	349

Source: *RD* 1994 No. 29 p. 7

After three years of *system shifting,* public opinion polls showed large majorities (80 per cent support) for publicly-provided, publicly-financed services. However, there was no intention to expand the public sector by the incoming government. On the contrary, it was clear that the public expenditure deficit and the national debt would have to be rectified by a combination of expenditure savings and tax and contribution increases.

Economic fortunes

Economic growth showed signs of improvement even in the last year of the Bourgeois government and continued to grow by an average of 2.5 per cent each year until the end of 1998 (*RD* 1998 No. 13b p. 4). Industrial production had grown faster and labour market costs had declined more than any other developed country between 1992 and 1997 (*DN* 22/5/99). The state of public finances improved but the need to encourage the country's small business sector remained an issue. The balance of trade improved, largely due to the depreciated value of the krona. There was a healthy surplus from 1995 until 1998 with a predicted surplus up to 2002 (Ministry of Finance 1999 p. 35). However, Sweden's OECD ranking in terms of GNP per capita failed to rise. Sweden lay in eighteenth place in 1997 – the lowest ranking of any of the Scandinavian countries (OECD 2000).[2] Another worrying feature of the economy was that while export markets were improving rapidly, the domestic market remained sluggish. Unemployment came down slowly but seemed unlikely to meet the government's target of 4 per cent open unemployment by 2000. Inflation remained under 3 per cent throughout the period but concern was expressed about pay rises by SAF and OECD. Both claimed that there was a need for a more flexible labour market with reforms to employment rights, lower unemployment benefits and wider pay differentials. Productivity remained low in comparison with other OECD countries.

Foreign share ownership in Swedish companies increased to over 30 per cent in 1996 from 14 per cent in 1992. Increasing numbers of Swedish workers were also employed by foreign companies. Meanwhile large Swedish companies threatened to establish their headquarters abroad. While this could be seen as evidence of growing diversity and internationalisation it was also clear that companies like Ericsson were very critical of government policy. The Minister for Industry and Commerce, Tomas Östros, saw the threat as pressure to lower tax rates, reduce the size of the public sector and to reverse redistribution policies. One writer saw the whole process as one in which a small nation like Sweden no longer mattered in the game plan of corporate finance

(Anderson 1999 p. 32). "Swedish" companies no longer owed allegiance to their country of origin.

Government policy did become more enterprise friendly. Alongside attempts to reduce the public deficit, measures to improve economic growth were introduced in 1995. Part of the package was concerned to reduce company taxation and the state pension fund was allowed to provide industry with more risk capital. Taxes on energy use and environmental damage were used to replace "taxes" on employment, while extra investment was put into wind power (*RD* 1995 No. 34 p. 3). Another part of the package was concerned with tightening up the rules on unemployment benefit and providing extra resources to higher education.

Political events

After a number of months had passed, the Social Democratic government negotiated an agreement with the Centre party – an agreement which worked well, if not to Centre's advantage electorally or in terms of its declining membership. This provided the country with stable government for the following three years. The important task to hand was to bring a degree of discipline to public sector finances and this was clearly something both parties were able to work on together. Hostility between the Centre and its previous allies – the Liberal and the Conservative parties deepened. The fact that the Centre party could be an integral part of a Bourgeois regime for three years and subsequently co-operate for a long period of time with the Social Democrats is quite remarkable and testimony to the consensual aspects of the Swedish system.

For the Conservative party, the years 1994 to 1998 were difficult. Their leader, Carl Bildt, took a couple of years leave to act as a negotiator in the Balkans dispute. When he returned to the fray, in 1997, the initial results were promising. His party enjoyed front-running popularity in the opinion polls with the support of 35 per cent of the electorate. Bildt tried to inject a bit of caring and compassion into his party's image. He even promised what opinion polls had said the public wanted – to pay no more than 50 per cent of their earnings in income tax. But to no avail. The argument that public expenditure and taxation were too high; that Sweden like Atlantis would sink even further; that the 2.2 million employed in the private sector were having to support 4 million dependants in the public sector would have little effect in the 1998 election (Bildt 1998). He wanted more privatisation and deregulation, the electorate did not. By September 1998, the Conservatives would find that yet again they had barely moved beyond their usual 20 per cent support.

For many Social Democrats, their government was to be a disappointment. They would argue that the leadership had moved to the right and had adopted neo-liberal ways of thinking. Both prime ministers – Ingvar Carlsson, who retired early in 1996 and his successor, Göran Persson – saw the maintenance of sound public finances as a priority; both tried to cement stronger links with industry and commerce; both sought to improve the conditions in which small companies could thrive. Persson, in particular, expanded the influence of the "modernisers" within his own circle of advisers. He was well aware of the way in which the forces of globalisation and internationalisation had limited the autonomy of governments. In the last year before the election he tried to create a new vision for Sweden drawing on the need to promote information technology, lifelong learning, small businesses and a sustainable environment (Persson 1998). If Carlsson had, in 1994, sought to rally the electorate behind equality and feminism, Persson, in 1998, tried the same with ecological issues. He wanted the "People's Home" to be an ecological model for the rest of the world.

Traditionalists, who tended to have stronger links with the trade union movement, were more concerned to defend the public sector and maintain benefit levels. Persson was also able to satisfy their demands due to the expected budget surplus in 1999. At the party Congress in September 1997 ministers were divided over whether to prioritise increased social spending or lower taxes. The former won the day. The announcement of increased spending on child allowances, student grants, education and health was applauded. Not only did it satisfy most sections of the party but it was intended to show the electorate that the Social Democrats remained the party of the public sector. It was also hoped that this increased spending would recapture the support of those who in opinion polls were giving their support to the Left party.

EU

The biggest single change to take place in Sweden between 1994 and 1998 was the decision to enter the EU. Negotiations had proceeded well under the previous government. The Social Democratic leadership gave its support to the yes campaign in the referendum, alongside the Bourgeois parties. The Left party and the Environment party campaigned against entry. The referendum in November 1994 demonstrated the ambivalence of Swedes to the EU. With an 82 per cent turnout, 52 per cent voted in favour and 47 per cent against. The majority of women were against entry, as were the overwhelming majority of working class people. Many remained convinced that membership was a threat to national autonomy and the welfare state. In the elections to the European Parliament the following year, the tide of opinion was already beginning to turn. Only 42 per cent of the electorate participated. The Social Democrats received 28 per cent of the vote, while the Left party gained 13 per cent and the Environment party 17 per cent (*RD* 1995 No. 29)! Subsequent opinion polls showed the Sweden to be the most hostile of member countries towards the EU (*DN* 10/12/97).

One of the principal reasons for the increasing success of the Left party was its clear opposition to the EU. This opposition was often very nationalistic in tone. Left party members, interviewed by *Dagens Nyheter* in 1996, had few qualms about flying the national flag on the national day as part of a campaign to get Sweden out of the EU. When their aim was accomplished, they claimed, their flags would not be put away in wardrobes. "We will raise them on our red cottages, where we shall catch herring and drink schnapps)" (*DN* 6/6/96). Swedish nationalism, which had already become inflamed by the issue of immigration and refugees, was further deepened by the alien threat of the EU.

According to one journalist, there was also a religious dimension to Sweden's hostility towards the EU. It was seen as "a Catholic project which threatened our Protestant values" (von Sydow 1998); the subsidiarity principal which informed EU policymaking derived from Catholic teaching. It was not difficult for countries which already accepted supranational religious authority, von Sydow argued, to consider the possibility of accepting supranational political power. It was no coincidence, she claimed, that Protestant countries – Sweden, Britain and Denmark – had decided not to take part in monetary union. She went on to argue that there were many policy differences which followed religious lines, but that with the unification of Germany and the ideological prominence of individualism and free market economics, Protestant influence was growing.

A study carried out in 1998 – three years after entry – suggested that the direct effects of membership on social policy had been minimal (Gould 2000). More important was the indirect effect of trying to fulfil the convergence criteria for membership of EMU. Some denied the impact was that great. Social Democrats, for example, who had been in favour of EU membership argued that the cuts to public and social expenditure might have happened a little more swiftly because of the EMU convergence criteria, but said they would have occurred anyway due to domestic and international pressures. They argued that Sweden could no longer rely on running a deficit or currency devaluation to sustain its public sector. It needed a period of budgetary restraint. Unemployment, it was argued, would thereby be reduced and welfare benefits and services would be financed more easily. Other Social Democrats were not so sure. The Social Affairs Minister, Margot Wallström told a conference held in 1997 jointly with LO, that joining EMU would probably damage Swedish welfare (*DN* 15/5/97). The Taxation Minister thought further tax reductions to come into line with other EU countries "would break this country" (*DN* 15/6/97). Sweden, he said, had higher taxes in order to maintain "a strong society ... We have higher ambitions for the public sector and the social insurance system, than many other countries."

These fears were echoed in the consultation process concerning a Commission of Inquiry's report on the implications of European Monetary Union (Ds 1997:22). A range of organisations with some responsibility for socially related matters expressed misgivings about joining. These included the National Boards for Employment and Social Affairs, LO and TCO, and the Associations for County Councils and for Municipalities. There was a concern that EMU was almost solely about financial rectitude and inflation control. Unemployment, poverty and social inequality, it was argued, were of little concern to those responsible for economic policy. Moreover, there seemed to be no democratic control over the European Central Bank which could ensure a consideration for the political and social consequences of its actions. Higher unemployment coupled with lower social expenditure could only mean growing inequality. How could you expect the unemployed to move to areas where there were jobs when this meant learning a new language and adapting to a new culture?

More trenchant critics of the EU tended to be on the left consisting of many Social Democrats, together with members of the Left and Environmental parties. These were much clearer about what the loss of national autonomy in economic policy meant. The leader of the Left party thought the convergence criteria were bringing Sweden down to the level of other European countries. An Environment party MEP wrote that following the EUs currency policy had led to the growth in unemployment.

> We managed to tear down in less than ten years a welfare state that took generations to build up (Gahrton 1997 p. 70).

Thus, membership of the EU was generally regarded as partly responsible for the erosion of the Swedish welfare state. It might have been felt that certain changes were inevitable anyway; that international forces were principally responsible; or even that the Swedish government was itself to blame because of its willing complicity with EU economic policy. But in one way or another the EU was seen as a factor in hastening the process of social disarmament.

Public and social expenditure

The new budget process, which had been designed to make expenditure cuts easier to implement, was due to change from January 1996. Government income and expenditure plans were to be placed before the Riksdag at the beginning of the parliamentary year (September) and decided upon by the following January. The intention was that the whole process should become more disciplined. The power of government in the budgetary process was strengthened and that of the opposition parties weakened. Ceilings were placed upon areas of expenditure and motions in the Riksdag to increase expenditure could only be made if they were accompanied by proposals to make cuts of a similar size in the same area (*RD* 1996 No. 13a p. 6).

The first budget of the new government was introduced early in 1995 to cover an eighteen-month period until the new timetable could be introduced. From the beginning it was clear that the deficit should become a surplus by 1999. While large cuts were to be made to public sector and welfare benefits, part of the deficit was to be made up by raising taxes and contributions.

As can be seen in Table 4.4, public expenditure had declined to 62 per cent of GDP between 1994 and 1998. In the next two years it was expected to fall a further 3 per cent to 58 per cent (*RD* 1997 No. 14 p. 4). Social expenditure fell a little to 33.3 per cent by 1998 and public sector employment was just below 30 per cent of the workforce. But while the budget deficit had disappeared, the national

Table 4.4: Public sector indicators (1995–8)

	1995	1996	1997	1998
Public expenditure as % GDP*	67.3	65.8	63.9	62.4
Social expenditure as % GDP**	35.2	34.5	33.6	33.3
Public employment as % total labour force ***	30.3	29.7	29.5	29.4
Public sector deficit as % GDP*	–7.8	–2.1	–1.1	2.2
National debt as % GDP*	78.0	77.2	77.0	75.4

Sources: *The Swedish budget 1999; **Välfärdsfakta social 2000; ***Statistical yearbook of Sweden 1998.

debt remained above 70 per cent. By 2001, it was predicted that there would be a large budget surplus and that the national debt would be only 65 per cent of GNP (*RD* 1998 No. 13a p. 7). In 1998, Sweden still had the largest public sector in the EU. Final consumption was 26.6 per cent compared with less than 22 per cent for most other countries (Eurostat 2000). Taxes and social security contributions also remained comparatively high at 54.1 per cent in 1997 when most other member states were below 47.5 per cent (Eurostat 1999).

A continuing debate throughout the Social Democratic period of office was the alleged impact of high taxation on economic performance. At different times, OECD, the IMF and the EU all called for lower taxation and public expenditure. Sweden remained at the top of the international league for taxation. There was also constant pressure from the business sector and the Centre-right parties to place more effort on reducing taxation. Social Democrats and LO representatives continued to deny that there was any clear evidence that economic performance and rates of taxation were in any way connected, yet in 1997 tax relief was given to small businesses in the hope that they would grow and create employment (*RD* 1997 No. 14 p. 6).

If the intention of the 1990 tax reform had been to simplify the tax system, the consequence of trying to bring the budget into balance had resulted in several new additions and complications.[3] In particular the tax on high income earners of 20 per cent was increased to 25 per cent in 1995. In the circumstances, it might have been expected that the Finance Minister would have wanted to reduce taxation in the run up to the election in 1998. On the contrary, tax cuts had to wait. Instead resources were devoted to schools, health and social care (*RD* 1998 No. 13b p. 4). This might have been more calculated than at first appeared to be the case. Svallfors' studies of public opinion over two decades suggested that even more Swedes were in fact willing, in the 1990s, to pay additional taxes for education, health care and the care of the elderly than they had been in 1981 (*DN* 28/7/98).

1998 election campaign and result

Opinion polls showed that the fortunes of the political parties varied during the years 1994–98. There was a time when the Conservatives broke the 30 per cent barrier and left the Social Democrats trailing. The Social Democrats fell to just below 30 per cent a few times and never rose beyond 40 per cent. The Conservatives uniquely achieved 35.5 per cent in August 1997. The biggest consistent change was the rise in the support for the Left party. Discontent with the Social

Democrats seemed not to benefit the Centre-right but its radical rival. Support for the Left party grew to 15 per cent in 1995 and to 13.5 for the Environmentalists in 1996. The only surprise in the 1998 election was the sudden upsurge of the Christian Democrats (see Table 4.5).

In the run-up to the election each of the smaller parties called for an alliance with the Social Democrats who flirted with each of them in turn. In the event, the Social Democrats did badly, but remained the largest party. What was clear, however, was that the Left party had benefited from Social Democrat desertions. The two socialist parties combined had 48.4 per cent of the vote. While many assumed that Persson would try and come to an agreement with one of the Centre parties or even the Conservatives, it was to the Left party and the Environment party that he was to turn for support. The Centre and Liberal parties joined the Environment party close to the 4 per cent margin while the Conservatives yet again had to be content with their usual result.

Demographic changes

Before we examine Swedish welfare in the chapters which follow, it is important to remind ourselves of a some important demographic features that are relevant to social policy. Sweden has a population of 8.8 million in a country twice the size of Britain. It has a population density of only 20 persons per square kilometre compared with 239 for the UK and 378 for the Netherlands (Statistical Yearbook of Sweden 1998 p. 428). Nor does Sweden have the kind of conurbations which we associate with many other advanced industrial countries – Greater

Table 4.5: The Election of 1998

	% vote	No. of seats
Bourgeois parties		
Conservative	22.7	82
Centre	5.1	18
Liberals	4.7	17
Christian Democrat	11.8	42
Socialist parties		
Social Democrat	36.6	131
Left	12.0	43
Environment	4.5	16
Total	97.4	349

Source: *DN* 22/9/98

Stockholm has 1.7 million people while Gothenburg has 800 000 and Malmö only 500 000.

The worsening dependency ratio

Another characteristic of the population for many years has been the high percentage of elderly people. Some observers have actually implied that this simple demographic fact may have been a significant reason for Sweden's low economic growth in the last three decades.[4] Certainly, it must have had some impact on the economy in comparison with countries like Japan, which at the beginning of the 1970s had to find resources for an elderly population of just 7 per cent in contrast to Sweden's 14 per cent. By 1991 almost 18 per cent of the population was over 65 and just less than 5 per cent over the age of 80 (see Table 4.6).

Both of these percentages are expected to increase by 2010, when quite a few other countries like Japan and Britain will have caught up. By 2030, nearly a quarter of the population will be over 65 and 8 per cent over 80. If the welfare system is finding it a struggle to meet the needs of elderly people now, how is it going to manage in the twenty first century? This is clearly not a problem for the Swedes alone, but how they are coping and will cope in the future may have lessons for us all. If an ageing population really does slow down economic growth, there will be many other countries experiencing the problems Sweden has faced for many years.

Apart from the problem of coping with an ageing population, Sweden found itself facing a baby boom from 1989 to the mid-1990s. In the early 1980s, 90 000 children were born annually. By 1991 this figure reached 124 000 (Statistical Yearbook of Sweden 1998 p. 47).

Table 4.6: Elderly population (in '000s and as a percentage of the total population)

	1991	2010 est.	2030 est
Age group	('000s)		
65+	1532	1737	2229
65–79	1152	1237	1490
80%	380	500	739
(% of total population)			
65+	17.7	19.2	23.9
65–79	13.3	13.7	16.0
80+	4.4	5.5	7.9

Source: adapted from Statistical Yearbook of Sweden 1994 and 1998

Although by 1996, the figure had reverted to 95 000, the implications of the early 1990s blip for social and educational expenditure were being realised later in the decade and would continue to have an effect for some years to come.

Immigrants and refugees

Another important change with social, economic and political repercussions has been the change in Sweden's ethnic balance. Early accounts of the Swedish welfare state often referred to the homogeneity of its population. Shortages of labour in the 1960s and 1970s led to large numbers of immigrants from southern Europe. Refugees from the Middle East, South America and Africa came later. The fall of the Berlin wall and the conflicts in Yugoslavia resulted in a further wave of refugees prompting widespread public concern and a more restrictive approach to immigration by the Bourgeois government. However, in 1993 and 1994, thousands of Bosnians sought refuge in Sweden and 50 000 were admitted – proportionally much more than any other European country. By 1996, over 900 000 people in Sweden had been born overseas compared with only 100 000 in 1945 (*DN* 17/10/96). Sweden's non-Nordic population constituted nearly 8 per cent of the population, with half from other European countries and half from the Third World.

Table 4.7: Ethnic minorities in Sweden ('000s and percentages) 1996

Place of origin	Total	Swedish citizens	Aliens	Born in Sweden
Scandinavia	334	170	121	43
% of population	3.8	1.9	1.4	0.5
The West				
Europe	333	152	157	24
North America	24	10	12	2
Total	357	162	169	26
% of population	4.1	1.8	1.9	0.3
Third World				
Africa	52	24	25	4
South America	49	29	19	0
Asia	227	119	94	14
Total	328	172	138	18
% of population	3.7	1.9	1.6	0.2
Final total	1019	504	428	87
% of population	11.4	5.7	4.8	1.0

Source: Adapted from Statistical Yearbook of Sweden 1998 pp. 64–7

A number of policies were introduced in the 1990s to encourage integration. Nevertheless, the economic difficulties of the last decade and the problem of unemployment led to increasing manifestations of ethnic conflict – racially-motivated assaults, racial discrimination, widening inequalities and the emergence of neo-nazi and anti-immigrant political parties. In response, governments have adopted a very restrictive immigration policy with compulsory finger-printing of all new arrivals and even introduced incentives for repatriation. At the same time they have created measures to help newcomers financially and to counter discrimination.

While the establishment – senior politicians, military leaders and even the monarch – have commendably and unequivocally opposed racism and while many ordinary Swedes have disrupted neo-nazi and racist demonstrations, two thirds of the population in 1992 disapproved of the level of immigrants and asylumseekers being admitted and large proportions of the population expressed fears about immigrants living on social assistance, the cost of providing for refugees, the character of those entering the country and their propensity to commit crime (*DN* 18/10/92).

Commentaries

In the early 1990s a neo-liberal hegemony seemed to be emerging in Sweden. The perceived failure of the Social Democrats led to a new confidence in the market, privatisation and competition. The old solutions were not working. The new, untried ones might. A spate of publications criticised excessive public spending, inflated social benefits and the inefficiency of state administration. Ståhl *et al.* argued that economic growth lagged behind other countries like those in the Far East; that cheap goods from Eastern Europe made Swedish wages and benefits unsustainable; that unless the power of the trade unions was curbed and public expenditure drastically reduced, Sweden would share the same fate as some South American economies (Ståhl, Wickman and Arvidsson 1993). They went on to say that Sweden had gone from being a *social state* in the 1960s, to a *taxation state* in the 1970s and a *debt-management state* in the 1980s and 1990s. Another economist, Eklund, regarded the public sector deficit as having serious structural weaknesses. It would not simply go away as the economy improved (Eklund 1993). Södersten, who had played a key role in the tax reform of 1990, castigated the public sector as an inefficient and intolerable burden on the country. Health and social services, he wrote, were overstaffed and too many people found it easy to live on benefits (Södersten 1992). The political right and many economists made similar suggestions as to how the problems should be tackled. In particular it was felt that government was vulnerable to pressure from too many interest groups; institutional forces were too powerful; the budgetary process was insufficiently disciplined; and three-year parliaments were too short for governments to act in the long term interests of the country. Many of these were cited in the Lindbeck Commission which had been set up to propose solutions to the economic crisis (SOU 1993:16).

These and similar arguments continued to be made in the mid-90s after the Bildt government had fallen and the Social Democrats had resumed office. Some of them, however, were a little difficult to sustain in the light of the previous government's experience. It was not so easy to advance market ideas and solutions when a government committed to them had presided over the most serious recession the country had experienced; when the private banking sector had needed state aid to survive; and mistakes by the National Bank had further worsened the public sector debt (*DN* 3/11/96). The much vaunted simplification of the tax system, which had been encouraged and endorsed by leading economists had also worsened the economic situation (*RD* 1995 No. 38). In 1995, it was still possible to criticise the failure of previous governments and the new Carlsson government for a lack of budgetary control. Cuts to public and social expenditure, announced at the beginning of the budgetary year somehow disappeared as the process continued (*DN* 8/3/95). After 1996 however, the new budgetary reforms began to bite; the agreement between the Social Democrats and Centre in a four-year parliament bore fruit; public and social expenditure did come down; and the public deficit and national debt were also reduced.

Those on the left, of course, complained that the electorate had not thrown out the Bourgeois parties only to be betrayed by the neo-liberal policies of Social Democratic modernisers. Early in the new government's period of office leading local Social Democrats warned the government not to make any further cuts to their services. In their view the electorate at the local level had rejected neo-liberal thinking even more strongly than at the national level. The Conservatives had been routed. It was clear that good quality health, welfare and education – publicly-provided – had been what the voters had wanted (Arvidsson *et al.* 1995). LO, around the same time, warned the government to make no further attacks on the security system and to leave unions and business to negotiate their own affairs (Jonsson 1995). Later, other union figures attacked the obsession with competition and urged the government to accept that it was not always appropriate for the provision of certain services and was often counter-productive (Erlandsson *et al.* 1997).

Rudolph Meidner, one of the architects of the Active Labour Market Policy back in the 1960s, argued that capitalism had won. In an interview in *Dagens Nyheter*, he said that the Swedish model had been built on the premise that it was important for the state to set up institutions and enact policies which would limit the power of capital. All of this had been abandoned.

> Today nothing exists of the restrictive policy which brought stability. There is nothing left of the thoughts of co-operation between state, unions and capital; nothing left of the solidaristic pay policy. Now there is nothing other than naked profitability and internationalisation. Everything else is finished (cited in Bratt 1997)

He claimed that large Swedish companies could now threaten the Finance Minister where in previous generations co-operation had prevailed. He said that wage earners' money invested in pension funds could be used for speculation against their interests; and that the monopoly bourgeois press made it impossible for LO to complain about this for fear of seeming to open up the wage earner fund debate.

Other Social Democrats seemed to be willing to admit that there had been mistakes in the past for which their governments had been responsible. Villy Bergström, who like Meidner had been employed as a researcher for LO, admitted early on that there had been a lack of control over the public sector in the 1980s which had led to a labour shortage and inflation (Bergström 1993). He subsequently demonstrated that the explosion in public expenditure had been largely due to transfer payments (Bergström and Vredin 1997 pp. 234–6). He also thought the Social Democrats had been too ambitious in their attempts to achieve social equality and had not recognised the problem of reduced incentives. Unlike Meidner, he thought that government attempts to control the economy had often resulted in excessive rules. Moreover the tax system had favoured large over small businesses. His overall conclusion was that the Swedish model had traditionally sought to achieve a balance between equality and efficiency. In the 1970s and 1980s, he claimed, governments had leaned too much towards the former. In the 1990s, efficiency had become the priority.

He seemed to have little doubt that the pendulum would swing in the opposite direction over time. The last words in his paper were, "Long live the Swedish model." (ibid. p. 247)

If the Swedish model has survived, part of the reason must be the electoral behaviour of the Swedish people and their attitudes towards the welfare state. Two thirds of the population disagreed that government should reduce rather than increase social programmes (Andersen *et al.* 1999 p. 245). Andersen *et al.* argued that support was greater for some services and benefits than others (health services, old age pensions, unemployment benefit and child care rather than social assistance and housing allowances) and among some social groups (working class, public sector workers, women) but generally it remained high. Svallfors, who had monitored public opinion on a range of issues for two decades, explained this by arguing that in every society there was a "moral economy", a set of dynamically-changing values which set limits on what government could do (Svallfors 1996 p. 17). Those who ignored this moral economy, did so at their peril. He rejected various interpretations of what had happened to the Swedish welfare state. There had been no retreat, as some had claimed. Nor was there evidence of, what he called, Korpi's "heroic" view of a society struggling towards socialism. He also rejected the "cynical" view that the welfare state persisted because of the self-interest of those who were employed by it or who received benefits from it. In his view the moral economy of the Swedes was little more than a striving for integration and the avoidance of marginalisation. People acted in their own self-interest but they recognised a wider, public interest. "Rational calculation and a normatively based set of rules exist side by side." (ibid. p. 20) Svallfors argued that a gap had grown between the opinion of Sweden's private sector élite and wider public opinion. The Swedish welfare state was part of the people's national identity. He warned that if membership of the EU deprived the Swedes of that, other, more destructive forces might come to define what being *Swedish* meant in the future (ibid. p. 221).

Summary and conclusions

The period 1991–94 required a strong government if it was going to effect a system shift. The Swedish electorate did not give such a mandate to the Bourgeois parties. Their subsequent failure was not entirely of their own making. In 1994, the Social Democrats were left with the job of not only clearing up the mess left by the Centre-right government but the mess they themselves had previously helped to create. By the end of their period of office in 1998, they had certainly achieved a more sustainable public sector. Their achievement was, however, in no small part due to some of the reforms initiated by their predecessors. Those on the Left might complain that too much ground had been conceded but few could deny that some change had been necessary. Those on the right certainly insisted that not enough had been done but it was no longer easy to claim that a system shift was necessary to put things right. The electorate was not happy with cuts and privatisation and had not opted for parties promising lower taxation. Nor by the end of the 1990s was it possible to point to countries like Britain and the USA and claim their people's security was better served by a diet of markets and competition. Whatever advantages may have accrued to countries adopting the neo-liberal approach, there were clear disadvantages to be set against them. As for the dynamism of the Asian Tiger economies and Japan – after the financial debacle of the 1990s – they could no longer be regarded as models for the future.

The electoral behaviour of Swedes would suggest that the majority continue to prefer a society which provides a high degree of collective security. However, as their economy has become more internationalised, their sovereignty more Europeanised and their population more homogenised, many Swedes have also become fearful of threats to their national identity.

5
Social Insecurity: Benefits and Services

Welfare and the People's Home in the words' correct meaning no longer exist in Sweden. It is a finished chapter in Swedish history.

(Arne Thorén 1997)[1]

Introduction

A recent comparative study of Nordic states described what was known as the Nordic welfare model as having the following characteristics (Kautto 1999 p. 13):

- The scope of public social policy is large
- An emphasis on full employment, accompanied by active labour market measures
- A high degree of universalism
- Income security based upon flat-rate and earning-related benefits
- High social expenditure as a proportion of GDP and high taxation
- Low income inequality
- Gender equality

Sweden certainly conformed to these criteria prior to the 1990s and had been much admired for the high value of its social benefits and the comprehensiveness and quality of its state-run services.

When the Bourgeois government was elected in 1991, it hoped to achieve a system change. Its aim was to return to "fundamental security"; to reduce income related benefits; to rely more on the private sector; and to create more freedom of choice. The Social Democrats in 1994 hoped to overturn whatever the coalition had achieved. However, both governments in the 1990s felt impelled to reduce total social expenditure. The former through ideological conviction and the latter out of economic necessity. This chapter will examine the outcome in terms of developments in social insurance, social services, social assistance (SA) and health care. Health care and social insurance are covered because they are regarded as major contributors to the reduction of inequality (Wilensky 1975). Social services are included, partly because as they are responsible for dealing with vulnerable groups and their problems but also because, in Sweden, a very broad section of the population use them for child care and the care of the elderly.

The administration of social insurance is the responsibility of the National Social Insurance Board which operates through local offices. Social services, which in addition to providing care and support to a wide range of groups also administers SA, are the responsibility of 288 local municipalities or district councils. Health care is run by the 26 county councils.[2] Both social services and health care are supervised by the National Board of Health and Social Welfare (Socialstyrelsen). These national boards are accountable to the Ministry for Health and Social Affairs which has ultimate responsibility for national policy and budgetary issues.

Social insurance

This section will cover sickness insurance, early retirement pensions, parental benefit and child allowances. It will not include old age pensions or unemployment insurance as these will be dealt with in Chapters 6 and 7.

The "base amount"

An important feature of social benefits in Sweden is the *base amount* which represents 20 per cent of the average industrial wage and is used as a yardstick for a wide range of cash benefits. For example, the upper income limit for the calculation of sickness benefit is 7.5 times the base amount. Those earning below 7.5 times the base amount were entitled to a sickness benefit amounting to a certain percentage of their gross income. Those earning more than this figure were only entitled to the same percentage of this upper limit. Basic pensions, disability pensions and guidelines issued on SA levels were all calculated with reference to the base amount. The base amount was originally raised every year in line with the consumer price index. However, for most of the 1990s the base amount was not raised in line with prices. Between 1991 and 1998, its value declined by 12 per cent (*Vår trygghet* 1998 p. 23).

Sickness benefit

There were numerous changes to sickness benefit during the 1990s. These occurred in part to reduce social expenditure but partly because the experience of the 1980s suggested that many people were abusing the system. By the end of the 1980s sickness benefit, which was taxable, amounted to 90 per cent of income (on incomes up to 7.5 times the base amount). When combined with an additional 10 per cent from negotiated agreements with employers, many workers could be sick and be no worse off than when they were working. The single waiting day (a period before which benefit could not be claimed) had been abolished in 1987. Concern had been growing for some time about the high amount of absenteeism due to sickness in Sweden compared with other similar countries but only when economic problems began to mount did the motivation to tackle the problem arise.

There were six major attempts to change the system. The first under the Social Democrats in 1991, the next two under the Bourgeois government and the rest under the Social Democrats. As can be seen from Table 5.1, benefit was reduced to 75 per cent for the first three days of sickness. In 1993, a single waiting day was reintroduced and compensation was reduced for the second and third days and those in excess of 90 days. Subsequently, compensation was further reduced to 75 per cent by the Social Democrats who then raised it again, in 1998, after considerable pressure from within the labour movement. The Bourgeois government had also introduced the idea of sickness pay, payable by employers, for the first 14 days of sickness. The Social Democrats increased this to 28 days, but again were pressured into a reversal in 1998.

Table 5.1: Compensation levels for sickness benefit and sickness pay as a percentage of income

Days of sickness	March 1991	Jan. 1992	April 1993	Jan. 1996	Jan. 1997	Jan. 1998
1	75	75	0	0	0	0
2–3	75	75	65	75	75	80
4–90	90	90	90	75	75	80
90–365	90	90	80	75	75	80
365+	90	90	70	75	75	80
Days of sickness paid by employers	0	14	14	14	28	14

Sources: Adapted from Svensson and Brorsson 1997, *Vår trygghet* 1996–98

These changes seem to have achieved the two things they were designed to do. Absenteeism and costs fell quite dramatically (Svensson and Brorsson 1997 p. 77; Palme and Wennemo 1998 p. 27). This had been achieved without damaging the basic principles of the system. Two other trends need to be mentioned. One is a tightening up of definitions around sickness and related benefits, the other is an increased emphasis upon rehabilitation. Employers and the Social Insurance Board were expected to co-operate over rehabilitative measures where it was thought that sickness leave might be reduced as a result.

Disability pensions

Disability pensions were originally intended for those who for medical reasons became unable to work. Under pressure from LO, the law was changed in 1970 to include older workers, who "are judged as to whether they have the ability or opportunity to continue to earn a living through work they have previously done or other suitable work" (cited in Berglind 1994). In 1978 there were 273 000 people (6 per cent of the workforce) receiving a state early retirement pension (Statistical Abstract of Sweden 1985). By 1991 this had grown to 323 000 and was regarded as a major problem. Labour market reasons for receiving an early pension became invalid in October 1991 (Ståhlberg 1997 p. 56), but the numbers continued to grow. They reached a peak of 411 000 in 1994 (9.5 per cent of the workforce) and have come down only a little since then (Statistical Yearbook of Sweden 1998). Eligibility rules were sharpened by the Bourgeois government and the Social Democrats with the result that the number of new cases declined steadily by a third after 1993 (Palme and Wennemo 1998 p. 18; SOU 2000: 3 p. 80).

Parental benefit

Parental insurance was introduced in Sweden in 1974. Both parents were entitled to leave while a child was under four years of age. In addition, leave could be claimed when a child was sick for up to 60 days each year until the child was 12. The benefit was originally fixed at the same percentage of income as sickness benefit and it has followed much the same pattern during the 1990s. A major change introduced by Bengt Westerberg, the Social Affairs Minister in the Bildt administration, was to make one month dependent upon the father taking up the benefit (with the added inducement of a slightly inflated amount).

A flat rate benefit existed for low income parents, but as a concession to the Christian Democrats it was replaced in 1994 by a Care

Allowance designed to encourage a parent (in all likelihood the mother) to stay at home permanently with young children and was conditional upon them not sending their child to a day nursery. This was seen by many women as a reactionary step to keep them out of the labour market and was abolished by the succeeding government.

Child allowances

Child allowances during the 1980s maintained their value at around 20 per cent of the base amount. An allowance was given for every child under 16. Those over 16 but still in full-time schooling received a student allowance. In 1989, large families – with more than three children under 16 – received 190 per cent of a single allowance for the fourth child and 240 per cent for the fifth. When the 1990 tax reform (see Chapter 3) was introduced families with young children were compensated with higher than average increases in child allowances. The Bourgeois government postponed this rise when it came to office but otherwise continued to maintain the value of the allowance. The Social Democratic government reduced their value in 1995 (as part of a strategy to eliminate the public sector deficit) and removed the additional allowances for *future* large families. When the need to cut social expenditure was no longer regarded as necessary, the allowance was raised again and the additions for large families restored (Elmér *et al.* 1998 p. 98)

Social services

Social services in Sweden were integrated in the Social Services Act of 1981. The framework legislation replaced the previous detailed and prescriptive laws on child care, SA and the care of alcoholics that had been enacted in the 1950s. The new legislation which had been passed by a Centre-right government, but had all party support, expressed the aim of meeting the needs of individuals while respecting their integrity. The new integrated departments of social services were to be responsible for services to the elderly, the disabled and day care for children. They were also responsible for cash support in the form of means-tested SA. Under separate legislation, social workers had powers to take children and adults with substance misuse problems into compulsory care. The care of the elderly will be covered in Chapter 6 while the care of substance misusers will be dealt with in Chapter 9.

During the 1990s, municipalities were prevented from raising their local taxes by central government, yet they were encouraged to take on the extra responsibility of running schools and to accept alternative ways of organising child care and the care of the elderly. On the whole the trend was towards community care rather than institutional care; voluntary care rather than compulsion. In addition, the Bourgeois government was keen to introduce greater reliance on the voluntary, informal and private sectors and create more choice and competition in service provision. However, the Minister for Health and Social Affairs, Bengt Westerberg, was also determined that Sweden's high welfare standards for the whole population be maintained if not improved.

Care of people with disabilities

The care of those with disabilities seems to have benefited considerably from the influence of Westerberg. Not only did the care allowance for parents with disabled children rise by 30 per cent only months after the election but even bigger changes were afoot (Kjellander 1991). In 1993, on the basis of a Commission on Disability a new law (LSS – the law on support and services for the functionally impaired), which came into effect at the beginning of 1994, was passed to give more rights to people with disabilities and their carers. In particular, the disabled were to have the right to choose a personal assistant, to be paid for by the municipalities and central government. County councils were given new obligations for rehabilitation and to provide advice, support and various services such as short-stay respite care (*RD* 1993 No. 17 p. 10). Although the legislation was criticised for being too hasty in closing down institutions and for not implementing some of the Disability Commission's recommendations, it was supported by all parties. Municipalities were likely to bear most of the costs of these reforms since many disabled people were being released from institutional care into the community. Some of the costs were to be borne by central government, others were to be paid for by a transfer of funds from the counties which no longer bore the costs of institutional care.

Unfortunately, Westerberg underestimated the total cost of his reforms. His SEK 2.4 billion "grew to SEK 4.1 billion in 1996 and SEK 4.5 billion in 1997" (*DN* 28/10/97). The Social Democratic government tried a number of times to change the rules to keep their own costs down; this only added to the insecurity of the disabled who had assumed that the new legislation was giving them rights. Municipalities and counties were criticised for not following LSS by Socialstyrelsen, by voluntary organisations representing disabled people and by Gerhard Larsson who had headed the Disability Commission. In some cases they were taken to court, but with little effect since the local authorities continued to defy the law (*DN* 6/10/95). Only in 1998 did the Social Affairs Minister, Margot Wallström, begin to fine local authorities where they failed to fulfil their duty (*DN* 2/8/98).

Another measure introduced in 1997 was the adaptation of public transport facilities to make travel more accessible for those with disabilities. Central government improved on its previous grant of 50 per cent towards the costs involved by an additional 25 per cent. In spite of measures like these, critics felt the Swedish system had failed those with disabilities. A year before, Larsson complained that the British had already implemented measures – to promote participation by, and equal treatment of, people with disabilities – which the Swedish authorities had been considering for some time without much action. He feared that Sweden would soon lag behind other countries in the EU (Larsson 1996). Others argued that people with disabilities in the USA had a greater right to equal treatment than in Sweden (Anderberg and Jönsson 1997). This was partly rectified in 1998 when the government proposed a new law which would prohibit direct and indirect discrimination against disabled people at work (*RD* 1998 No. 22 p. 8).

Socialstyrelsen also criticised municipalities for their treatment of the mentally disordered (Grunewald 1997). In 1995, it had been estimated that up to 40 000 mentally disordered people needed help and support in the community but two years later only 1000 individuals were getting it. "It seems that municipalities are sabotaging the law. Scandalous and catastrophic for the individual!", wrote the representative for Socialstyrelsen (ibid.). An editorial in *Dagens Nyheter* suggested that for many years the mentally ill had also been caught in a Catch-22 situation. Many were incapable of applying for help and, therefore, did not receive any; those that could were deemed to be healthy enough not to need it (*DN* 28/12/98). Socialstyrelsen estimated that 12 000 people in Stockholm and 50 000 in the whole of the country were not getting the help they needed (*DN* 11/8/99).

Child care

Soon after coming to power the Bourgeois government took steps to make it possible for profit-making child care agencies to be set up. Private and co-operative child care were entitled to receive state grants. This sector was not the subject of extensive privatisation in the 1990s in any of the Nordic countries (Lehto *et al.* 1999 p. 124). However, between 1990 and 1998, the proportion of children receiving private child care in Sweden rose from 4 to 12 per cent (SOU 2000:3 p. 119).

The need for expanded child care provision was recognized even by the Bourgeois government, largely due to the persistence of the Social Affairs Minister and the unexpected increase in the birth rate referred to at the end of Chapter 4. In the 1990s, one solution to increased demand for child care was to increase the size of groups cared for (*RD* 1993 No. 28). In 1993, it was decided that all parents who wanted child care for children between the ages of l and 12 years should have it and that the municipalities should ensure that it was available within a few months of application by the parent(s).

The law came into force at the beginning of 1995. Many municipalities failed to comply with the new legislation and had waiting lists as a result (*DN* 14/12/94 and 9/3/96). Others managed to comply by increasing the size of classes, reducing the numbers of teachers/minders or by raising their fees to parents. Large differences in the charges made by different municipalities began to arise with the result that many parents found their children excluded from day care because fees could not be paid (Johansson 1993). This was clearly unacceptable in a country where social opportunities were based upon equal opportunity and equal access (see Table 5.2).

Another way of reducing their liability to provide a place for all children for many municipalities was to deny a place to parents who were unemployed or on parental leave. Socialstyrelsen calculated that in 1996 48 000 children of unemployed parents and 83 000 of children whose parents were on study leave, were denied a place in a day nursery (*DN* 27/1/97). The Board continued to publicise this issue throughout 1997. The Education Minister agreed that it should be "the

Table 5.2: Monthly cost of sending two children to a day nursery for 8 hours a day: in Swedish krona (£)*

	Family A: gross annual income SEK 336 000 (£26 000)	Family B gross annual income SEK 480 000 (£37 000)
Stockholm municipalities		
Most expensive	3 349 (258)	3 788 (291)
Least expensive	2 292 (176)	2 292 (176)
Sweden's richest cities		
Most expensive	2 823 (217)	4 033 (310)
Least expensive	1 971 (152)	3 084 (237)

Source: *DN* 24/2/98
*Assuming £1=SEK 13

need of the child" which was paramount in determining whether or not a place was allocated and threatened to change the law if the municipalities did not change their practices (*DN* 31/10/97).

Even accepting the difficulties outlined above, Sweden's children continued to fare well in comparison with other countries. A consultant engaged by the Children's Ombudsman claimed that even with all the changes and cuts to benefits and services affecting children, a greater proportion of public sector resources were devoted to children than in any other comparable Western country (*DN* 4/9/97). Even compared with other Nordic countries, the Swedes devoted a greater percentage of its GDP to child care (Lehto *et al.* 1999 p. 118). The proportion of children receiving day care continued to increase throughout the 1990s. During the previous decade, provision had expanded so that 63 per cent of children under the age of 6 received some form of day care (Swedish Institute, 1992). By 1998, this figure had reached 72 per cent (SOU 1999:97 p. 102).

Ironically, by the time that the waiting lists in most municipalities had disappeared – towards the end of the Social Democrat's period of office – the decline in the number of young children in the population was creating a different problem for the authorities. They were having to consider what to do with a surplus of day nurseries and their staff (*DN* 30/11/97).

Social assistance

Another area which created problems of cost, equity and justice was that of means-tested social assistance (SA). The rising numbers of those on SA was a source of concern both to central government and the local municipalities who administered the benefit. In 1980, only 4 per cent of the population had been living on SA, but by 1994 that figure had risen to 8 per cent and by 1997 to 8.5 per cent (see Table 5.3). In 1998 this figure fell to 7.7 per cent. The real costs had more than quadrupled between 1980 and 1994 and had doubled between 1990 and 1997. Unemployment was seen as a principal cause of these increases. Increasing numbers of refugees were also cited since many of these found getting work extremely difficult. Other contributory factors were the numbers of single parent and divorced families.

One of the characteristics of SA in the past had been the short amount of time for which it was claimed. From 1983 until 1992, the average was just over four months. This figure rose constantly until 1996 after which it remained constant at five and a half months.

Table 5.3: Social assistance 1991–98

	Those dependent on SA (a) Individuals No. 000s	%	(b) Households No. 000s	%	Cost at 1997 prices SEK million
1980	418	4.1	178	3.7	
1990	517	6.0	277	7.9	5 833
1991	538	6.2	297	8.7	6 387
1992	589	6.7	328	9.5	7 768
1993	671	7.6	373	10.1	9 214
1994	715	8.1	392	10.5	10 615
1995	721	8.2	389	10.3	10 870
1996	753	8.5	403	10.7	11 930
1997	749	8.5	403	10.7	12 377
1998	692	7.7	367	9.6	11 446

Sources: Statistical Abstract of Sweden (1986) (for 1980), Socialtjänst 1999:5 (for 1990–98)

However, a Commission investigating the development of social services showed that the numbers of households dependent upon SA for lengthy periods (at least 24 months in a three year period) had increased from 32 000 in 1990 to 150 000 in 1996 (SOU 1999:46 p. 19). The largest increase was among young people under the age of 25. One quarter of all long-term dependence occurred in such households in 1996 compared with 10 per cent in 1990.

Faced with growing costs, both central and local government tried to keep them under control. Under the Bourgeois administration, SA rates were affected by the reduced value of the base amount, since Socialstyrelsen recommended that a single adult's benefit be calculated at 116 per cent of the base amount. Moreover, 90 per cent of local authorities were found to be paying at rates below this *existence minimum*. The variations were as wide as from 46 per cent to 135 per cent of the base amount. As a result it was recommended by the Commission on Social Services that SA be reduced to 100 per cent of the base amount but that all local authorities should be made to respect this figure (*RD* 1993 No. 14 p. 5). Variation also existed within one local authority where researchers found that your benefit depended very much on the official in charge of the case. Officials were asked to respond to a number of hypothetical claims. Decisions resulted in an award as low as SEK 250 a month and as high as SEK 11 657 for the same case (Hydén, Westermark and Stenberg 1995 p. 35). A case accepted as legitimate by some was rejected by others. The same research also showed there had been a change over time with cases accepted in 1990 being rejected four years later. It was thought that officials were more likely to check up on a claim and to doubt a claimant's honesty in 1994 than in 1990 (*DN* 15/1/96).

Part of the problem was that the legislation of 1981 only required municipalities to provide those entitled to SA with a *reasonable living standard*. Socialstyrelsen had admittedly been more explicit in its guidelines. But not only had many local authorities ignored these but they had refused to accept the decisions of courts which found in favour of claimants. The situation was resolved in 1997 by an amendment to the Social Services Law (*RD* 1997 No. 7 p. 4). Using Socialstyrelsen's revised norms, which had in turn been based upon calculations by the Consumer Board rather than the base amount, the amendment required that SA include a standard amount for all claimants and an amount which would vary according to the individual's circumstances. The standard amount for 1998 was to be SEK 2 887 (£222) a month for a single adult. This was arrived at as detailed in Table 5.4. In addition claimants would receive money for housing, fuel, home insurance, health care fees (see below), acute dental treatment, spectacles, *trade union subscriptions and unemployment fund contributions* [my italics] (see Chapter 8).[3] While the new standard might have been more realistic in terms of affordability, it represented an absolute cut for most claimants (See Table 5.5).

Socialstyrelsen had claimed in its defence that the old norms overcompensated for price rises (*DN* 8/10/96). The Association for Municipalities agreed, arguing that earnings had risen more slowly than SA rates and that many low paid people had lower living standards than those on SA. The national norm was set by central government, but it was the municipalities which bore the cost.

Table 5.4: Revised national norm for SA for one adult per month (1998)*

	SEK	(£)
Food	1 374	(106)
Clothing	461	(35)
Recreation	291	(22)
Hygiene	170	(13)
Spending money	110	(9)
Newspapers/TV licence	481	(37)
Total	2 887	(222)

Source: *RD* 1997 No. 7 p. 4.
£1 = SEK 13

Table 5.5: Changing SA norms, SEK per month

	1996	1998	% change
Single adult	3 451	2 887	–16
Couple	5 712	4 853	–15
Couple + two young children	9 342	7 537	–19
Couple + two young and two older children	13 008	11 826	–11

Sources: *DN* 6/10/96 and 13/12/97

Moreover, municipalities were having to bear the maintenance of those who previously had been supported by national social insurance schemes. The Association's solution was to demand less state involvement in SA (*DN* 10/5/96).

Socialstyrelsen's contribution to this debate – apart from recommending lower norms – was to argue that too much was being expected of a system intended to help people with temporary difficulties facing acute problems. SA costs, it suggested, were inflated by the large number of refugees who had come to Sweden in the 1990s, at a time when there were few jobs for those with little or no Swedish. In a series of articles, senior administrators argued that groups such as single parents, elderly immigrants and refugees and the young unemployed should be paid for either by central government or by a system separate from SA (Begler 1995; Begler *et al.* 1996; Begler 1997). Central government went some way to recognize this by providing extra resources to municipalities that had large numbers of immigrant families. Municipalities were also encouraged by Socialstyrelsen to pay refugees *Introductory Compensation* rather than SA, as the former was not governed by the national norm and could therefore be paid at a lower rate (Begler 1995).

Whether or not SA claimants had been overcompensated in the past – and this was disputed by researchers (Salonen and Sunesson 1996) – the new national norms represented significant and sudden reductions in the standard of living of the poorest members of the community. Poverty was not only being experienced by more and more people in Sweden – the numbers of homeless people were growing and begging on the streets of Stockholm was becoming more widespread – but the experience was becoming more degrading as eligibility rules were tightened up. At the same time as the national norms were being reduced, the government was also insisting that Departments of Social Services demand that SA be denied to those below the age of 25 who refused to undertake work experience or improve their vocational skills (*RD* 1997 No. 7). Claimants often complained that "going to the social" was debasing. This was illustrated in a number of interviews conducted for a comparative project on long-term unemployed people (Clasen, Gould and Vincent 1998 p. 172).

> "Go to social services? I've been there three times and it was a fruitless experience. It feels like a stigma." (lone parent, female). "You feel as though you are begging." (single, female) "I'd rather live on nothing than live on social assistance." (lone parent, female) "I felt shat upon. I applied for emergency help and it took a whole month before I got any money." (single woman) "It makes you so angry when you go to social services." (couple with children, female) "[Unemployment benefit] feels better than to say I go to social services. Some aren't ashamed of it but I am. I haven't told my son that I go to the social. I keep it in the dark." (lone parent, female).

However both the long waiting times they experienced and the insulting treatment by officials were exacerbated by cuts in the administration of SA (*DN* 4/4/97).

While there was considerable pressure upon the government to reverse its cuts to social insurance benefits as soon as the economy improved, there seemed little likelihood of the same pressure being exerted on behalf of SA recipients.

Health care

Finance

Health care services expanded considerably during the 1970s and 1980s to the point that they were consuming 10 per cent of GNP and employing 10 per cent of the work force. While the system had a good reputation internationally, there was widespread suspicion that its cost was not entirely justified. It was felt by some that there was overemployment of staff, including doctors; that there was too great a reliance on hospitalisation, particularly of the elderly and the mentally ill; that waiting lists were far too long. These criticisms which grew during the 1980s were given added urgency by the country's economic difficulties. Cuts led to only 7.9 per cent of GNP being devoted to the health service in 1994 – the last year of the Bourgeois government and to 7.2 per cent in 1997 under the Social Democrats (*Välfärdsfakta* 1999

p. 56). However, some of this fall was due to the transfer of elderly care to the municipalities. Figures showing per capita expenditure on health care published for 1994 showed Sweden lying in seventeenth place out of the OECDs 22 member states; just above Britain (*RD* 1996 No. 33 p. 6). In the 1980s Sweden had ranked second only to the US.

Health care charges to visit a doctor and for prescriptions rose considerably between 1988 and 1991 and between 1991 and 1994 in order to both reduce costs and to discourage overuse or abuse of the system (*Vår trygghet* 1988–98). Since the last year of the Bourgeois government through to 1998, fees have remained fairly stable with patients paying SEK 100–130 (£8–10) for a visit to a doctor; SEK 50–100 (£4–8) to visit a physiotherapist, psychologist and so on. There was a ceiling to what one individual had to pay in a 12-month period of SEK 900 (£70). Prescription costs rose more steeply with patients paying SEK 120 (£9) in 1994 and SEK 160 (£12) in 1996. After 1997 the actual cost of medicines had to be paid up to a value of SEK 400 (£30) with discounts operating up a maximum of SEK 1300 (£100). Children and young people up the age of 19 were exempt from these charges. Prescription charges in total amounted to around 20 per cent of what the state spent on medicines.

Even before the Bourgeois government's period of office, attempts were made to reduce spending and make the system more efficient. Internal markets based upon pricing mechanisms began to develop. The resulting rationalisation and cost-cutting necessitated hospital closures and staff redundancies. The private sector began to expand. While increased competition and a greater reliance on market mechanisms might have resulted in some efficiency improvements, there were less desirable consequences as well – fewer examinations of patients and unnecessary referrals to specialists (Blomberg, 1993; Johansson 1992). According to Brunsdon and May, freedom of choice, efficiency and accountability were not just neo-liberal slogans but something many sections of the population wanted, especially women and disability groups (Brunsdon and May 1995 p. 15). The Social Democrats, in 1989, accepted "a lexicon and logic that certainly suggested the use of the private sector 'quality management' conceptions if not the phrase 'market forces' " (ibid. p16). The economic crisis faced by the Bourgeois government gave an added impetus to those reforms. Hospital beds, staff numbers and salary costs were significantly reduced.

Cuts to health care were also considerable in the first two years of the Social Democratic government. In 1995, the Association of County

Councils claimed that health care would face an overall 10 per cent cut by the end of the twentieth century. Having cut employment by 50 000 in the previous four years, it estimated another 30 000 would have to go by 2000 (*DN* 21/9/95). Nor was the turn of the next century likely to prove any better. A Commission examining the future costs of health care concluded that, the cost of meeting health needs would grow 5–6 per cent by 2010. It did not think that resources could be found within the existing system through rationalisation and reorganisation. That had been done in the 1990s with considerable success, but there would not be the same scope for similar savings in the future (*RD* 1996 No. 33 p. 6). The degree of rationalisation can be illustrated by the fact that although hospital beds had declined by 50 per cent between 1989 and 1998, care times had also been reduced, enabling the volume of treatment to remain constant (SOU 2000:3 p. 150).

Stockholm was hit hard by cuts in 1995. The big four acute hospitals had to reduce their staff by between 25 per cent and 40 per cent (*DN* 14/6/95). Wards were closed and outpatient care reduced. The market-oriented nature of the Stockholm model of the 1980s had to give way to a mix of autocratic decision making and the need for co-operation for survival's sake. Subsequently the Minister for Social Affairs claimed that the changes in Stockholm came too late and occurred too rapidly. By 1997, with the improvement in public finances she was able to claim that extra resources would be made available to health care again (Wallström 1997). But by the summer of 1998, there was considerable discussion about the "crisis" facing health care with severe shortages of hospital places for acute medicine. Both the Inspectorate and Socialstyrelsen expressed anxiety about the pressure the system was under. These developments were mirrored by increasing public dissatisfaction expressed in terms of formal complaints to the county authorities. In 1995, there were 12 000 complaints and by 1998, these had increased to 17 000 (*DN* 13/3/99).

Personnel

In the summer of 1993, a proposal was made to introduce *husläkare* (family doctors or general practitioners) into the system and an intense debate ensued. Some aspects of the proposal together with the resentment that had built up over staffing cuts resulted in a major strike by doctors early in 1994 (Brunsdon and May 1995 p. 20). The problems facing hospitals were compounded in 1995 by a seven-week strike over pay by nurses. The strike finished with a compromise but one which was far from meeting the nurses' demands. The effect on waiting lists, x-ray examinations and operations took over six months to resolve. Dissatisfaction among nurses led many to leave the profession over the next few years or to work for agencies. Specialist doctors were attracted to Norway. Moreover, staff shortages of both nurses and doctors compounded by staff cuts led many of those remaining in the service to become burnt out.

Family doctors, freedom of choice and the decline of the private sector

Prior to the 1990s, there had been an overemphasis in Swedish care on the hospital sector with primary health care being relatively under developed. Each time a Swede visited a medical centre or a hospital s/he could be seen by a different doctor. The *husläkare* system was partly intended to provide patients with a degree of continuity in their primary care but also to give them some choice. Individuals would be able to choose their own public or private sector doctor from a local list. Since this was going to create a need for 4000 doctors, who were either newly trained specialists in general medicine or retrained specialists from other fields, the cost was going to be considerable. The socialist opposition argued that it would damage the preventative work of the existing system of medical centres (*vårdcentral*). It seemed a strange innovation none the less at a time of public austerity. The following April New Democracy, with the socialist bloc, voted against *husläkare* but by then more than 70 per cent of the population had already registered with one (Johansson 1994).

More controversially, the Bourgeois government proposed to make the establishment of private practices for specialist doctors and physiotherapists much easier, a measure strongly opposed by the socialist bloc in the Riksdag (*RD* 1994a No. 1 p. 15). The government's intention was to improve competition and choice for patients. Counties would have to recompense private practitioners for their services and patients would pay slightly higher fees than they would to doctors employed by the county. The Social Democrats and the Left party took the view that the costs would be difficult to control. Moreover, counties could find themselves losing patients, and therefore resources, to doctors who contracted out of public service. The expansion of private medical practices and physiotherapists that took place in the following year was considerable. However, when the new government was elected in 1994, one of its first acts was to make an agreement with the counties a prerequisite for establishing a practice, thus enabling them to stop the supply of specialists in areas where there was already a plentiful supply (*RD* 1995 No. 1a p. 23).

The private sector had enjoyed a degree of expansion in the 1980s when it rose to 10 per cent of total health care expenditure (Lehto *et al.* 1999 p. 114). It reached a peak of 16 per cent in the mid-90s after which it declined. The decline was partly the result of the worsening economic climate but was reinforced by the hostility of the Social Democrats. Stockholm county council investigated private practices suspected of fraud; Socialstyrelsen was given the same powers to supervise private practice as it exercised in the public sector; and county councils generally began to demand that patients could only make use of private sector doctors if they had an official referral from the county. None of this was conducive to expansion. By the end of 1996, the number of doctors in private practice who received payment from the counties had declined by 14 per cent (*DN* 30/12/96).

But if the experiment with private medicine was coming to an end, the principle of choice was by no means abandoned. It remained possible for individuals to choose their own family doctor even if s/he practised outside the area in which the individual lived. In 1998 it was also decided that patients should have the right to more information and choice in the hospital treatment they received (*RD* 1998a No. 36 p. 16). Oddly, primary care seems to have been spared the drastic cuts affecting hospitals. Resources remained almost unchanged between 1992 and 1998 (*RD* 1998 No. 11 p. 7). In an international comparison of European general practitioners showed that the Swedes worked less hours and saw fewer patients than their counterparts in other countries (*DN* 5/5/97). They were also better educated, better equipped and were able to give their patients more time.

Inequalities

It is widely accepted that the 1990s saw growing inequalities in Swedish society. An LO report in 1997 claimed that if existing developments were to continue Sweden would share the same inequalities as those in existing in Britain and even the USA (*DN* 2/9/97). Figures for 1989–95 showed that the poorest decile had experienced a 33 per cent decline in real income compared with less than 2 per cent for the richest decile. Moreover families with children were more likely to have suffered compared with those without. And one parent families were more likely to experience poverty than other households (Linnell 1998 p. 7). While it was accepted that unemployment explained many of these differences, declining welfare benefits and rising welfare fees were also to blame. Vogel, a researcher who has specialised in social inequality for many years, argued that old age pensioners – men and women – had been relatively well protected because of ATP (the state earnings-related pension scheme). Others had not fared as well. He cited evidence from Socialstyrelsen which suggested that poverty in 1998 affected 7 per cent of the population compared with 3 per cent at the beginning of the decade. He agreed that there had been an increase in marginalisation.

> Statistics show clear signs of the effects of unemployment and public expenditure cuts. Those with labour market problems, certain kinds of welfare clients and families with high maintenance costs, had decidedly worse development in their living standards or even a worsening of those standards than the rest of the population (Vogel 1998).

Young people in particular had suffered partly because there were no jobs for them and partly because they were, as a consequence, only entitled to the lowest level of benefit. However, Vogel still thought that Swedish living standards remained high in comparison with other countries and that the inequalities in Sweden and the other Scandinavian countries remained higher in comparison with the rest of Europe. "The Swedish model", he said, "has wavered but not fallen" (ibid.).

With patient fees rising faster than prices, there was evidence that the least well off could not afford to visit their doctors. The low-paid, least educated, single mothers and the unemployed were the hardest hit. In the view of Margaret Persson, the social democratic chair of *The Committee for Public Health Targets*, health was becoming a class issue (*DN* 20/1/97). Class differences in children's health were widening. A government report showed that whereas in 1989 only 7 per cent of manual and non-manual men had suffered from anxiety, six years later the percentage for non-manual workers had increased to 10 per cent, but for manual workers it had risen to 16 per cent (*RD* 1997 No. 34 p. 18). There were also claims that the rich and the upper class received preferential treatment in health care (Bergh *et al.* 1997; Jonsson and Kuritzén 1998).

Ethnic minorities

The experience of ethnic minorities in Sweden is as varied as their countries of origin. As was seen in the previous chapter a third of the "foreign-born population is from neighbouring Scandinavian countries". It makes little sense to include these people in calculations about the relative advantages and disadvantages experienced by non-Nordic ethnic minorities. Moreover, many of those who came from other European countries – particularly in the 1960s and 1970s when employment opportunities were so plentiful – seem to have become relatively well integrated into Swedish society, sharing similar living standards and opportunities as the indigenous population.

Much stronger differences exist between Swedes and those immigrants and refugees who came to Sweden in the 1980s and 1990s. Studies published by Jan Ekberg in the mid-90s showed that their poverty was three times greater. Whereas 8 per cent of Swedish households had disposable incomes which were less than half the national average, the figure amongst the most recent arrivals (1988–90) was 28 per cent (*DN* 27/3/94). A more recent survey of immigrants from Chile, Iran, Poland and Turkey, published by Socialstyrelsen, illustrated the varied backgrounds and experiences of different minority. With the exception of the Turks, those interviewed had better educational qualifications on average than Swedes. Of those who were employed, many felt that they were over-qualified for their jobs. These were often stressful, poorly paid, with few opportunities for further training and they provided little work satisfaction. As a much higher percentage were unemployed than the indigenous population, many were living

Table 5.6: Average income, unemployment rate and poverty by country of origin

Country of origin	(a) Average income for those in work	(b) Unemployment rate*	(c) % in poverty
Sweden	225 000 men	7	11
	154 000 women	8	11
Poland	193 000 men	27	20
	124 000 women	32	22
Chile	155 000 men	24	23
	1–1 000 women	34	24
Turkey	105 000 men	33	91
	75 000 women	43	94
Iran	112 000 men	51	42
	76 000 women	53	46

*Standardised for differences in age structure.
Source: Column (b) Invandrarprojektet 1998: 1 p. 72, Columns (a) and (c) Socialstyrelsen-rapport 1999:9 pp. 123 and 144.

on social assistance or had been awarded disability pensions. The percentage living in poor households was determined by standards set by Socialstyrelsen (see Table 5.6).

Ekberg claimed that many of those who came to Sweden in the 1980s not only faced a healthy job market but also had a good educational background (*DN* 27/3/94). Why then did they experience such great disadvantages? His explanation was that the Swedish economy was in the process of a transformation from an industrial society to a service society where language and cultural communication was of greater importance than previously (*DN* 9/11/96). This was hotly disputed by Mauricio Rojas – who emigrated to Sweden in 1974 and subsequently became a lecturer at Lund University. Rojas argued that Swedish employers were taking a short-sighted view of their economic interests when they preferred native Swedes to those from minority backgrounds. While it was easy in a time of mass of unemployment to build a monocultural workforce, to neglect the potential of a multi-cultural workforce in a globalised economy was a costly mistake (Rojas *et al.* 1997).

His poor view of employers was matched by his criticism of the "integration industry" – those employed by the state to "help" ethnic minorities adapt to Swedish society. He criticised them for their social engineering approach and their need to "put people's lives in order" rather than allow difference and creativity to flourish. He attributed this narrowness in part to Sweden's long history as a homogeneous society. In this respect he clearly felt that Sweden's way of dealing with newcomers was inferior to that of countries like the USA and Britain and that it was well underway to creating an "ethnic underclass".[4] This view was reinforced by evidence of the increased housing segregation in Stockholm, Gothenburg and Malmö experienced by ethnic minorities during the 1990s (SOU 2000:3 p. 57).

Conclusions

This chapter has summarised some of the principle developments in a wide range of welfare services and benefits. While the Bourgeois government had intended a system change, it had insufficient time and too many problems to be able to achieve this goal. The public finances inherited by the Social Democratic government were in worse shape than those they had bequeathed in 1991. The Social Democrats approached the task with discipline and even ruthlessness, but they were only looking for cuts not a system change. As Ståhlberg argued, supported by Palme and Wennemo, the changes to the social security system were implemented to deal with immediate problems, they were technical rather than systemic (Ståhlberg 1995; Palme and Wennemo 1998). In a review of Nordic welfare states generally it was concluded that, "The Nordic way of organising welfare production and distribution adapted fairly well to changing circumstances" (Heikkilä *et al.* 1999 p. 272). This chapter bears out these conclusions.

There can be little doubt that had the Centre-right parties remained in power in 1994, they would have pursued the goal of creating a system based upon basic security – providing for essential needs while leaving most employees to make there own additional arrangements for pension and sickness insurance. It is reasonable to assume that the electorate had decided in 1994 that it wanted no such change. And while the Social Democratic government was single-minded in creating a healthier set of public finances, it restored many benefit and expenditure cuts as soon as it was prudent to do so. It was under constant pressure from LO and TCO, from social workers, doctors and nurses. Socialstyrelsen had to acquiesce in many of the changes, but in its supervisory role often pointed out the adverse consequences of government policies. When the government went into the 1998 election campaign, it could have prioritised taxation cuts but explicitly set out the case for reviving health care, education and care for the elderly. This was in line with public thinking. For many, the People's Home remained just that. It can even be said that it was being run more efficiently and was more cost-effective. But this did little to help the long-term unemployed, those on social assistance or recent influxes of refugees. This also was in line with public thinking. Some people were becoming excluded from the People's Home.

6
Grey Policies: Caring for the Elderly

> An increase in political participation of pensioners has been observed at all government levels during the past ten years. Sweden's pensioners show all the signs of grey activism.
>
> (Mark Blake 1997 p. 59)

Introduction

Sweden has been proud of the way in which it has provided for its elderly population. So generous have the benefits and services been that one economist in the 1970s wondered whether "too much was being done for the elderly" (Wilson 1979). This could not have been an issue for many countries. Health care and social services – on which elderly people depend disproportionately – were provided free or with minimal charges. The pension system gave most elderly people an income close to that enjoyed while working. However, with 18 per cent of the population above the age of 65 and nearly 6 per cent over 80, the 1990s were bound to present difficulties. Demographic pressures added to the emergence of economic problems. The rise in unemployment, the related costs, and the perceived need to reduce social expenditure, meant that provision for the elderly would come under scrutiny like other aspects of the welfare system.

In this chapter we will examine the two major policy changes affecting the well-being of elderly people – the Ädel reform of 1992 which affected the provision of health and social services and the new pension system which will be introduced in 1999. Alternatives to state provision will be discussed – particularly the private sector and some of the problems accompanying expansion. The chapter will conclude with some consideration of the role of pensioners' groups in challenging many of the changes that have been introduced.

Health and social services

Ädel reform

The Social Democrats had, during the 1980s, already moved towards a preference for community care and closed down many institutional homes for both the elderly and the mentally ill. Sheltered housing, day care centres and home helps were provided to make this possible (Daatland 1997 p. 155). By the end of that decade only 9 per cent of pensioners were not living in their own homes: 3 per cent were in nursing homes where they were deemed to need medical attention; 3 per cent in old people's homes because they were in need of care and support; and 3 per cent in *servicehus* a form of sheltered housing attached to which were a wide range of services to meet people's daily needs. At the beginning of the 90s the Social Democratic government introduced a major reform in the care of the elderly by making the municipalities responsible for all residential provision for old people. This involved many of the services, like geriatric hospitals, that had previously been provided by the health care authorities. In practice it meant the transfer of 31 000 places and 50 000 employees (SOU 1999:97 p. 116). The aim of Ädel reform was, according to the recent Commission which examined the whole social services sector:

> ... an emphasis upon the social elements of caring. A good home adapted to an individual's needs should make it possible to remain at home, to maintain one's social network and strengthen independence. (ibid.)

The municipalities also became responsible for co-ordinating provision. On completion of medical treatment, they were expected to provide either accommodation and/or services which would enable elderly people to leave hospital. Failure to do so meant they had to recompense the counties for the additional expense they incurred (Fernow 1992).

The reform of elderly care came into force at the beginning of 1992 – soon after the election of the Centre-right government. The transition, therefore, occurred just as the new government was promoting more private, voluntary and co-operative care. In addition to the tasks originally set for the municipalities, the new system was expected to adopt principles of competition, choice and flexibility in meeting the needs of elderly people. Unfortunately Ädel reform was also introduced in the same year as Sweden's economic crisis came to a head and local authorities were not allowed to increase local taxation. With each successive round of budget cuts, the elderly experienced less resources and increased charges. The Bourgeois government reduced the value of the basic pension over successive years. It also raised the standard amount that pensioners had to pay towards the cost of their housing.

Initially, Ädel reform itself seemed to function quite well. Less people were being cared for in institutions but the closing down of the latter was sometimes criticised for being hasty and premature. More housing was provided for community care and better compensation for carers of elderly relatives. A concerted effort was made by Bengt Westerberg, the Social Affairs Minister to increase the building of new accommodation for elderly people suffering from dementia, mental illness and physical disabilities. Group homes were increased by 25 000 and 20 000 places were provided for long term care. Not only was this considered a useful Keynesian stimulus to the building industry but was considered a priority in spite of the economic problems faced by the government.

However, charges for services sometimes rose enormously, with the poorest complaining the most (*RD* 1993 No. 30 p. 5 and 1993 No. 31b p. 8). Fees for some nursing homes and old people's homes doubled. At the end of 1993, Socialstyrelsen criticised municipalities for charging elderly people so much they were left with less money to spend than the norm for social assistance (*DN* 7/12/93). When males on higher pensions needed care in a nursing home the situation of their female partners on low pensions became impossible. Many authorities were making no adjustment for such situations. Socialstyrelsen also criticised the wide variations in local authority charges, saying that many of them were not justified by differences in costs. In a study of Stockholm municipalities the following year, Socialstyrelsen said that services for the elderly had become fewer, worse and more expensive – with relatives increasingly having to shoulder more caring tasks (*DN* 8/9/94).

Two years later – under the Social Democrats – Socialstyrelsen was still making the same criticisms of local authorities; that charges were too high, variations were too great and no account was being taken of couples where one needed long term care and the other was left to manage at home (*DN* 5/10/96). In the 1996 budget, the Social

Democratic government had actually removed a further SEK 2billion from elderly care but the new Minister for Social Affairs, Margot Wallström, claimed that other groups had suffered even more. Subsequently, she insisted that it was right that the elderly should be prioritised even at the expense of other groups (Wallström 1996). In 1997, Socialstyrelsen published a damning criticism of the Ädel reform (*RD* 1997 No. 37a p. 3). It claimed places in the health care sector had been reduced by 25 per cent in the 1980s and by 40 per cent in the 90s but that municipalities had not built up replacement services in the community to the extent required. They not only lacked resources; there was waste and confusion over the parallel provision of home help services and home nursing care; and staff lacked medical competence. Wallström took particular notice of Socialstyrelsen's critical evaluation of the implementation of the Ädelreform. She accused counties and municipalities of evading their responsibilities and insisted that they stop reducing personnel. The Liberal party and the Christian Democrats were anxious to prevent a deepening crisis in the care of the elderly and gave their support to the government. Even the Conservatives, in their approach to the 1998 election, while promising cuts in taxation and expenditure, felt obliged to say that they would provide more resources for the elderly (*DN* 28/10/97).

By 1998, Wallström was able to promise an increase in resources to employ more personnel in elderly care (Wallström 1998). The proposition put to the Riksdag in the spring was partly a response to the revelations of neglect within the private sector (see below), and partly a sign of the growing consensus among all political parties that something had to be done. Municipalities were expected to ensure that elderly people had enough to live on after they had paid their various service fees; staff were to receive better training; more support was to be given to relatives; more money for special housing and meeting places. The total package of SEK 700 million went some way to restore the cuts made earlier by the government (*RD* 1998 No. 14 p. 14).

At the end of the decade, the Commission on Social Services summarised the inadequacies in Ädel reform.

> A major part of discussions in the 90s has been about weaknesses in the chain of care, deficiencies in transferring information between the responsible authorities, deficiencies in medical measures – above all medicinal matters – and doubts about whether it is always the individual's best interests which decide where and how comprehensive care needs can best be satisfied. Moreover, the shared

responsibility for rehabilitation, aids and medical care at home continue to cause problems (SOU 1999:97 p. 117).

The persistence of these problems in spite of additional resources from both the Bourgeois and Social Democratic governments led to Socialstyrelsen and Länstyrelser (the county agencies responsible for the co-ordination of government policy at a local level) implementing stricter supervisory procedures of the care of the old and disabled at the end of the decade (SOU 1999:97 p. 118). Yet in 1997, research showed that 20 per cent of those above the age of 75 discharged by geriatric hospitals failed to receive adequate care from their local municipalities (*DN* 11/11/98).

Home helps and other services

In 1991, 16 per cent of over 65s were receiving home help service. This declined steadily until 1997 when the figure was 8.4 per cent. Figures for the over 80s were 38 per cent and 22.8 per cent respectively (Pettersson 1995; Socialstyrelsen 1998:9). While the overall figures compared well with other countries, within Sweden there was considerable variation between municipalities with some providing for only 5 per cent of the over 80s and others 40 per cent (Thorslund *et al.* 1997 p. 200). Moreover, it was the older pensioners who now received more help than previously. Priority was also given to people living alone (ibid. p. 201). Fewer were getting help, but those who were, were getting more. Basic services to 37 per cent of all clients (such as cleaning and food provision) accounted for only 5 per cent of total home services while the 10 per cent of clients in need of more comprehensive care consumed 40 per cent of resources (SOU 1999:97 p. 119). The actual volume of home help services remained relatively unchanged from 1993 until 1997 (Socialstyrelsen 1998:9 p. 23).

As with charges for long term care, Socialstyrelsen was critical of the variations in charges for home help services. In a study of fees charged in Stockholm, it was found that the cost of nine hours help to a pensioner with a gross income of SEK 16 000 a month was SEK 1 800 in the most expensive local authority and SEK 450 in the least expensive – a fourfold difference (*DN* 5/10/96).

The rights of elderly people

Municipalities tried to cope with their own economic problems in a variety of ways, not always respecting the rights of elderly people as they did do. The freedom of local authorities to set their own charges had, according to a senior official in Socialstyrelsen, resulted in a consequent loss of legal rights for both the elderly and the disabled (*DN* 5/10/96). There was sometimes confusion as to which authority was responsible for care – the county or the municipality. Each could disclaim responsibility leaving the individual or the relatives to sort out the problem. The Association of Municipalities (Svenska Kommunförbundet) even tried to make appeals against local authority decisions more difficult (*DN* 6/11/96). A Commission examining ways of improving the quality of elderly care complained that too often elderly people were treated badly and with disrespect, but that neither they nor their relatives dared to complain for fear of even worse treatment (*RD* 1997 No. 18 p. 9).

The same Commission investigated the right of elderly people to move from one local authority area to another and found that municipalities refused to provide special housing for elderly people who moved into their areas from outside. Half of the applications for such assistance in 1995/96 were turned down. Not only did some elderly people want to move nearer relatives but no doubt they also wanted to avoid some of the costs of living in expensive local authority areas. The Commission recommended that elderly people should have the right to move where they chose and that, if some municipalities and counties suffered disproportionately, an adjustment could be made to their state grant (*RD* 1996 No. 36 p. 3).

Alternatives to state provision

Sweden's reputation as a welfare provider in the past emphasised the importance of state provision. Families and voluntary organisations had always played a role but it was the public services that were looked to as the main provider. As municipalities pruned their budgets, so relatives found themselves playing a greater role in looking after the elderly and the disabled. Local authorities began to look more and more to the caring potential of voluntary organisations. But perhaps the most dramatic change in Sweden's welfare mix has been the expansion of the private sector.

Fernow, as early as 1992, claimed that the provision of a range of services (window cleaning, house cleaning, shopping) by private companies had created an alternative to municipal home help services but that the elderly themselves seemed to prefer public provision (Fernow, 1992). At times there were protests by public sector workers and elderly people as private companies took over services for the elderly in the early years of the Bourgeois government. Significant financial savings were advanced as a principle reason for privatisation but it was also argued that new ideas and greater efficiency would result.

Even under the Social Democrats private provision for the elderly increased. In 1993, only 2.3 per cent elderly people were receiving private home help services and 5.4 per cent were in privately provided special accommodation. By 1997, these percentages had almost doubled and Sweden had more privatised care for elderly people than any other Nordic country (see Table 6.1).

In Solna, a suburb of Stockholm – where a third of all elderly care was in the private sector – a nurse revealed a high degree of neglect, poor conditions and mismanagement in Polhemsgården, a privately-managed home in October 1997. The local authority immediately took the home back into public management. In the scandal that followed, the relatives of an elderly man who died while in care in Polhemsgården filed an official complaint with the police. It was subsequently revealed that a disproportionate number of deaths had taken place in the first few months of the home's existence. There were insufficient staff and not enough personnel with medical training. Blame was firmly placed not only on the home itself but also on the municipality. Newly appointed officials presented a programme to improve elderly care in April 1998 but admitted that the new measures would not affect privately run homes (*DN* 3/4/98).

Szebeheley, in an analysis which was critical of a tendency to conceal the class and gender implications of terms like *welfare pluralism* and *welfare mix*, examined changes which had taken place in a district of Stockholm (Szebeheley 1999). She confirmed that there had been a clear shift in the 1990s from publicly provided care for the elderly to informal and privately provided care. But she also pointed out that the private option was more marked among the middle-class elderly while

Table 6.1: The percentage of all those receiving help receiving it from private sector 1993–97

Year	Home help service	Special accommodation
1993	2.3	5.4
1994	3.4	7.1
1995	3.6	8.3
1996	2.5*	9.3
1997	4.2	10.2

*Insufficient data provided.
Source: Socialstyrelsen 1998:9 p. 18

working-class elderly people had to rely on their families (usually daughters). She summed this up with the phrase, "Marketisation for the resource rich and informalisation for those with less resources" (ibid. p. 25).

Dilemmas and choices

The Solna scandal – coming as it did at a time when there was a growing awareness of a crisis within the system and only months before a general election – helped to focus public and political attention on the issue. It added impetus to the need for more resources, which to a certain extent, the government was able to provide. While Polhemsgården could hardly have helped the cause of privatisation, the leader of the Liberal party was right to point out that there were also examples of neglect and mismanagement in the public sector. It had been clear for some time that cutbacks had resulted in a shortage of staff both in terms of quantity and quality. Not only were many of those employed to look after elderly people under increasing stress as their workloads increased, but they were less able to do their work adequately. At one level this meant that they could not provide their clients with sufficient attention: they carried out their tasks and moved on, and could not stop to chat. At another, there were indeed many examples of physical neglect with research showing that increasing numbers of elderly people suffered from bed sores through inadequate help (*DN* 16/1/98). There was already a gap between needs and resources in the 90s; that gap was likely to grow in the next century.

Thorslund and Parker had argued that as much as possible had already been done to improve the effective and efficient use of existing resources (Thorslund and Parker 1995 p. 209). As they saw it, unless more resources were forthcoming, health care and social services would be unable to meet many of the basic needs of elderly people in the future. More and more, decision making would become a question of priorities within the elderly care sector and within the social sector as a whole. In a subsequent paper, Thorslund and his colleagues, suggested that health care authorities were more used to making priorities on the basis of research and evaluation than social services (Thorslund, Bergmark and Parker 1997 p. 203). This was partly because social services had much more diffuse and less easily measurable goals but partly because they "denied" the need to prioritise and lacked the necessary information. Thorslund worried that the *ad hoc* nature of existing decision making might have "unanticipated consequences" (ibid.). If present trends continued, he argued, wider differences would exist between a plurality of providers and inequalities in care would continue to increase.

Johansson disagreed that more resources were the answer (Johansson 1997). He sympathised with the view that existing resources could be used more efficiently. What was lacking was leadership, an improved incentive structure and good management. Above all, he felt that Ädel reform had failed to inspire a vision of social care which "saw people as a whole, with their own value, as participants in a social context" (Johansson 1997 p. 282). He concluded:

> The quality of caring for the very ill at their life's end is the highest testimonial for a system of elderly care. To make it a reality does not primarily depend upon resources but the ambition to develop elderly care with a different vision of humanity. (ibid. p. 282)

Old age pensions

The old system and the need for change

If demographic and economic factors had serious implications for the care of the elderly, they were also an important consideration in deciding what sort of pension system Sweden could afford for the future. The existing system had been introduced in 1960 and was widely regarded as a key measure for retaining the support of middle-class, as well as working-class people, for the welfare state. It was composed of a number of elements – a basic flat rate pension, a supplementary pension, a state earnings-related pension (ATP) and a negotiated occupational pension. The basic flat rate pension existed as a matter of right for any Swedish citizen who was resident in Sweden. Prior to 1993, it was equivalent to 96 per cent of the base amount (see Chapter 5) for a pensioner not living with another pensioner and 78.5 per cent each for two pensioners living together. After 1976, those pensioners not entitled to ATP were given a supplementary pension which grew in value over time to over half the value of the basic pension.

The maximum ATP was paid to those for whom employers had paid contributions for thirty years. ATP was based upon the fifteen best years of earnings and, together with the basic pension, provided a pensioner with a pension equivalent to over two thirds of their previous income up to a ceiling of 7.5 times the base amount. In addition white collar workers, blue collar workers, state employees and local government employees were covered by agreements reached between their trade unions and employers' association for additional occupational pensions which could provide a further 10 per cent of their income in retirement. For many, the need to augment these arrangements with private pensions simply did not exist.

However, neither the basic pension, the supplementary pension nor ATP were for the most part funded. They were largely based upon the pay-as-you-go principle whereby the present generation of employees paid for the present generation of pensioners. As long as the proportion of pensioners remained low and economic growth high, the financing of the system worked well. Problems arose as the proportion of pensioners increased and economic growth fell below 2 per cent. Calculations made by Ann-Charlotte Ståhlberg in the early 1990s showed clearly the difficulties the system would face in the future (Ståhlberg 1991 p. 220). Her projections indicated that the percentage of the employers' payroll devoted to state pension contributions would remain stable at just above 20 per cent with an annual economic growth rate of 2 per cent but would rise to over 50 per cent if there were no economic growth at all!

At that time, Sweden was experiencing very low and even negative rates of economic growth. Moreover with pensions being linked to prices and wages rising at a lower rate, it was clear that pensioners' incomes were likely to rise at a faster rate than those who were financing them. Other anomalies had also become apparent over time. Manual workers' contributions were often well in excess of the 30 years required for full ATP. Senior white collar women gained most from a system which required only 30 years of contributions while female blue-collar workers benefited least (Ståhlberg 1995 p. 13). It was also clear from official calculations that the proportion of employers with incomes over 7.5 per cent the base amount was growing (Ståhlberg 1995 p. 11). The long term effect of this trend would reduce the status of ATP. It would become a basic pension for many which would need to be supplemented by occupational or private pensions. The system could therefore be seen as having unforeseen implications both for redistribution and for solidarity. For all of these reasons, it was widely accepted that reform was required.

Consensual politics

The new system was agreed upon by five of the political parties by the end of 1997 (Social Democratic, Conservative, Liberal, Centre and Christian Democratic) and approved by the Riksdag in the summer of 1998. It was to come into effect in 1999 with the first pensions to be paid out in 2001.

The early signs of a consensus were not promising. In 1991, the Social Democrats suspected that the Centre-right government wanted to move away from the state earnings-related system towards a basic security model, leaving individuals to make their own private arrangements for additional pension benefits. This was denied by Carl Bildt, the Prime Minister. An all-party parliamentary working party was set up which, from the outset, established contact with trade unions and pensioner organisations. It was hoped that a set of proposals would emerge by autumn 1992. This was seen as unrealistic by the Social Democrats, which was understandable given the major issues which had yet to be agreed. The Bourgeois parties clearly wanted a greater emphasis upon a funded element which would both show a greater correspondence between what an individual contributed and subsequently received from the system and at the same time boost Sweden's savings and investment rate. The Social Democrats preferred a pay-as-you-go system which included an element of income redistribution. Subsequently they were alerted to the need to broaden this concern to ensure that there was a just distribution of the benefits between the sexes (Hedborg and Thalén 1993). A major difference concerned contributions paid by the well-off. Under ATP, contributions were paid by employers on behalf of high income earners which were earnings-related, but there was a ceiling for the maximum pension they could receive. The Bourgeois parties argued that if there was a ceiling for benefits there should be a ceiling for contributions; the Social Democrats, that the existing arrangement was intended to be redistributive (*DN* 20/10/93).

A preliminary set of proposals was published in February 1994 and was sent out on *remiss* (the consultation process). There was broad agreement that the old system needed reform but there were objections to different aspects of the new proposals. The trade union federations (LO, TCO and SACO) were unhappy about a recommendation that there be a shift from employer to employee contributions. The employers' federation (SAF) and the Industry Association (Industriförbundet) did not like the idea that employees should be compensated for their contributions with higher pay. Others – including the National Bank, the National Audit Board and the Social Insurance Board – were worried that the new scheme remained under financed and would have damaging implications for both public finances and the economy (*RD* 1994 No. 14 pp. 6–7). The new system was finally agreed upon in principle in May leaving some undecided details for future deliberation

(*DN* 3/5/94). The change towards employee and employer contributions was to take effect from 1 January 1995.

However, the debate rolled on. After the election of a new government in 1994, dissatisfaction emerged about various aspects of the new pension scheme. There were worries about the new replacement rate with some suggesting that in place of the old system's 67 per cent, future pensioners would only receive 50 per cent of their income. LO continued to pressurise for the dropping of employee contributions. There were many delegates at the 1996 Social Democratic party congress who objected to some aspects of the new arrangements. By the end of the year there were still a number of unresolved technical, legal and political issues. Dissatisfaction from the majority of the local branches of the Social Democratic party led to the party leadership seeking to renegotiate some aspects of the five-party agreement much to the dissatisfaction of the other four. The Conservative leader complained:

> A major agreement, on a major issue of the future, of major significance to the great majority of the Swedish people is threatened by internal disintegration within the Social Democratic party. I do not understand how Social Democrats can talk of social stability or taking responsibility for welfare when they are threatening to tear up the most important agreement on the greatest issue. (*DN* 10/1/97)

It didn't happen. By April 1997, a clear timetable was agreed for the introduction of the new system. There was one more major crisis over the employee contributions before final agreement was reached in January 1998.

The whole process had taken nearly seven years – from the appointment of the parliamentary committee at the beginning of one government's period of office to the decision of the Riksdag at the end of another's. During that time there were many conflicts, delays, threats and crises. But the will to reach a consensus persisted throughout. No one political view had prevailed, no one set of interests had dominated the process. The Bourgeois government had included the Social Democratic opposition and had routinely consulted the unions and pensioner groups. The Social Democratic government had in the end put the agreement above the pressure from its own rank and file. Each side of the political divide had tried to find a long term affordable solution to the country's way of providing decent old age pensions for the whole population.[1]

The new pension system

Under the new arrangements, a guaranteed pension (GP) will be paid to all adults resident in Sweden for 40 years (from the age of 25). For those without a right to an income-related pension (IRP) the GP will correspond to the old basic pension plus supplementary pension. Those with an entitlement to IRP amounting to *less than* 100 per cent of GP will receive an amount which will raise their pension to the GP level – hence the guarantee.

Contributions to IRP will be made by individuals throughout their lifetimes and their pension will be based upon their total contributions. What pensioners receive will be dependent upon the growth of wages in the economy. The pension will also be dependent upon the life expectancy of particular age cohorts. Total pension assets will be multiplied by coefficients reflecting current economic and demographic trends. There will, therefore, be no entitlement to a fixed percentage of earnings. As with the previous system however, only incomes up to 7.5 times the base amount will bear pension rights.

Contributions will amount to 18.5 per cent of a person's income. This will be made up of 16 per cent payable by employers and employees (the proportions of which have yet to be decided) into a pay-as-you-go scheme and 2.5 per cent into funded schemes. Funding arrangements will be supervised nationally. Individuals will be able to choose the fund in which they want their contribution invested.

> For those who do not choose a fund, the money will be deposited in the premium savings fund of the National Pension Insurance Fund. (Pension reform in Sweden 1998 p. 8.)

Contributions will be paid out of earned income but in certain circumstances, individuals will be credited with contributions paid for by the state:

- parents who look after small children
- people on national service
- recipients of disability /early retirement pensions

Individuals will be able to choose to retire as early as 61 or as late as 67. The earlier you retire, the lower your IRP pension will be, the later, the higher the IRP. The GP will be paid when you reach the age of 65. Instead of a separate system of partial pensions, individuals may choose from the age of 61 to take a quarter, half or three quarters of their IRP entitlement. The new system, unlike the old one, will not have to finance disability pensions. One of the problems faced by the previous funding mechanism had been the growth in the numbers of people retiring early for health reasons.

The new system will not affect those already in retirement. For those born between 1938 and 1953, their pensions will be a mix of the old and the new system. Those born after 1953 will be part of the new scheme.

How it will work

Palme has argued that the new system was a genuine compromise between the Bourgeois parties and the Social Democrats (Palme and Wennemo 1998 p. 22). The former would have preferred a greater emphasis upon private pensions and funding but had to accept that public expectations supported a largely public system. The latter had abandoned the commitment to a definite percentage replacement rate and no individual funding. This compromise between political parties, however, did not mean that argument about the new system would cease. On the contrary, ever since the agreement on principles was reached in 1994, there has been considerable debate about the costs and benefits, the winners and losers.

Government figures had suggested that if economic growth of about 2 per cent was achieved, IRP would provide a level of income replacement similar to ATP (*RD* 1998 No. 1 p. 3). Others argued that the government had used favourable assumptions to give this impression (*RD* 1998 No. 15b pp. 4–5). Using different assumptions (1–2 per cent growth, 2.5–3 per cent interest accruing to the funded part of IRP) it was suggested that IRP would provide a 6–10 per cent lower replacement rate than ATP. A Ministry of Health and Social Affairs spokesperson in response claimed that the government had made no predictions, it had merely used examples (Oscarsson 1998 p. 21). It did not deny the revised calculations made by the journal however.

A similarly pessimistic conclusion was reached at an earlier stage of the debate when it was alleged by an economist speaking at a meeting of the women's section of the Social Democratic party, that on average IRP would be 12 per cent lower than ATP (*DN* 24/2/94). Calculations made by the federation of academically-qualified workers, SACO, showed on the contrary that most employees would be better off (*DN* 11/4/94). On another level, it seemed to be the case that less educated working-class women were going to benefit from the new system but not their more educated, middle-class counterparts. This seemed to be supported by the fact that the leader of TCO expressed hostility to IRP as being anti-education, while the leaders of three manual worker unions with large female memberships thought IRP "good for women" (Arvidsson, Pettersson and Svensk 1994). These conclusions would also seem to be shared by Ståhlberg who wondered about middle-class support for the new system.

> The present ATP design chiefly favours large middle classes (or, more accurately, intermediate level white collar workers). It remains to be seen whether this group will show solidarity by supporting a system in which it no longer enjoys a comparative advantage. (Ståhlberg 1997 p. 51)

The debate about which groups would be winners and which losers and the likely overall income replacement rate continued without resolution in the years running up to the final legislation. One firm conclusion seemed to be that in the end everything would depend on the country's economic performance, the other was that as highly qualified women had benefited from ATP, so their working-class counterparts would benefit from IRP.

Changes to the existing system 1991–98

Changing the pension system was a dominant feature of welfare debate in the 1990s but the effect will not be known for some time. The more pressing need to reduce social expenditure inevitably led to a consideration of what scope there was for savings within the existing system. The value of the basic pension was reduced under both governments. The basic amount on which the pension was calculated was not raised in line with prices for a number of years (see Chapter 5). Moreover, instead of the pension being calculated as a percentage of the whole base amount, from 1993 it was calculated as a percentage of 98 per cent of the base amount. With membership of the EU on the horizon, eligibility for the full basic pension was also changed. All Swedish citizens had been entitled to a basic pension but as part of negotiations for membership of the EU, the rule was changed so that individuals had to live in Sweden for 40 years – a measure which would adversely affect elderly immigrants.

The Bourgeois government also considered the possibility of raising the retirement age to 67. The immediate savings looked tempting but would have been reduced by increased claims for early retirement pensions and unemployment benefit. Moreover, the Centre party had made a reputation for itself in the 1960s as the party in favour of lowering the retirement age to 65. The idea was abandoned.

The abolition of the partial retirement pension was discussed at length from early in the Bourgeois government's reign. Here too, it was argued that the savings would be counteracted by increased expenditure on other benefits. The Social Democrats complained that any discussion of partial pensions should be included in the cross-party talks on the wider issue of pension reform. New Democracy also refused to support the idea, and the proposal was dropped. Ironically, current expenditure was increased by thousands of applications for partial pensions by people anticipating that their chance of applying later might be lost. The same thing happened when in 1992, the government proposed raising the age of entitlement to partial pensions and reducing the level of income replacement. Finally, in 1994, an agreement was reached with the Social Democrats that the age for claiming a partial pension be raised to 61 and the income replacement rate be reduced from 65 per cent to 55 per cent (*DN* 14/5/94). It had taken the whole of the government's period of office to reduce one small part of the welfare budget to make minimal savings.

This constant changing of pensions policy and regulations led to more Swedes taking out private pension insurance. There had been considerable expansion in the 1980s because of favourable tax regulations but uncertainty about the future of the state pension system led to a further increase in the early 1990s. Around 5 per cent of adults had taken out a private pension in 1984 compared with over 20 per cent in 1993 and 25 per cent in 1996 (*DN* 10/8/95 and 28/12/96).

Social assistance and pensioner poverty

Did the various changes that took place in the 1990s mean that pensioners were worse off by the end of 1998, and if so by how much? These questions are difficult to answer as statistics on income are more readily available than those on the effects of increased charges for health care and social services.

In the 1970s, observers of Swedish welfare were impressed by the low numbers of elderly people on SA and in poverty. Wilson stated that, "Only 3 per cent of pensioners in any year have recourse to SA and then only to cover exceptional needs." (Wilson 1979 p. 37) Whereas pensioners constituted 57 per cent of all SA recipients in Britain, they amounted to only 4 per cent in Sweden (Greve 1978 p. 2). In the 1990s the percentage never rose above 2 per cent.[2] Using a different kind of measure the Household Income Survey (HINK) showed the percentage of different age groups, that – when "certain" household expenses were taken into account – had disposable incomes under the SA norm. It would seem to have declined considerably for all groups, as shown in Table 6.2, with the exception of men between 65 and 74, for whom the percentage was already very low.

The relatively good standard of living enjoyed by pensioners in Sweden was reinforced by responses to a question asked in SCBs annual survey of living standards. When asked whether they could raise SEK 12 000 to meet unexpected expenditure, only 15 per cent of those between 65 and 84 said they could not – the lowest response for any age group (Socialstyrelsen 1994:10 p. 76). Pensioners, like other groups did feel the effects of the lower basic pension and increased charges but this was partly compensated for by more people receiving a full ATP compared with previous generations. ATP was protected against inflation throughout the 1990s, whereas earned incomes declined in value.

The Finance Ministry produced annual calculations of income distribution changes which showed that pensioners suffered less than other age groups. Young people fared much worse as did families with children (*RD* 1994 No. 15 p. 6; Schuck 1996). In the early 1990s Finance Ministry figures showed that pensioner incomes had risen by 4 per cent. Even the adverse effects of the economic crisis in 1992 had been partially compensated for by raising housing allowances for the most needy (*RD* 1994 No. 1b p. 28). What the Finance Ministry's figures did not show was the effect on living standards of increased charges. Later

Table 6.2: Percentage of pensioners in households with incomes under the social assistance norm

	Age 65–74		*Age 75*	
	Women	Men	Women	Men
1987	19	3	40	28
1994	6	3	18	8

Source: Socialstyrelsen 1997:14 p. 94

figures from an investigation undertaken by the Ministry for Social Affairs showed that pensioners as a group continued to improve their real income between 1991 and 1998. In contrast three other groups – the young (18–29), young middle-aged (30–44) and older middle-aged (45–65) – had seen their incomes decline. More significantly, whereas in 1991, pensioners as a group had a lower income than the other three, by 1998, they ranked second to the older middle-aged (*RD* 1999 No. 7a p. 16).

Elderly immigrants

While elderly people generally in Sweden did not suffer too badly in the 1990s, the experience of the non-Swedish elderly was not so satisfactory. Research in both Gothenburg and Stockholm demonstrated that the non-Nordic elderly were much less likely to use home services or to have access to special accommodation than Swedes and Nordic immigrants (Gaunt 1996 pp. 345–6). A report from Socialstyrelsen was also very critical of the inadequate treatment received by elderly immigrants from local social services (*DN* 20/2/96). They not only received fewer services but also less information. Whereas 20 per cent of all elderly people received some help in the home only 6 per cent of elderly people from a minority background did so. Moreover, of 21 municipalities, only three made the effort to produce literature in the language of their minorities. Many elderly immigrants simply did not know what was available to them.

One study of pensioners showed a more promising picture. In the years 1978, 1991 and 1993, immigrants as a whole were as likely as Swedes to have pensions (Ekberg 1996). Moreover, the differences in their value were not too dissimilar. Indeed for women, those from ethnic minorities fared slightly better than their Swedish counterparts. Understandably, when comparisons were made in 1991 between immigrants who came to Sweden at different points in time, it was clear that those who had arrived after 1980 – and who were, therefore, more likely to be from the Middle East and Africa – were much less likely to receive pensions and those who did had much lower pensions. Much of this disadvantage could be explained simply by the fact that they did not have adequate contribution records. Less easy to explain were the disproportionate numbers of older immigrants who had received disability pensions. While this may have been due to poor health, it might also have been an indicator of labour market exclusion.

Grey politics

If pensioners as a whole did not suffer as badly as other groups in society, this may have been due in part to their political organisation. As Schuck has pointed out:

> It is easy to forget this growing division between old and young when demonstrating pensioners fill the streets and a pensioners' party is under way ... well-organised groups have a better opportunity to protect their interests (Schuck 1996)

Sweden's "well-organised groups" are part of the country's *folkrörelse* (people's movement) tradition. People's movements come in many forms but they typically consist of a number of organisations which are organised at a national and a local level, have common aims and strong mutual links, and co-operate to put pressure on local and national politicians. Nationally, there are four main organisations which represent the interests of elderly people – the PRO (National Organisation of Pensioners), the SPF (Sweden's Pensioners' Association), SPRF (The National Association of Sweden's Pensioners) and the RPG (National Association for the Community of Pensioners). Together, they claim a membership of 700 000 – nearly half of all elderly people – which had increased significantly in the early 1990s (Blake 1997 p. 57). Their representatives sit on the pensioners' national advisory committee (PK) which meets four or five times a year with ministers and civil servants. PK was established in 1991 after a Commission had recognized that pensioners had "weak political influence relative to member strength" (ibid.). Most municipalities have local advisory committees where the pensioner organisations put forward the views of elderly people on a wide range of issues. Pensioners also have discussions with investigative commissions, the Central Bureau of Statistics and Socialstyrelsen on matters affecting the welfare and interests of elderly people.

Right from the beginning of the Bourgeois government, PRO and SPF made representations to government about the adverse effects of its policies. In October 1991, they were demanding to meet with ministers in order to influence the first budget (*DN* 16/10/91). They campaigned for the compensation they had been promised for the losses they suffered as a result of the 1992 crisis agreement between the government and the opposition Social Democrats. In particular they pressurised for, and got, increased housing allowances. Nor was the government hostile to pensioners. The Assistant Minister for Social Insurance expressed his aim that no pensioner should have to claim social assistance and claimed that he gave considerable weight to the views of pensioners.

His Social Democratic successor expressed the same view when speaking at the 1996 PRO congress. Two weeks later 12 000 pensioners – representing all the associations – marched in Stockholm, protesting about government policies (*DN* 27/9/96). Increasingly strident statements were being made about the neglect and discrimination being experienced by the old. It was said that the major political parties were ignoring them. For over a decade the Swedish Pensioners' Interests party (SPI) had campaigned in local elections with some success, but in 1996 it decided to fight the next election to the Riksdag. Its problem was to unite its potential support. Elderly people made up over 20 per cent of the electorate. Theoretically, the 4 per cent minimum to gain entry into the Riksdag was achievable. The problem was disunity (Thorén 1997). There were a number of other smaller pensioner parties campaigning on care issues. Moreover the two main pressure groups PRO and SPF favoured the Social Democrats and the Conservatives respectively.[3] There were problems too with the SPI programme which in some respects was quite reactionary (*DN* 11/5/96). It was one thing to unite pensioners on pensioner issues but quite another to get them to agree on issues like foreign aid and immigration. In the event SPI won only 1 per cent of the votes in the Riksdag elections of 1998.

In interviews, carried out by the author, representatives of PRO, SPF and RPG felt that they had achieved a great deal by working through the existing party system and saw no need for a separate party. They had become stronger and more active in the 1990s and had co-operated with each other at a national level to campaign on behalf of their members. They had resisted an attempt by the Bourgeois government to set up a separate *base amount* for pensioners and in getting the Social Democratic government in 1998 to restore the system of calculating the basic pension with reference to the *whole* of the base amount. However, they were resigned to not restoring the 12 per cent cut in the value of the basic pension. They felt they had also been successful in getting financial support for dental costs – an important health issue for the elderly – and in resisting proposals for care taxes for the elderly. They were all agreed that while pensioners receiving ATP had come through the last decade relatively unscathed, those without ATP had suffered a great deal.

It was clear from the interviews that the success of pensioner groups, however, lay not simply in direct action but also in the institutional arrangements which made consultation with interest groups a matter of course. Moreover, these were in turn backed by a consensus among all the political parties and in the population as a whole, that the elderly had a right to a decent standard of living and high quality services, largely provided by the public sector.

Conclusion

Writing about the welfare of elderly people in a comparative perspective, the Norwegian, Daatland, wondered whether support for the Scandinavian welfare system would survive. The public's trust in the welfare state had been developed at a time when the economy was strong and the population homogeneous. Now that this was no longer the case, "solidarity may crumble and the support for common, collective solutions may weaken" (Daatland 1997 p. 160). This was written in the context of cuts, targeting and privatisation of benefits and services for the elderly. These trends might, in his view, "reflect a more pluralistic and heterogeneous population" (ibid.). This would seem to be a rather pessimistic conclusion in the light of this chapter. It is true that services and benefits for the elderly have deteriorated but they remain quite robust. The private sector in care and in pensions is still dwarfed by public provision. When neglect and mismanagement in a private nursing home were revealed, it caused outrage. When pensions were reformed, much of the old system was retained.

Pensioners' interests and their welfare have been protected by their own political actions. Moreover, it cannot be said that their complaints have been dealt with unsympathetically. From within the machinery of the state, Socialstyrelsen was always ready to champion their cause against struggling local authorities. Within both governments, even the Centre-right coalition, ministers were sympathetic to the needs of elderly people. Ministers had their own problems and constraints but they tried to protect the elderly.

Part of the explanation for this may be the fact that the majority of elderly people are women and the majority of their carers – whether in the informal or the formal sectors – are women. And, as we shall now see, women in Swedish society, are also a formidable force in Swedish politics.

7
The State of Women

> When it comes to equality, Swedish men are the best in the world.
>
> (Inger Segelström 1999 p. 9)[1]

> Access to political equality and democracy has improved: the large disparity between women's and men's participation and representation has disappeared, and the organisation of the Swedish welfare society has enabled women to achieve a higher level of influence and autonomy.
>
> (Bergqvist and Jungar 2000)

Introduction

Traditionally, social policy has been about the kinds of services and benefits which have been discussed in Chapters 5 and 6. But in recent years the subject has been widened to incorporate other aspects of "the social". In particular, the subordinate status of ethnic groups, people with disabilities and women have led to a concern about discrimination and disadvantage. Social policies have been implemented to improve the situation but in turn they have been criticised either for not going far enough or for reinforcing the very patterns of behaviour they claim to oppose. Welfare in this sense is very much bound up with the notion of equality; equality with whites, with those without disabilities, with men. In the struggle for their own identities, groups which have suffered systematic discrimination sometimes seek to go beyond mere equality to creating an alternative set of values and institutions. This has certainly been the case with some parts of the Swedish women's movement.

We will begin with an overview of the principal measures which have contributed to the high status which women seem to enjoy in Sweden and show how this is linked with the public sector and women's role in political life. This will be followed by an account of the continuing gender inequalities within Swedish society and how feminists assess what has been achieved. The chapter will conclude with two other social issues which symbolise women's subordination – violence against women and female prostitution. Concern about the latter resulted in the passing of a law which criminalised those purchasing a prostitute's services and the question will be raised whether this was a blow for women's liberation or another example of *putting people's lives in order*.

Published material in this chapter will be complemented by interviews carried out with representatives of the women's sections of the political parties and of four extra-parliamentary women's organisations.[2]

Women and the welfare state

Throughout Sweden's industrialisation, women drew attention to a wide range of gender and social issues. It is possible to argue that Scandinavian women generally have enjoyed higher social status than their counterparts in other countries throughout this century. The concern for the family shown by the Population Commission in the 1930s certainly improved the social situation of women. Incentives were provided for "family formation: marriage loans, affordable housing for families, prenatal and postnatal care, social transfers for poor mothers (both married and single)" (Hobson *et al.* 1995 p. 2). Hirdman – in her book *Att lägga livet till rätta* (putting people's lives in order) – described how the socialist utopias of the nineteenth century and the social engineering approach of the Myrdals in the 1930s, filtered by the pragmatic politics of the Social Democrats, improved the home life of ordinary Swedish families. The "need" to increase the birth rate was used as a justification for improving the health of children, encouraging women to take on employment and taking a progressive line on contraception, abortion and sexual behaviour. In the reports of the Commission and the writings of the Myrdals:

> We find ... another emancipatory strategy for women: to seek to raise women's value through raising the value of the home, through

> raising the status of housework. We see this stressed again in another report ... where it was argued that boys should be given instruction in school kitchens as a means of teaching them the value of housework. (Hirdman 1989 p. 158)

For all the emancipatory rhetoric, Hirdman claimed, it remained clear that women were intended to remain the chief homemakers within households dominated by men.

The real breakthrough seems to have occurred in the 1960s and 1970s when Social Democratic governments took on gender equality as a major social goal (Persson 1990 p. 223). Over the next few decades, enormous strides were taken to improve women's independence. Extensive childcare provision made it easier for mothers to be employed. Parental leave made it possible for women to combine the dual roles of child-rearing and employment. The dual taxation system and the right to work part-time were also important (Hobson *et al.* 1995 p. 5). The high rate of employment among women in turn enabled women to "earn" their own rights to social insurance benefits. Women in other countries were more likely to be dependent on means-tested social assistance than their Swedish counterparts (Sainsbury 1993). Many unemployed women in Sweden were entitled to earnings-related unemployment benefit; women who were sick were entitled to earnings-related sickness benefit; and elderly women received a state earnings-related pension. Moreover, extensive state provision of care for elderly people and those with disabilities, provided them with greater support and respite than elsewhere.

Since these policy measures were largely the result of developments in the 1970s and the 1980s, what did the experience of the 1990s imply for the status of women in Swedish society? To the extent that women's status had been enhanced by welfare services and benefits, cuts in social expenditure had a serious effect. There was a concern about what was happening to the public sector generally and the implications of welfare privatisation. What effect would EU membership have on women's interests? What could be done about continuing gender inequalities in Swedish society? How much political power did women actually have? What was to be done about violence against women? What was to be done about prostitution? Alongside traditional concerns about economic independence and political influence, there also emerged a more postmodern concern about what Eduards calls "bodily integrity" (Eduards 1997a p. 23).

Women and the public sector

There can be little doubt that there is a strong correlation between the size of a country's public sector and the status of its women. The public sector is more likely to provide jobs in education, the caring professions and administration – all employment areas in which women tend to dominate. Sweden's public sector remains one of the largest, if not the largest, in the world. The expansion in the public sector which had occurred in the 1970s and 1980s had provided considerable employment for women. It was hardly surprising, therefore, that many women were concerned about the possible consequences of a Centre-right government in 1991.

> The woolly alternative [to the Swedish welfare system] – privatisation and female charity in civil society – can only terrify. The 90s utopia of the right does not fundamentally have good intentions in the relationship between state and citizen. The chief actor in the new utopia is not even a person. It is an institution called the Market. And it isn't even *Swedish* [my italics] (Hirdman 1993 p. 37).

We have already examined many of the changes which took place within the welfare state 1991–94. Coupled with the changes introduced by the Social Democrats we can now see that tough though they were, they did not result in a system change but rather system erosion. Sweden at the end of 1998 still boasted a welfare system dominated by a large public sector. This does not mean that women's fears were unjustified. Indeed, it may be that it was partly due to their concern and pressure that the system changed so little. In the interviews, all – even those from the Bourgeois parties – agreed that women had been adversely affected by cuts to social and public expenditure. Oddly enough, they also all agreed that women had also benefited from some forms of privatisation. The example commonly offered was of nurses – who had been made redundant by the county health authorities – setting up their own agencies and selling their services back to state hospitals at higher rates of remuneration. Women were beginning to make more of a success of the private sector.

Women, politics and power

Women had already made considerable progress politically prior to the 1990s. Representation in parliament and government had increased in the two previous decades. Large proportions of women were members of political parties and trade unions. In 1987, when roughly 16 per cent of elected posts to public bodies consisted of women, a Commission on Women's Representation recommended that by 1992 representation should have increased to 30 per cent, by 1995 to 40 per cent and by 1997 to 50 per cent (SOU 1987:19). The threat of a quota system was made should the Commission's goals not be realised. While the absolute goals have not been achieved, women's representation has improved enormously as a result.

Although the proportion of women in parliament declined to 33 per cent in the election of 1991, there were eight women in the Centre-right government – 38 per cent of ministerial posts (Raaum 1995 p. 34). Nor were they in "soft" posts. The finance minister, the justice minister and the minister for foreign affairs were all women. In the 1994 election, 40 per cent of members of parliament were women and 50 per cent of cabinet posts went to women, largely because of a decision by the Social Democrats to ensure that every other candidate on the party's slate was a woman. Subsequently, there were large percentages of women sitting on parliamentary standing committees (44 per cent), investigative committees (36 per cent), state agencies (43 per cent) (SOU 1998:6 pp. 138–40).

During the 1990s, women in both the Social Democratic party and the Left party campaigned for as much, if not greater, emphasis upon a gender perspective as opposed to a class perspective, within their respective parties. It also became customary in the 1990s for the Equality Minister to meet regularly with women members of the Riksdag to discuss matters of concern to all women. These meetings were subsequently widened to include extra-parliamentary groups. They inspired a high degree of co-operation which often resulted in joint pressure on government and joint motions to the Riksdag. Across the parties a watchful eye was kept on the under-representation of women in all spheres and public attention was brought to any deficiencies. In spite of this obvious success, there was a lot to be watchful about, particularly in the media. Sweden might have had its first woman prime minister but for the press.

When Ingvar Carlsson, in 1995, announced his intention to stand down the following year, Mona Sahlin, Carlsson's deputy and Minister for Equality, became the frontrunner for the post. Sahlin's succession seemed certain until the media alleged irregularities in her use of a cash card issued for official purposes. Although a subsequent investigation cleared her of any intention to defraud, she had by then been forced to resign her post and to withdraw her candidacy.[3] It would be simplistic to suggest that the media campaign against her was inspired by a simple reluctance to accept a woman as a prime minister, but it is equally clear that the frenzied pursuit of her and attacks on her were sexist in nature (Boethius 1995, Sahlin 1997). As many anxious women had – according to Boethius – asked of Sahlin's previous treatment at the hands of the media:

> Isn't this a message to every young woman in Sweden that she should behave herself damn correctly if she wants to have anything to do with politics and absolutely not assume political power (Boethius 1994)?

If there were ambivalent attitudes towards women and power in the media, the leadership of the trade union movement was also finding it difficult to cope with the need for greater female representation on its governing committees. On the one hand, it is clear that due to membership of, and representation through, the trade union movement, women's power has been strengthened. In 1975, 34 per cent of LO members and 49 per cent of TCO were women. In 1996/97 these percentages had increased to 46 and 60 respectively (SOU 1998:6 p. 141). On the other hand, women found male attitudes contradictory and their own pursuit of power difficult. How, asked one woman, could male work-mates talk about the equal value of all people during the day and go to porn clubs in the evening? (*DN* 12/10/93) Fewer women than men were given union responsibilities; fewer were elected to senior positions; and in consequence, fewer represented the union on external agencies and official bodies (see Table 7.1).

In the last days of the Centre-right government, a new Commission (KMU – the Investigation into Women's Power) was set up to investigate women's power in Swedish society. The new government found

Table 7.1: Women's representation in LO 1988–95

	% of women 1988	% of women 1995	% change 1988–95
Members	44	46	+2
Delegates to previous congress	23	26	+3
Representatives on governing committee	17	23	+6
Representatives on negotiating delegations	17	23	+6
Departmental officials	5	9	+4

Source: *DN* 13/4/96

itself in deep water when it appointed Olof Petersson to lead the investigation. Women researchers were outraged and claimed there were plenty of women (in particular Inga Persson of Lund University), whose life's work had been devoted to the issue of women and power, who would have been better suited to the post. As a result, in 1995, the government's appointee stood down (under protest) and Kristina Persson, a Social Democratic county governor, took his place. KMU had to report within two years and as a consequence relied upon existing research rather than carry out its own. Most of the 13 reports were published in 1997 and the final one *Ty makten är din* (Because power is yours) (SOU 1998:6) early in 1998. The reports contain a wealth of interesting data about not just the macro level of gender power differences but also the micro level of the home. The accounts of the research are fascinating but the conclusions of Persson, the lone investigator – as we shall see below – were rather disappointing.

No discussion about the influence and power of women in Sweden would be complete without some mention of the nature of the women's movement in Sweden. The term *women's movement* has an international resonance but in Sweden there is a direct link with the whole tradition of *folkrörelser* – popular movements. This has already been referred to – in relation to grey power – in the previous chapter. In the interviews it was clear that the *folkrörelse* model, as much as any international influence, had enabled Swedish women to influence policy and politics at local and central government levels. As one respondent put it, women had traditionally taken a major role in voluntary organisations anyway. They were used to the *folkrörelse* way of co-operating, influencing and networking. Action sometimes took the form of demonstrations; it communicated itself through a complex network of organisations; it informed itself through study circles and conferences; and it resulted in a high degree of consciousness, cohesion and consensus. As with the politics of the elderly, there was an attempt to form a women's party. As with the elderly, it failed because it was found that co-operation between groups and across parties was the more effective mode of operation.

Women and the EU

Having attained a considerable degree of influence and power in their home country, many women came to see the EU as a threat to many of the gains they had made. They were horrified at the lack of power women had within the EU. How could women's interests be advanced they asked when there were so few of them in the European Parliament, the Commission and the Council of Ministers? The majority had fears prior to the referendum on entry – they voted against entry – and continued to express anxieties once Sweden had become a member. Women, it was claimed, had lost jobs in the public sector; child care provision had been cut; and much elderly care privatised. Women in other European countries – especially Catholic ones – were seen as being on the "margins of the labour market" and more likely to experience poverty, more likely to have part-time work, less likely to have social insurance benefits (SOU 1993:117 p. 239).

In the view of Gertrud Schymann, the leader of the Left party, Swedish women were becoming more like their European counterparts and "the situation will be worse with EMU" (Schymann 1995 p. 13). It was accepted that in some ways the more legalistic approach to gender equality within the EU might have complemented Sweden's more family policy approach, but by itself it could not create the degree of integration and status which had been achieved by women in Sweden (Hobson and Takahashi 1997). Even the legalistic approach was seen as having deficiencies. A Commission appointed to investigate equality regulations in the EU concluded that it endorsed a narrow and minimal approach which focused on pay levels. Swedish legislation, it was argued, had gone further by including other aspects of employment and by encouraging positive discrimination to bring women up to the level of men (*RD* 1996 No. 14 p. 12).

Gender inequality in the 1990s

It is one of Sweden's proudest boasts that the UN has declared it the most gender equal country in the world. This reputation alone provides a strong impetus to maintain the position. Even the Centre-right government felt it important to demonstrate its concern about gender inequalities. Through Bengt Westerberg – who as well as being the Minister for Health and Social Affairs was also Minister for Equality – it recommended that pay differentials be investigated and reported on annually with a view to sharpening Equal Opportunities legislation (*RD* 1994 No. 5 p. 5). It set up KMU with the aim of finding ways to further reduce the gender inequalities in Swedish society. Earlier, it had instructed another Commission to investigate the likely gender outcomes of EU membership (SOU 1993:117).

The Social Democratic government claimed that gender equality would be one of its chief priorities and that all policies would be examined for their gender implication. Some municipalities, like Vaxsjö, claimed to have implemented this practice at a local level. When Sahlin was Minister for Equality she organised a three-hour workshop for her cabinet colleagues on gender issues. Yet criticism was aimed at the government for failing to prioritise gender sufficiently. Even state agencies like the Labour Market Board were criticised by the government Audit Office for failing to implement adequately their own, internal, equal opportunities policies (*RD* 1995 No. 36 p. 12). The KMU itself stated that Sweden was *not* a country of gender equality – the public sector exploited women; gender inequalities at work were increasing; the difficulties of lone mothers were becoming worse; and men "like corks" always floated to the top (SOU 1998:6). This will be illustrated in the following sections on employment, unemployment, the family and welfare.

Employment

A greater percentage of women are employed in Sweden than in other countries. In 1996 70 per cent of women were employed and 73 per cent of men (SOU 1998:6 p. 81). This fact suggested a greater degree of equality than actually existed. Sweden is also known to have one of the most gender-segregated work forces among industrialised societies. According to the KMU, 54 per cent of women were employed in the public sector and 46 per cent in the private sector. In contrast, only 21 per cent of men were employed in the public sector while 79 per cent were in the private sector. Moreover, within the public and the private sectors, women were much less likely than men to achieve senior positions (Table 7.2).

Few women got to the top in the private sector where technical education was an important criterion for promotion (SOU 1998:6 p. 2). When Sweden was compared to other countries, women were seen to have less power in the private sector. Whereas 95 per cent of top

Table 7.2: Percentage of women among employees and senior staff 1995

	Employees	Senior staff	Difference
Private sector	37	20	–17
Public sector	72	43	–29
County Councils	81	48	–33
Central government	44	23	–21
Municipalities	62	51	–11

Source: SCB, cited in *RD* 1997 No. 37b p. 7.

American companies and 41 per cent of British companies had at least one woman on the Board, only 22 per cent of Swedish companies were in the same position (ibid. p. 102). Even when women did achieve senior positions, they received lower salaries than their male counterparts. Professions dominated by women were also more likely to be less well paid than professions dominated by men. Nevertheless, whereas in 1975 only 10 per cent of women had incomes higher than their male partners, by 1993, the figure had risen to 20 per cent. Among young women, the percentage was 44 per cent.

Throughout the 1980s and 1990s however, women's *hourly pay*, in comparison to men's, had been relatively stable at 80 per cent; *average pay* for women in 1996 was 68 per cent of men's (Ministry of Labour 1998).[4] While this was better than many other countries, there was little evidence of the gap diminishing. When, however, the Centre and Left Parties in 1997 suggested that the law on equal pay needed revision, the Riksdag rejected the proposal (*RD* 1997 No. 9 p. 3). The tradition in the past, according to Hobson, had been to leave questions of pay levels to the labour market partners – with little effect (Hobson *et al.* 1995 pp. 4 and 7). Moreover, it remained true that more women than men were likely to work part time which had implications for pay, prospects and pensions. Two thirds of those in permanent jobs who worked in excess of 40 hours a week were men, and one third were women. The reverse was true for those working less than 34 hours a week (SOU 1998:6 p. 86).

Unemployment

Early in the 1990s when unemployment first began to rise, it was men who suffered most with the loss of jobs in manufacturing. But as public sector cuts took their toll, women in the public sector took the main brunt. Yet even in 1996, it was still the case that men were more likely to be unemployed. The rate for men was 8.5 per cent and for women 7.5 per cent (SOU 1998:6 p. 81). However, when hidden unemployment and underemployment were taken into account, 17 per cent of women were affected in comparison to only 13 per cent of men (*RD* 1996 No. 13b p. 10).

Faced with the likelihood that large-scale unemployment was going to be around for some time, various proposals were put forward for its alleviation. Neither economic growth, nor the expansion of the public sector, were on the cards. Alternative proposals therefore emerged. One proposal, which had the support of many women on the left, was to reduce working time. For many years they had argued specifically for a six-hour day, to no avail. But with the onset of mass unemployment new demands were made. This subject will be dealt with in more detail in Chapter 8. What is important to stress at this point is that the impetus behind such proposals came mainly from women. Against the wishes of the Social Democratic leadership, female delegates had forced the issue onto the agenda at the 1997 party Congress. It was agreed that it was a matter, which should be left to the labour market partners on the understanding that if little progress was made, legislation would be passed.

Another proposal, intended to provide more work for women, met with divided reactions from those on the left. In Swedish it was referred to as the *pigdebatt*[5] – the maidservant debate.

The "maidservant" debate

As the supply of jobs decreased and as income differentials widened in the 1990s, proposals to make it easier to employ people to work in one's home as cleaners, and to perform other sevices in the home, emerged. Employers contributions and VAT made it expensive to employ people legitimately. The services were, therefore, provided through the informal economy or not at all. Reductions in the taxes on such services, it was argued, would both stimulate more jobs and enable those working illegally to do so legally. Some of the debate about the various proposals that emerged concerned technicalities; whether tax reductions or subsidies would achieve the desired effect. Others were about whether there was scope for reducing taxes when public services were being seriously eroded. But more important than these was the ideological issue of whether it was right to subsidise the affluent so that they could employ servants. For many socialists, it was an issue of whether the regrettable inequalities which were already widening should be further encouraged by making it easier for the affluent to get cheap help in the home. It was seen as a return to the days of the past. To clean an office was one thing, to clean up after the rich in their own homes was another.

The Bourgeois parties tended to favour a subsidy and the Socialist parties were opposed. The Chair of the Social Democratic Women's Association, Inger Segelström, argued that:

> Well-paid women and men, directors and yuppies shall not use our limited tax resources to increase their well-being. Many women cannot afford such services (*DN* 5/6/96).

One correspondent to *Dagens Nyheter* put it slightly differently:

> Why haven't these people got the time or strength to clean for themselves? There are normally three reasons: too big a house or flat, too many ornaments, poor distribution of labour in the home ... I've cleaned at home and elsewhere in my time. Now I'm worn out and as my aches increase and my strength declines, I get rid of those objects which make cleaning more difficult. My pension is 4,613 kronor (£350) a month after tax. What is left over after my rent and the newspapers will certainly not be sufficient to subsidise home services. I'm very conscious of the fact that no matter how bad I feel, I've got to look after myself. (*DN* 11/3/98)

The Commission that had been appointed to examine the issue in 1996 published its report with a set of proposals early in 1997. But the matter was shelved before the end of the government's period of office.

Housework

Who did the housework was, of course, an important issue in other respects. KMU devoted a considerable amount of space to the division of labour within the home. Research carried out at the beginning of the decade showed that men continued to do much less work in the home than women and tasks tended to be gender related. Women devoted 33 hours a week to domestic jobs compared to 20 for men (cited in SOU 1998:6 p. 40). When it came to tasks such as cooking, cleaning and washing, women contributed 17 hours to men's 6 hours.

A survey of the division of labour in Swedish homes estimated the number of *equal, semi-equal, conventional* and *patriarchal* couples (SOU 1997:139). Looking at the three tasks of cooking, washing and cleaning, it was found that only 13 per cent of couples shared tasks equally. In 24 per cent of the couples there was a sharing of two of the tasks (semi-equal); in 36 per cent a sharing of one (conventional); leaving 27 per cent where women did almost everything (patriarchal). The most *equal* categories were young people without children and those with small children. While this might suggest a generation change, it might simply reflect men's willingness to share in the early stages of setting up a home. In two thirds of couples with school-age children and older couples without children, they were either in the *conventional* or *patriarchal* categories.

Progress towards an equal sharing of domestic tasks in Sweden was clearly proving a long struggle. As the final KMU report said, men simply did not have "the ability and will to see what needs to be done, take the initiative to do something or show a sense of responsibility" (SOU 1998:6 p. 49). This was reinforced by the finding that men who were unemployed – but whose partners were employed – were not likely to do much more housework than when they were in work. It is also interesting to note that the seeming equality of highly paid couples was not the consequence of men doing more in the home but of women doing less by employing poorer women to do the dirty work.

Parenting

Patterns of domestic responsibility were repeated when it came to caring for children. On average Swedish women spent 47 hours a week with their children and men only 18 (ibid. p. 50). And while it was true that an insurance based system of parental leave had been beneficial for many women, it did not seem to have resulted in an equalisation of parenting. Men took a very small proportion (0.5 per cent) of the total days leave back in 1975 (ibid. p. 51) and while the figure had risen to 10 per cent by the early 1990s it had remained static for some time. Hobson suggested that the parental leave taken by men was not necessarily to discharge their child-rearing responsibilities but to extend their holiday entitlement (Hobson *et al.* 1995 p. 17). Men always had the excuse that "the family" stood to lose more money if they took the leave. Thus one form of inequality was used to justify another. This was reinforced by the reluctance of many employers, particularly in the private sector, to look favourably on male employees taking parental leave (SOU 1998:6 p. 117).

Social policy

Women of course did suffer from job cuts in the public sector. They were also hit by the cuts to sickness, parental and unemployment benefits, pensions, child allowances and social assistance. The lower one's income the more difficult it is to cope with such reductions. Hobson also claimed that women suffered from cutbacks in hospital and institutional care. Cutbacks in resources for community care meant that an even greater share of care of the elderly and those with disabilities fell upon women (Hobson *et al.* 1995 p. 12).

In percentage terms, women derived more of their income from the welfare state but in absolute cash terms there was little to choose between the sexes (SOU 1998:6 p. 155). In terms of the amount of cash men and women would seem to have gained about the same as each other. Of course, when it came to social insurance and pensions, earnings-related benefits were bound to reflect the greater income of men.

> There exists therefore an inequality between men and women that is built into the transfer system which is rooted in the sexual division of labour within the family, a sex differentiated labour market and pay differences between men and women. (ibid. p. 148)

In spite of Bengt Westerberg's efforts to advance the cause of gender equality, the last year of the Centre-right government saw an attempt by the Christian Democratic party to encourage more mothers to stay at home to take care of their children. A care grant – *vårdnadsbidrag* – of 2000 krona a month (£200 at that time) was proposed. This was to be financed by higher charges for municipal day care and a reduction in parental benefit from 90 per cent to 80 per cent of income (*RD* 1993 No. 25 p. 5). According to Hobson, there was "a wave of protest" from women, but the measure was passed by the Riksdag in Summer 1994 (Hobson *et al.* 1995 p. 10). Unfortunately for the Christian Democrats, the new government abolished the measure on achieving office.

If the Christian Democratic side of the coalition tended to be reactionary, the same could not be said for the Liberal influence of the Minister for Health and Social Affairs. Not only did he establish a number of initiatives to promote gender equality but took the practical step of encouraging men to take up at least one month of the 12 months parental leave allotted to parents of young children. If they did not, it could not be taken by the mothers. An additional incentive was that the *pappamånad* (dad's month) as it came to be called was paid at 90 per cent of income when the other months were reduced to 80 per cent. Westerberg also introduced a guarantee of a place in child care for all children up to the age of 12 (*RD* 1994 No. 1c p. 14).

Single mothers were said to have been well favoured by policies in the 1970s and 1980s. Full employment policy combined with widely available childcare had made it possible for single mothers to achieve economic independence. They received preferential treatment in queues for childcare. Hobson argued that they were better protected than in other countries and stood less chance of experiencing poverty. They were included in "the policy framework developed for working parents" (Hobson and Takahashi 1997 p. 116). She expressed a fear that the policies of the Centre-right coalition, with their emphasis upon privatisation and cuts to benefits and services, would widen the gap between women in two earner families and single mothers (ibid. 1997 p. 117). A joint report published in 1996 by the ministries of employment, education and social affairs confirmed that their situation had deteriorated in the 1990s. They were more likely to be receiving social assistance, their living standards had declined and their labour market situation had deteriorated, both in comparison with women in couples and with lone fathers (*DN* 17/2/96).

Another group of women whose situation seems to have deteriorated was that of women with disabilities. The Disability Ombudsman, Inger Wästberg, claimed that women were receiving lower benefits and less rehabilitation than men (*DN* 7/1/96). She urged the government to ensure that future statistics were collected and analysed by sex to check on such deficiencies. Research in Lund University confirmed Wästberg's view. Malena Sjöberg claimed that in almost all of the cases she examined, functionally impaired women received less benefits than men in the same situation.

> Whether it concerns sickness benefit, rehabilitation, disability pension, disability compensation of personal assistance compensation it is clear: your sex decides how much you get (Novak 1998 p. 6).

It was also claimed that changes by the Bourgeois government to work injury insurance which demanded stricter proof for, and reduced the amount of, benefit, had affected low paid women more than any other group (Carlén 1999 p. 22). As a result of such revelations, the Ministry of Social Affairs has initiated a gender programme for social welfare and demanded that social insurance boards analyse "their proposals and activities from a gender viewpoint" (Lindén 1998 p. 20).

Violence against women

While it may be the case that Sweden leads the world in gender equality, we have already seen a number of examples of where women remain in a subordinate position to men. As one kind of inequality was alleviated or removed, so other issues became more obvious and demanded attention. Problems which had been concealed, or had simply not been regarded as problems, emerged. The systematic nature of inequality and social injustice was revealed. Swedish feminists in the 1990s became more aware of the ways in which women were oppressed through violence and sexuality. This section will deal with the issue of male violence against women – an issue to which other countries had responded before Sweden did so. The following section will deal with an area where Sweden sees itself in the vanguard – making the purchase of a prostitute's services an imprisonable offence.

The awareness of violence against women seemed to have arisen as a result of overseas experience according to the view of one trenchant critic of the Swedish state. Amy Elman is the American author of *Sexual subordination and state intervention* in which she compared the different ways in which women expressed their demands and the different ways in which the authorities responded to them. Elman's own position was that of a feminist who was suspicious of the state and believed women needed to engage in self help rather than get embroiled in compromises with state agencies. She argued that few of the "women friendly" measures implemented by the Swedish corporatist system had been driven by feminist demands. They were either motivated by the desire to improve the labour market or to make men's lives easier. When women's liberationists (non-feminist women, in her view, who were merely concerned with equal opportunities) made demands, they did so from a position of weakness. Women's groups in Sweden and the female sections of political parties were too dependent upon the existing male dominated power structure to express adequately what women really needed. Elman cited her Swedish colleague Maud Eduards who claimed that the political parties, in particular, had been "remarkably efficient in co-opting both women and women's demands" (cited in Elman 1996 p. 29). State finance and support was only granted on certain conditions, one of which was that criticism of government policies was restrained.

Rape and sexual violence were regarded as "immigrant" problems and "Sweden's battering and rape programmes and reforms are best characterised as weak and reserved" (ibid. pp. 92 and 118). Although some shelters for battered women were initiated by women rights activists with close connections to the Social Democratic party, Elman claimed that they objected to both feminist ways of thinking and to lesbian involvement. They "operated out of a more conventional social-service approach to battered women" (ibid. p. 40). There was no private funding; there was an over reliance on volunteers and paid staff were available for limited hours only. When the principal Stockholm refuge was vandalised it remained closed for "several months" (ibid. p. 53). In the research on battered women she carried out with Eduards, in the late 1980s, it was claimed that the problem had been ignored by those who wanted to believe Sweden was a haven of equality. Violence against women was something which Swedish men did not do. However when Elman and Eduards investigated the views of women in refuges, they found 80 per cent of both batterers and victims were Swedish (Elman and Eduards 1991 p. 415). Respondents criticised police, prosecutors and social workers for failing to help them. The police did not believe them; prosecutors were reluctant to issue protection orders; and social workers gave them poor advice.

There can be little doubt that there was something of a change in the 1990s – perhaps as a result of the sort of criticism alluded to. Eduards has described the development of refuges in the 1980s and the various organisational and ideological conflicts between different women's groups and between the groups and the local authorities. By 1995, she said, there were 133 shelters – the vast majority affiliated to ROKS (the Swedish organisation of emergency shelters for battered women). ROKS certainly saw itself as a feminist organisation fighting against "male domination and superiority" (Eduards 1997b p. 143). It was not solely concerned with domestic violence:

> Violence against women, the sex trade, rape, incest and other sexual forms of assault, together with pornography, are the ultimate consequences of the visible oppression of women in society. All forms of this repression are different only in degree, and not in kind (cited in Eduards 1997b p. 143).

Eduards claimed that that the number of shelters had grown and that the funding had improved considerably. She insisted that "shelters had arisen from the women's movement" (ibid. p. 144) and that they were voluntary in nature in spite of their dependence on public money. She also described the effects of public sector cuts upon the shelters. Some jobs had gone and some shelters had closed. At the same time the number of cases of domestic violence was increasing.

The Centre-right administration demonstrated its concern when Bengt Westerberg appointed a Commission to investigate violence against women in 1993. Eduards clearly thought the new Commission an improvement on previous inquiries partly because it was chaired by a woman. Most of its members were women and it was informed by feminist discourse (Eduards 1997b p. 166). In 1994, before the publication of its final report, it recommended the establishment of a centre for women at Uppsala University's teaching hospital. The centre was to take care of women who had been raped or abused, on a 24-hour basis, providing overnight accommodation for women and their children. It was special in that it was also intended to be a centre for research and development with the aim of disseminating advice and help to other organisations (*RD* 1994 No. 18 p. 10). In 1997, a new emergency centre for women was established in Stockholm to deal with the special problems faced by immigrant women (*DN* 16/6/97).

The final report of the Commission broke new ground with a formulation of a new crime – the disturbance of *kvinnofrid* (women's peace). This went further than just outlawing violence. It dealt with men's controlling behaviour such as hiding house keys and the telephone or preventing women from "meeting with friends and relatives," (*RD* 1995 No. 25 p. 8). The Commission also proposed:

- that rape and sexual abuse be placed on the same footing
- increased punishment for sexual mutilation
- improvements in crime statistics which would result in more details about victims' sex, age, nationality and relationship to the criminal
- more women's centres, with improved facilities and financing
- investigations to be carried out by the prosecutor rather than police
- more research and advertising
- activation of more specialist work within social services

Legal experts expressed concern about the practicability of the new law on women's peace but most of the remiss responses were positive (*RD* 1996 No. 23 p. 11).

The climate on women and violence had certainly changed. Statistics suggested that cases of violence against women in the home, on the streets and at work were on the increase. Reported assaults had risen 30 per cent in the 1990s according to a report by the Crime Prevention Council (Begler and Andersson 1998). While some of the rise was assumed to be due to a greater willingness by women to take legal action, the trend was worrying. The Liberal party said it wanted to see tougher sentences on such crimes than did the Social Democrats (*DN* 16/3/98). A Centre party spokesperson wanted to know why there was no vision of zero tolerance[6] when it came to the abuse of women (*DN* 25/4/98). When a number of legislative changes were announced at a press conference, three women ministers presented the details – the Minister for Social Affairs, the Justice Minister and the Minister for Equality. This was not an attempt to pretend that Sweden had no problem. As Ulrica Messing, the Minister for Equality stated clearly:

> Every year, thousands of women in our country are exposed to mistreatment and sexual abuse. The most dangerous place for a woman

is the home. Abuse occurs throughout all social classes (*DN* 19/12/97).

There was to be a new law on harassment at work – employers were expected to prevent and take action on harassment or be liable to claims for compensation (*RD* 1998 No. 15a p. 20). The recommendations of the Commission on Women's Peace were to be enacted (*RD* 1998 No. 6 p. 4). And lastly, the purchase of the services of prostitutes was to become a criminal offence.

The interviews carried out, by the author, with representatives of women's organisations confirmed the view that awareness of violence against women as an issue had increased. It was well established on the political agenda and drew on the combined support of women in all parties. Credit was given to a recent campaign launched by Länstyrelsen called *Operation Women* in which posters appeared in public places, the underground railway system and on buses attacking the cowardly nature of violence. What was unusual about the campaign was that those speaking out were significant establishment male figures. A number of respondents however, felt that neither the attitudes of the public nor the behaviour of the police, social workers or the judiciary had changed sufficiently.

Much had been done, but there was a long way to go. Many of the respondents cited the same figures: that in the previous week 3 women had been murdered; that 20 000 women were battered annually and between 30 and 50 women were murdered. Some suggested that the rise in reported cases was due to greater awareness of the problem and the help available. Others suggested that there was a large hidden figure and that violence had increased. It was, according to the spokesperson for the Liberal party, "the price we pay for equality". Many complained that resources in some municipalities were insufficient. The former chair of ROKS, Ebon Kram, cited municipalities which were unwilling to provide a place in a refuge for women battered in other local authorities. Municipalities had reduced their grants to refuges by 40 per cent in recent years, she said. Some refuges were unable to employ staff, rent sufficiently large properties or provide a decent range of activities.

Prostitution

The Commission on prostitution was appointed in 1993. Only two years earlier two researchers had informed the government that prostitution in Sweden's large cities had declined by 40 per cent during the

1980s (*DN* 13/9/91). By 1994, it was on the increase. High unemployment, recession and the breakdown of Eastern European economies were regarded as the principal causes of the increase (*DN* 30/3/92). The Commission's final report was published in 1995 and recommended the punishment of those buying the services of a prostitute *and* of prostitutes themselves (SOU 1995: 15). The proposal was based upon three clear arguments. First, it was felt that the sex trade was in conflict with the notion of equality between men and women. How could the sexes, it was asked, be of equal value in a society that allowed women's bodies to be sold. Second in other European countries, like Germany and Holland, where prostitution had been accepted, it had increased. It was suggested that 75 per cent of German men had at some point purchased sex whereas only 10 per cent of Swedish men had done so. Third, the social costs of prostitution in terms of disease and crime were damaging to society as a whole. Moreover, most prostitutes were exposed to cruelty and rape, developed mental disorders and had a negative self-image. Sweden had to show that prostitution was unacceptable.

Only one Commission member – the manager of a residential home for prostitutes and substance misusers – argued that prostitutes themselves should not be punished.[7]

> In my view, society ought ... to take the side of vulnerable women in the fight against the inhuman and unworthy trade in sex. Not by continuing to punish the women – as has happened throughout history – but by placing the responsibility on those in the superior social position, namely the male buyers. (ibid. p. 241)

Over the next few years, it was this view which prevailed. It was supported by most women's organisations and opposed by the police, the prosecution services and the judiciary on the grounds of impracticability. The National Association for Sex Education and the National Federation for Lesbian and Gay Rights were also opposed to the criminalisation of either punters or prostitutes. At the Social Democratic party Congress in 1997, it was agreed that prostitutes' clients alone should be punished. The Chair of the Association of Social Democratic women, Inger Segelström, declared:

> It is fantastic. It is the first visible proof that every other politician is a woman ... What is unbelievable is that the men were with us all

> the way. We had lobbied intensively to get men to take part in the campaign and they did (*DN* 14/9/97).

As part of the new law on *Women's Peace*, passed in 1998, only those purchasing a prostitute's services were to be punished by a fine or up to six months in prison. The measure – originally inspired in the 1980s by ROKS – had become a mainstream political issue. The vote in the Riksdag was 2:1 in favour. Most of those voting against were Conservatives and Liberals who thought that the measure would only result in driving the problem underground (*RD* 1998 No. 19 p. 24).

This was reflected in the interviews. A few thought criminalisation would have adverse effects, some thought that both the selling and buying of sex should have been penalised but most supported the punishment of punters. All thought the sale of women's bodies was incompatible with the respect due to women in a gender equal society. The more liberal view associated with other European countries in general, and the Netherlands in particular, was unacceptable.[8] One respondent implied that prostitution was acceptable to the Dutch because of their history of colonial exploitation. The idea that prostitution might be thought of as voluntary, as a job, like others, which a woman chose, was anathema to the Swedish mentality. "We don't discuss whether or not people want to be prostitutes," declared the Conservative respondent. "What sort of freedom was it to choose to sell your body?" asked another. It seemed to be generally accepted that most prostitution could be regarded as forced. Women were forced when they were too young to decide for themselves, as immigrants by fear of repatriation, when poor by basic material needs, while addicts were compelled by their drug habit. Behind all of them stood the demands and appetites of the procurers, the pimps and the punters.

There were a number of elements in this debate apparent from both the interviews and a review of the literature (see Gould 2001), the significance of which is a matter for conjecture: a fear of the foreign, the absence of a liberal perspective and the drugs connection. Much of the concern about prostitution represented a fear of the foreign. Early in 1998, the newspaper *Expressen* had published an interview with two women social workers in Stockholm who claimed that more and more prostitutes were coming to Sweden from the Baltic countries and Russia.

> Without exaggeration, one can say that there is an invasion of foreign girls ... They are exploited by pimps, mistreated by their

> clients and spread life-threatening sexual diseases ... Girls from the East have no tradition of using protection. Condoms are simply too expensive in their own countries. *They are used to unprotected sex and bring this tradition further into Sweden.* (*Expressen* 1998)

Although many of interviewees mentioned the number of prostitutes coming from Eastern European countries after the fall of the Berlin wall, the child prostitution of Thailand and the existence of trafficking, only one of them – an expert advisor to the Commission – attributed the new legislation to such factors. In his view, the visit by the Commission to Riga, Tallin and St Petersburg was of crucial importance. The Commission knew that Helsingfors in Finland had experienced a phenomenal growth in street prostitution and bordellos. It witnessed the plethora of advertisements inviting punters to ring for prostitutes to come to punters' homes. It might be that for many feminists, the fear of "foreign invasion" was not a factor in their thinking about prostitution but it certainly preoccupied the press, the public and the Commission. Since the Commission estimated the number of prostitutes in Sweden to be around 2500, it was certainly not the scale of the domestic "problem" itself that was uppermost in their deliberations.

The absence of, and hostility towards, a liberal perspective was marked. Among feminists in the US, UK and EU, there are many who take a liberal approach to the prostitution issue but in Sweden hardly anyone suggested that prostitutes had the right to choose the work they did. One of the few liberal contributors to the debate about the sex buying law, Alexander Bard, complained that those in favour of penalising punters belonged "to the same dying school of thought as the Myrdals' *People's Home*. People are dumb and don't know what is best for them." (Bard 1999) Certainly a general assumption made was that prostitutes were victims – incapable of acting in their own interests. This was Segelström's view.

> We know that half the prostitutes on the streets do it to finance their drug misuse. We know through in depth interviews that many of them feel very bad. It is our duty to intervene. (*DN* 3/8/98)

This brings us to the similarity between the discourse on prostitution and that of drugs (see Chapter 9). Prostitutes, it was argued, were *forced* into the sex trade just as drug users had been compelled to take drugs. There were fears about foreign prostitutes *flooding* into the country from Eastern Europe and of *liberal* ideas and practices emerging from EU countries. The same fears had emerged in the debate about drugs. Again, as in the example of drugs, Sweden had not *capitulated* to prostitution. Sweden was *unique*, a *model* for other countries to follow.[9] It was important to send out a *signal* that prostitution was *unacceptable* in a gender equal society.

This approach was questioned by Katarina Lindahl, the General Secretary of the National Association for Sex Education. It was not right in her view:

> to send out signals when they hurt those they are meant to help and that is what I think this law will do. Prostitutes will pay the price so that polticians can send out signals against something from which society already distances itself (Brink 1999).

One is bound to ask why such a measure should have been adopted in Sweden when elsewhere it is barely on the political agenda. While, there can be no doubt that without a powerful women's movement and strong female representation in parliament and government, the prostitution issue would never have appeared on the agenda in the first place, it is also reasonable to assume that without the threat from the East, the law might not have been passed. Part of the reason would seem to be that it evoked a similar kind of threat to cultural values and national idenditity as the issue of drugs. Could it even be, that with Sweden having been shown to lag behind other countries in recognizing the problem of violence against women, there was a subsequent determination to show that it had now taken the lead?

Discussion

In the following discussion, like Hobson, and in contrast to Elman, I prefer to use the term "feminist" in a broad inclusive sense. Hobson has suggested that two feminist camps emerged in the 1980s with some regarding the Swedish state as women friendly and others seeing it as an example of *public patriarchy* (Hobson 1995 p. 3). Those who took the former view would regard Swedish gender policy as a "success"; those who endorsed the latter view, would see it as "segregated subordination" (Gustafsson 1997a p. 41). The 1990s saw these two sides come together, in a practical political sense if not theoretically. There are two reasons for suggesting this. First, there was a clear commitment by women on the left to issues of, what Eduards called, "bodily integrity" – issues around violence, pornography and prostitution. In the past, Eduards said, such issues had been ignored or downplayed. Second, economic recession, unemployment, public sector cutbacks, membership of the EU and the international forces of neo-liberalism seem to have concentrated the minds of those who had tended to devalue the achievements of social policy. Hirdman who had been in the public patriarchy camp was scathing in her attacks on the policies of the Centre-right government. She admitted that, "the two earner system had a range of positive consequences (besides being a socio-economic injection): it has undoubtedly created the most choice-free society in the world – for women" (Hirdman 1993 p. 36). Eduards admitted that "the relative empowerment of Swedish women brought about by two decades of paid work and social benefits, has created more agency among women" (Eduards 1997a p. 18).

In contrast to the pessimism of Amy Elman, Swedish feminists were optimistic. They still claimed Sweden was a gendered political order but felt confident that "bodily integrity" (which according to Eduards was "the foundation of an egalitarian social order"), was now firmly on the political agenda. Gustafsson felt that the women's movement was becoming much more pluralist and that it was that which made "the challenge to the patriarchal order relatively sustainable" (Gustafsson 1997b p. 174). There would certainly seem to be a strong awareness today among Swedish feminists, not only of the need for economic and political equality in the traditional sense, but also of the more subtle and routine forms of male domination and "the exploitation of the female body as the first site of control and subordination" (Eduards 1997a p. 123). This was demonstrated by the changes to the criminal law on violence and prostitution and the various reports of the KMU. There are, however, two worrying aspects of recent developments.

The first is that in spite of the excellent set of reports produced by the KMU, the proposals made in its final report were not very inspiring. They were strong on exhortation and weak on substance. There were the usual calls for more research and monitoring; more information and better communication; an intensification of the government's examination of the gender implications of all of its policies; a renewed emphasis upon gender equality in schools; and an "equality" mark of approval which firms with good gender equality practices can use in their branding.

The second is the criminalisation of prostitutes' clients. Few feminists outside Sweden have called for such a measure in their own countries. There is a strong view that the more underground you drive the sex trade, the more damaging it is likely to be for the women involved. There is also a view that if women choose to be prostitutes then that choice must be respected and that to suggest that all prostitutes are under the control of men is to stereotype them as victims. One has to ask, therefore, whether this is another example (a) of the Swedes taking a rational argument to its logical extreme regardless of the consequences or (b) of a moralistic tendency in Swedish society to say "we disapprove of this behaviour so it must be outlawed".

What was remarkable about the prostitution issue – and feminist politics in general in the 1990s – was the successful mobilisation of feminist opinion. The degree of co-operation amongst female Riksdag members and between extra-parliamentary groups was impressive. It was undoubtedly a major factor in preserving the main features of the Swedish welfare state. Women from all parties and all walks of life – even if they were critical of some aspects of state welfare – knew that the public sector had provided the material bedrock of their achievements. The interviewees – including those from the Bourgeois parties – were all happy to describe themselves as feminists. They did not, however, feel that this was the case for all women – some of whom felt that feminism had "negative" overtones. They were also worried that women's organisations generally were experiencing a decline in membership. The younger generation of women was in danger of taking Sweden's degree of gender equality for granted, not realizing, the importance of organisation in the achievements of the preceding generation.

Conclusion

Many observers inside and outside Sweden have called it the world's most gender equal society. In many respects this was, and remains, the case. In spite of cuts to services and benefits, Swedish women still benefit from generous arrangements for parental leave, they still have a plentiful supply of job opportunities and can rely on the state to take on a large part of care for children, the elderly and the disabled. Half[10] of the government consists of women ministers and 40 per cent of Riksdag members are women. Some feminists in the 1980s, however, argued that Swedish women had simply swapped male dominance for state patriarchy. In particular it was alleged that little attention had been paid to the many ways in which women in Sweden were controlled and dominated. They had been co-opted by established political institutions to give an appearance of power. Social policies had merely improved the operation of the labour market and women still took the major part of caring and domestic responsibilities. By the end of the 1990s a radical feminist discourse and practice had become much more widespread. Domestic violence and other forms of harassment had been firmly placed on the political agenda. Prostitution was seen as unacceptable in a society aiming at gender equality and the purchasing of sexual services by men was made a criminal offence.

Women have protected their strong position within the public sector and have advanced their power base inside all political parties. They are also said to have become more pluralistic in their organisation and influence. It is little wonder that they should defend the public sector given that that is the base of the considerable amount of power they wield in Swedish society. In the 1990s they used that power base to defend the welfare state and resist its erosion by domestic and international forces. At the same time they sought to advance their power and influence by calling for significant changes in society where women have been shown to be weak. Research and official investigations have demonstrated their lack of strength within the private sector; more was understood about the way in which men rose to the top more easily than women; the home as a site of inequality and oppression had been explored more thoroughly.

It is important to recognize, however, that many of the actions of the Social Democratic government were the outcome of initiatives taken by its Centre-right predecessor – and in particular Bengt Westerberg who combined the posts of Minister for Social Affairs and for Equality. The Social Democrats were not the only party in favour of gender equality. Other political parties and other politicians had also advanced the cause of women in Swedish society. All had responded to a powerful, indigenous, women's movement. Wherever you want to put Sweden on the continuum of state patriarchy and women friendly state, the 1990s saw a move in the latter direction.

8
Responses to Unemployment

> People thought that [the assassination of Olof Palme] couldn't happen here, but then a whole lot of things started happening that couldn't happen here.
>
> (Swedish journalist *Guardian* 1999)

Introduction

The postwar welfare state in Europe was made possible by governments' pursuit of full employment as a policy priority. The policy was abandoned by many countries in the 1980s in favour of a prioritisation of the fight against inflation. What surprised many commentators about the Swedes was their refusal to abandon the goal. Indeed by the end of the decade, the unemployment rate was below 2 per cent. From this point, however, the combined impact of deregulation policies, the slowdown in economic growth, tax reform and the rise of inflation, led to an acceptance by Swedish governments for the need to prioritise other economic goals. The perceived "need" to create a flexible labour market in line with international competitors also led to successive governments arguing that unemployment benefit levels should be lowered and employment rights weakened. Even the value and relevance of the *Active Labour Market Policy*, a cornerstone of the Swedish welfare state, was questioned. Not only was there considerable resistance to these trends but a major attempt was made to counter them with work-sharing proposals.

This chapter will begin with an examination of the characteristics of Swedish unemployment before discussing some of the changes which have been attempted in the areas of unemployment benefit, labour market policy, employment rights and the redistribution of work.

Unemployment and employment

It can be seen from Table 8.1 that total Swedish unemployment rose during the 1990s to a peak of over 15 per cent in 1994, the last year of the Centre-right coalition and thereafter fell slowly. The Social Democratic government set itself the goal of reaching 4 per cent "open" unemployment (that is total unemployment minus those on labour market schemes) by the year 2000. That figure will not be reached but the position at the beginning of that year was similar to that for 1992 – 5.1 per cent.[1]

At the peak of unemployment, over 7 per cent of the workforce (including disabled workers) were on labour market schemes – causing considerable headaches for Arbetsmarknadsstyrelsen (AMS, the labour market board). In 1995, Sweden's unemployment rate was higher than that of either Britain or Germany. In particular more young people were unemployed in Sweden (20 per cent) compared to Britain (16 per cent) and Germany (9 per cent) (Clasen, Gould and Vincent 1998 p. 7).

The duration of unemployment

The length of unemployment also needs to be considered. In Sweden, long-term unemployment is defined as those unemployed for over six months. In the mid-90s, people between the ages of 55 and 64 were the most vulnerable to long-term unemployment. According to the Department for Employment, half of those unemployed in this age group in 1993 were unemployed for more than six months – double the percentage for 16–24 years old (Ds 1994:108 p. 57). Unemployed males were more likely to be long-term unemployed (34 per cent) than

Table 8.1: Percentage of the workforce openly unemployed or on labour market schemes 1991–98

	Open unemployment	Labour market schemes	Total
1991	3.0	3.7	6.7
1992	5.2	5.4	10.6
1993	8.2	6.1	14.3
1994	8.0	7.1	15.1
1995	7.7	6.3	14.0
1996	8.1	6.4	14.5
1997	8.0	6.3	14.3
1998	6.5	6.0	12.5

Sources: Statistical yearbook of Sweden 1998, 1999, 2000.

unemployed women (27 per cent) (Socialstyrelsen rapport 1994:10). The sex differences between the young long-term unemployed had in the 1980s been minimal but by 1994, 41 per cent of young males (16–24) were long-term unemployed compared with only 24 per cent of young unemployed women (Ds 1994:108). Nevertheless, compared with other countries, Sweden's rates of long term unemployment were not at all bad (see Table 8.2).

Distribution of unemployment

Unemployment of course affects industries, regions and social groups differentially. The crisis in the early 1990s saw a 24 per cent loss of industrial jobs and 29 per cent in the building industry. Only 7 per cent of jobs in the public sector and 7 per cent in the private services sector disappeared (*DN* 26/2/94). Unemployment in the county of Stockholm during the 1990s was consistently 1 per cent lower than the national average while the country's northernmost county, Norrbotten, was consistently 2 per cent higher (Arbetsmarknadsdata 1999). Gender differences were similar with women 0.5–1 per cent lower than the average and men 0.5–1 per cent higher (ibid.). However, as we saw in Chapter 7, when hidden and under-employment were taken into account the position of women was considerably worse than that of men. Age too made a difference. Over 15 per cent of young people aged 18–24 were unemployed in 1993 but by 1998 this had been reduced to 6.9 per cent (ibid.). The official figures for older workers were very good in comparison but many had taken early retirement pensions.

Ethnic minorities

Ethnic minority workers were particularly badly hit in the 1990s. The unemployment rate in 1995 for workers born outside Europe was

Table 8.2: Annual rates of long-term unemployment (12 months and more) in Germany, Sweden and Britain as a percentage of unemployment 1995

%	Germany	Sweden	Britain
All unemployed	48.7	20.2	43.6
Unemployed males	45.9	23.4	49.6
Unemployed females	51.3	15.9	32.3
15–24 years	26.8	12.7	27.2
25 years and more	51.7	22.8	50.3

Source: Eurostat 1997.

three times that of those born in Sweden (Socialstyrelsen 1997:14 p. 26). An investigation into immigration and employment showed that whereas "European" immigrants to Sweden before 1970 did not differ much from Swedes in their employment profiles and contributed more in taxes than they received in state benefits, the reverse was true for non-European immigrants who had arrived more recently (*RD* 1996 No. 1 p. 6).

A later report from the Democracy Investigation Commission stressed the relationship between unemployment, segregated housing and political participation. It cited the data for different ethnic groups presented in Table 8.3. The report claimed that during the 1990s employment had been halved in the Stockholm estates where most of the population were from ethnic minorities. Women had lost jobs in health and social services and men had suffered because of the decline in the building industry. People were being excluded from the labour market, lived in segregated suburbs and took little part in Swedish political parties or interest group activity. The report criticised both economic and housing policies for exacerbating the problem of unemployment among minorities (*RD* 1999 No. 7b pp. 10–11).

Research from Lund University suggested that discrimination by employers, although part of the problem, was not the only factor (Scott 1999 No. 3 pp. 14–15). Kirk Scott argued that Information Technology had made language and cultural competence important prerequisites for new forms of employment. At the same time he implied that employers were reluctant to accept cultural diversity as part of their management philosophy. A 1994 law which had made racial discrimination at work illegal had been spectacularly unsuccessful in dealing with the problem. Only one case had reached the labour court and that had failed (*DN* 2/12/97). A new law prohibiting racial discrimination was passed in 1997 which required an employer to aim

Table 8.3: The percentage of different ethnic groups who were employed or owned their own businesses 1997

Swedish born citizens	74.5
Foreign born with Swedish citizenship	53.9
Non-Nordic minorities	34.7
1990s immigrants and refugees	10.0

Source: *RD* 1999 No. 7b pp. 10–11.

for ethnic diversity within the workforce and to take action against those found guilty of racial harassment.

The effects of unemployment

The monthly climb in the numbers of people laid off in the early 1990s was a major shock to individuals and to the system. Here was a society which had prided itself on full employment. How could you claim to be in favour of solidarity when 15 per cent of the workforce was out of work? How could you ignore the problem when researchers and state agencies produced evidence of the individual and social costs of the problem? Research carried out in three of Sweden's major universities into the effects of unemployment in the early 1990s was published by the Ministry of Social Affairs (Palme and Stenberg 1998). Unemployment was affecting people's physical health and was more likely to lead to heart disease and alcohol problems. As people's income deteriorated so did their mental condition. The welfare and education of the children of unemployed people also suffered. Diderichsen showed that Stockholm's unemployed constituted only 7 per cent of the county's population but represented 33 per cent of those who were mentally ill (*DN* 22/7/94).

The problem was not confined to industry or to blue-collar workers. Doctors and academics were losing their jobs; "secure" jobs in the service sector – public and private – were disappearing. The very term "mass unemployment" was new to Sweden. It was supposed to be a problem other countries suffered from. Young people were being alienated. The long-term unemployed and immigrants were becoming marginalised. Sweden too, it was said, was becoming a two-thirds, one-third society. "Marginalisation", "outsidership" and "social exclusion" were increasingly used to describe the situation of many of those without jobs and homes.

In interviews with politicians, officials and researchers carried out in 1995 by the author for a previous study, few denied that social exclusion existed or that long-term unemployment was an important factor in bringing it about (Clasen, Gould and Vincent 1998). While there were those who insisted that social exclusion was nothing like as bad as in the rest of Europe, largely because the Active Labour Market Policy had prevented it, others saw the problem as a growing one. Concern was expressed about the increasing segregation of immigrant communities, begging on the streets, the growing visibility of homelessness and the increasing demand on Salvation Army hostels. Some thought that perhaps social exclusion was, by definition, a consequence of long-term unemployment in a society – like Sweden – which had a strong work ethic. Others speculated on the possibility that long-term unemployment might be experienced more acutely by some groups than others. Was there a greater tendency for Swedes who were unemployed to become socially isolated compared with workers from more tightly-knit ethnic minority communities; was social exclusion worse for those unemployed in the North compared with the South; for older men (who lost their purpose in life) than for older women (who had alternative roles to fill their lives)?

Employment

Mass unemployment did not however affect only the unemployed. The employed feared for their job security and their employers took advantage of that fear. Aronsson at the Working Life Institute in Stockholm found that over a third of employees were working unpaid overtime. These were more likely to be men and more likely to be service workers (*DN* 28/4/97). A similar situation was found with banking employees where nearly half of those interviewed worried about whether they would be able to cope in the future (*DN* 28/3/98). Stress in the workplace was increasing. One study found that a quarter of those in "secure" jobs felt trapped. They were unhappy with their present employment but dared not risk changing jobs for fear that they would be more likely to be made redundant (*DN* 17/5/97).

There was also an expansion of part-time and temporary jobs in Sweden. According to LO, in 1991 there were less than 400 000 temporary jobs in the labour market; by 1998 that figure had increased to 553 000 or 8 per cent of the labour force (*DN* 19/6/99). In the past organisations had been able to cope with emergency situations by being over-(wom)manned. Those days were gone. Employees had to be more flexible and do more overtime. In the public sector there was a greater reliance on pools of workers who could be called on in time of pressure. The Central Bureau of Statistics found that "project" work (which tended to affect men) and temporary work (which tended to affect women) where workers were called when needed had doubled from 80 000 in 1990 to over 160 000 or 4 per cent of the workforce in 1996 (*DN* 6/8/97).

Pressure for the Swedish labour market to become even more flexible came from the OECD which had suggested that the greater part of Sweden's unemployment was structural rather than cyclical, that is it was unlikely to go down much more and in another economic crisis was likely to rise (*DN* 30/5/98).

Employment policy

The two governments tried various ways to reduce unemployment and reform employment policy. Although the Social Democrats opposed many of the Bourgeois government's policies, on their return to power they would propose something similar. The Bourgeois government wanted lower pay rises and was accused by LO of maintaining high levels of unemployment to force wage levels down (Edin and Carlsson 1993). Under the Social Democrats LO actually admitted that unemployment could not be fought as long as high pay awards were driving inflation upwards (Edin and Andersson 1997). In opposition the Social Democrats had initially accused the Centre-right government of making the crisis worse by cutting public expenditure (Larsson 1992). In government they accepted the necessity of doing so.

The persistence of high unemployment was *the* crucial issue for voters in the 1994 election. Over 50 per cent of most voters – men, women, different age groups – regarded unemployment as the most important issue facing the country (*DN* 21/9/94). When high unemployment continued and the Social Democratic government proceeded to continue with public expenditure cuts, it was criticised in turn by those on the left for exactly the same reasons as Social Democratic leaders had criticised the previous regime. To the chagrin of the left of the labour movement, the government had adopted neo-liberal policies. There was a growing acceptance of the need for wage moderation among modernising social democrats and LO. Even trade union researchers called for reductions in employers' contributions as a device for creating jobs. They argued that even if this caused a worsening of the public sector deficit in the short term it would be made good by the taxes and contributions resulting from the increase in employment (Lundberg and Zetterburg 1997). Such ideas and arguments had been rejected when put by the Bourgeois parties.

Unemployment benefit

While governments may have converged in their approach to unemployment, there was a basic ideological difference which pervaded Swedish debates about the causes of unemployment which came to the fore in discussions about unemployment benefit. Those on the right tended to emphasise the failings of the unemployed as individuals and the way in which employment policy could either reinforce or counteract those failings. Many individuals were said to prefer to live on benefits and/or work in the informal economy. They were poorly qualified, they were sick, they were unwilling to move to find work. The state needed to induce them to find genuine work. In contrast, those on the left argued that unemployment was caused by deficiencies in the economic structure. The only lasting solution to unemployment was the creation of real jobs. Both sides could agree on the need for labour market measures to induce or help the unemployed find work, but what was to be done about unemployment benefit?

Earnings-related unemployment insurance in Sweden – *a-kassa* – was a "voluntary" scheme administered by the trade unions but funded largely by contributions paid by employers to the state. For those not members of trade unions, AMS administered a flat-rate benefit (KAS) equal to the minimum entitlement of *a-kassa*. Prior to the 1990s, trade union members who became unemployed would, up to a certain income ceiling, receive *a-kassa* equivalent to 90 per cent of their pay. *A-kassa* lasted for up to 300 days (450 days for those aged over 55). It was possible for the unemployed to extend their period of benefit by joining a labour market scheme and subsequently claiming a further period of benefit – a process described critically by some as a *merry-go-round*.

> An unemployed individual can qualify for a 60 weeks spell of *a-kassa* by participating in a labour market programme ... As of 1986, five month's participation in practically any measure fulfils the work requirement. Furthermore, in 1983 insured individuals were given the right to relief work when their benefits were approaching termination; in 1993 this right to a placement in a programme was extended to include labour market training. (Agell *et al.* 1995 pp. 106–7)

One consequence of this arrangement was that large numbers of even long-term unemployed people did not have to depend on social assistance for their main source of income. In the early 1990s two thirds of the unemployed received *a-kassa*, with a further 7–10 per cent in receipt of KAS. Only around 25 per cent had to claim social assistance (SOU 1996:51). In Britain, these percentages were reversed (Clasen, Gould and Vincent 1998 p. 87). What was true for the unemployed as a whole however did not hold for all. Non-European immigrants (over 55 per cent) and young workers (over 30 per cent of 20–24 year olds) were the least likely to be receiving unemployment benefit.

As mass unemployment and Sweden's economic difficulties increased so the unemployment benefit fund moved from a small surplus in 1991 to a serious deficit in 1993. Pressures to limit the rights and sharpen the responsibilities of the unemployed grew. Calmfors and Herin argued, in evidence to a Commission investigating the unemployment insurance system, that the high levels of *a-kassa* were in part to blame for the worsening opportunities of the unemployed (Calmfors and Herin 1993). There was no incentive for those on high benefits to seek work when the pay they were offered was lower than their benefit. Moreover, there was no restraint on union negotiators to moderate their pay claims, since those made unemployed still enjoyed a similar standard of living to those in work. Calmfors, in another article, claimed that:

> The biggest problem from the point of view of incentives is the opportunity of an eternal *merry-go-round* between unemployment benefit and AMS measures (Calmfors 1995).

Other economists concluded that because of the system "people collect unemployment benefits several years in a row" (Agell *et al.* 1995 p. 124). The authors claimed that a disproportionate number of those on the merry-go-round were non-Nordic citizens, the disabled and those with low qualifications – people, who in the existing economic climate, were unlikely to find work anyway.

Korpi, however, argued strongly that there was substantial evidence to show that high benefits did not in themselves create unemployment (Korpi 1995 p. 119). Why, he asked, in the years between 1950 and 1990, when benefits were rising and opportunities to go on labour market measures plentiful, was unemployment low? And why in the 1990s when benefits were reduced did unemployment rise? The obstacle to employment opportunities, in his view, lay not in the benefit system but in the lack of demand for labour.

The Centre-right government accepted the need for reform and in 1993 reduced *a-kassa* from 90 per cent of income to 80 per cent. KAS and the maximum benefit claimable under *a-kassa* were reduced by over 5 per cent and five waiting days – before which benefit could be claimed – were introduced (*RD* 1993 No. 13 p. 24 and No. 22 p. 10). These measures were not supported by the Social Democrats or the Left party. From the beginning of 1994 employees had to contribute 1 per cent of their gross income employment to help reduce the insurance fund deficit (*RD* 1993 No. 32 p. 3). One of the final acts of the Centre-right coalition was an attempt to remove the dominance of trade unions in the administration of unemployment benefit. Participation in earnings-related unemployment insurance became compulsory. Employees who were not or did not wish to be members of trade unions would be part of a state administered *a-kassa* (*RD* 1994 No. 22 p. 8). Just as controversial was the new rule which entitled claimants to just two periods of 300 days of benefit, after which they could only build up further entitlement by becoming employed and making sufficient contributions again – a measure intended to end the merry-go-round.

When the Social Democrats were returned in 1994, one of their first acts was to abolish the state administered *a-kassa* and abolish the limit set upon claiming periods. It was not long, however, before the new government felt it necessary to show that it too needed to be tough about fraud and eligibility. Just before the election, a data register was to be set up under the auspices of AMS to prevent people claiming both sickness and unemployment benefit (*DN* 16/9/94). Subsequently, it was also proposed that those claiming unemployment benefit should be forced to keep in contact with the world of work. This could mean the form of employment they were previously used to or something quite different from their normal line of work. The government claimed that it was concerned about the possibility of workers losing their "competence". But the Labour Market Minister, added a moral dimension when he expressed the conviction that "rights and obligations must go hand in hand" (*DN* 6/12/94).

A Commission investigating this proposal reiterated the Minister's point and invoked the idea of a mutual "social contract" between society and the unemployed (SOU 1995:7 p. 17). In the past an individual's "availability for work" had meant an obligation to accept "suitable work or labour market measures" when offered. This principle, it was now suggested, was being abused through for example, work in the informal economy. The report went on to say that at a time when unemployment was so high that both jobs and labour market measures were in limited supply, the meaning of the concept "available for work",[2] had to be widened to prevent abuse on the one hand and passivity on the other. Benefit abuse became a much discussed issue in the 1990s in contrast to the decades of full employment when it was rarely referred to.

Another Commission was subsequently asked to examine aspects of unemployment insurance further: to consider whether young people under the age of 20 should have their entitlement to *a-kassa* withdrawn and the need for a clearer statement on the obligations of the unemployed to be available for work (*RD* 1995 No. 24 p. 3). Soon after the Commission was appointed the government reduced *a-kassa* from

80 per cent of income to 75 per cent – to take effect from the first day of 1996. The outcry and protests from the labour movement were so great that the decision was reversed after the Social Democratic party Congress in March 1996 and before the Commission had even produced its preliminary report. In a fit of pique, the government insisted that the cost of paying for this concession (SEK 700 million) would have to come from within the insurance system. Trade union members would have to pay higher contributions, have their entitlement to benefit based upon working for nine months in the previous year rather than five months, or put up with an extra waiting day for benefit. LO objected strongly. In their view, this would still have the effect of reducing *a-kassa* for a substantial number of people. The government claimed it was simply trying to find different ways of reducing the unemployment benefit budget.

When the Commission published its final report in October, it recommended that the *merry-go-round* be limited in duration to 600 days. LO and TCO were outraged and demanded that the report be scrapped. While some features of the proposed system were fairly generous, it was clear that one consequence of limiting the amount of time one could claim benefit would be that 40 000 would ultimately find themselves outside the system and, therefore, dependent on social assistance (SOU 1996:150). Three thousand union members demonstrated outside the Riksdag in Stockholm and the Prime Minister was booed and heckled at a major union congress (*DN* 18/10/96 and 19/10/96). The Minister for Employment, Margareta Winberg, received similar treatment in Gothenburg after saying that those in employment should pay higher contributions to *a-kassa* (*DN* 24/10/96).

On the limitation of the duration of benefit, the raising of employees' contributions and an extra waiting day, the government was forced to climb down. Much of the rest of the Commission's report was adopted. KAS was to be amalgamated with the *a-kassa* system, the minimum daily benefit raised and a new earnings-related benefit introduced for non-union members (10 per cent of the workforce). The difference between this and the Bourgeois government's similar proposal was that trade unions would continue to administer *a-kassa* which would remain voluntary (*RD* 1997 No. 19 p. 10).

The conditions to be met for claiming *a-kassa* also became tougher during the 1990s. Table 8.4 shows the number of hours and months it was necessary to work to be eligible for *a-kassa*:

All of the changes discussed above were intended to reduce public expenditure. The government had a number of choices: to reduce the

Table 8.4: Eligibility conditions for *a-kassa*

	1991	1993	1994	1998
Waiting days	0	5	5	5
Minimum number of months worked within previous twelve month period	4	4	5	6
Minimum hours worked per month	75	75	75	70

Sources: *RD* 1993 No. 13 p. 24; No. 32 p. 3; 1997 No. 19 p. 10.

value of benefits; to increase contributions; to make benefits more difficult to get (more waiting days, stricter eligibility rules); to make it easier to end people's entitlement (limits on duration). The real costs of each proposal would be borne by a different social group: the unemployed as a whole, the young unemployed, women, ethnic minorities, those in jobs. All the proposals were discussed *ad nauseam* and pressures brought to bear by organised interests. What pleased the right did not meet with the approval of the centre or the left. Opposition sometimes came from political parties, sometimes from the unions, sometimes from the Association of Municipalities, sometimes from AMS. The forging of the necessary consensus to get measures through took enormous amounts of time and effort.

There can be little doubt that many Conservatives in the earlier administration would have liked to see a more drastic reduction of *a-kassa*. A Commission report in 1993 did in fact recommend an income replacement level of 60 per cent. Later, under the Social Democrats, there were proposals recommending that income replacement percentages could be reduced in stages over time. An unemployed person would start with 90 per cent, some time later this would be reduced to 75 per cent and subsequently to 60 per cent. What is remarkable is that in the end it took such a long time for the two determined governments to achieve what seemed like relatively small changes. Was this a triumph for consensus politics, strong trade unions or an example of Swedish sclerosis?

Although, superficially, the main change during the whole period was the reduction from 90 per cent to 80 per cent, the myriad minor changes meant that the ambience of the system had changed from a very generous one in a period of full employment to a much more constrained one in a time of mass unemployment. Rules and regulations had been tightened up; AMS called claimants in for meetings in an attempt to discourage abuse; immigrant workers *had* to learn Swedish to receive benefit; holidays could not be taken since you had to be contactable by the Employment Service. In a report to the government by AMS, it was claimed that testing willingness to work was extremely difficult in a time of high unemployment (*DN* 27/9/97). There were too few jobs and measures available to meet the needs of the large number of claimants. Telling the difference between genuinely unemployed people and those who abused the benefit system was almost impossible. Striking the right balance between social justice, cutting public expenditure and discouraging false claimants was not an easy task.

Active labour market policy

The administration of labour market policies in Sweden is the responsibility of Arbetsmarknadsstyrelsen.[3] AMS is a semi-autonomous administrative board which is accountable to the Department of Employment. It was established in 1948 and until 1991 was run by a committee consisting largely of representatives of employer and employee organisations. AMS is a national organisation with a structure of regional and local offices. From the early 1960s it has implemented an active labour market policy, the chief characteristics of which were established by the economists Gösta Rehn and Rudolph Meidner. The Rehn–Meidner model gave AMS a crucial role not only in employment but also economic policy. Aware that Keynesian techniques of *general* demand management could have inflationary consequences, the active labour market policy was intended to operate *selectively*. Not only would labour market measures such as training and job creation schemes be expanded (to accommodate up to a maximum of 3 per cent of the labour force) as unemployment grew, and be reduced as full employment was restored, but efforts would be made to identify and rectify sectoral, industrial and local deficiencies in terms of labour supply and demand (Hedborg and Meidner 1984). In other words AMS had the task of seeing that the labour market worked efficiently. Its importance was such that it was regarded by many as the cornerstone of the Swedish model

AMS also embodied a moral dimension. Swedes have been critical of other countries' labour market policies in the past for the emphasis they placed upon *passive* measures – the receipt of cash benefits. In their view, the provision of *active* measures – measures which helped people to train for and find jobs – was as, if not more, important. While this modern version of the work ethic – called *arbetslinje* or the work line – had a broader political appeal than AMS' economic role, the corporatist assumptions of AMS came under increasing scrutiny in the 1990s with the international emphasis upon free markets, flexibility and deregulation. The Employers' Federation (SAF) disengaged from the state's administrative boards in 1991 in protest at what it saw as their domination by the interests of the labour movement. Subsequently the centre right coalition marginalised other AMS committee members by giving them a narrow supervisory role. In the early stages of mass unemployment fears were even expressed about whether AMS could continue to perform an effective role.

The main task of AMS was to provide training opportunities, relief work and job creation places for the unemployed. The numbers on the various labour market measures are listed in Table 8.5. As the numbers increased so the expensive schemes such as relief work and labour market training were contracted and new cheaper schemes such as a *Ungdomspraktik* (Youth Training) and ALU (Working Life Introduction) were introduced and expanded. In 1995 the municipalities took over

Table 8.5: The main categories of labour market measures and the numbers placed on them ('000s)

	1991	1994	1996	1998
Relief work	11	17	8	1
Public temporary work for older workers	–	–	–	8
Labour market training	59	60	46	42
Sheltered work (for the disabled)	80	80	80	82
Introductory placement	13	0	–	–
Youth training scheme	–	56	–	–
Working place introduction (API)*	–	–	32	19
Working life introduction (ALU)	–	45	52	39
Substitute for workers on training	1	13	10	0
Employment with recruitment subsidies (RAS)	5	23	12	0
Individual hiring support	–	–	–	11
Expanded trial employment periods	–	2	–	–
Start up grant	–	9	10	13
Computer activity centre plus other IT programmes	–	–	12	13
Local labour market measures for young people	–	–	13	12
Development guarantee for jobless youngsters	–	–	–	3
Employability Institute Programme (AMI)	–	–	–	8
Resource jobs				4
Total	169	305	274	255

Sources: Statistical yearbook of Sweden 1998, 1999, 2000

*API replaced Youth Training in 1995 and incorporated the Immigrant Training Programme from 1994.

the responsibility of young unemployed people and Youth Training was replaced by API (Working Place Introduction), which later included work experience measures for unemployed immigrants.[4] New schemes also included help with starting one's own business and computer training, while substitutes for those on educational or training leave, *vikariat*, were expanded. One constant feature of AMS measures were those for people with disabilities. These remained steady throughout the period at 80 000 per annum and consisted principally of placements with employers with salary subsidies (57.5 per cent) and sheltered work (40 per cent).[5]

AMS measures were complemented by provision for the long-term unemployed made by local municipalities. A major incentive for local authorities to do so was to reduce the size of the social assistance budget, as 50 per cent of this was attributable to unemployment (Klingensjö 1994 p. 13). Moreover, legislation required municipalities to provide temporary employment for those unemployed for at least 14 months (Auer and Riegler 1994). It was also possible for municipalities to establish projects that were wholly or in part financed through AMS. Recipients of social assistance were provided with 7000 placements in 1994 while an additional 56 000 placements were provided in collaboration with AMS (Ds 1995:12).

New AMS programmes were often the subject of considerable debate and controversy. The Centre-right coalition introduced a Youth Training scheme to cope with the thousands of unemployed young people between 18 and 25. LO opposed the scheme arguing that education or relief work were preferable alternatives. The scheme was subsequently criticised for failing to provide the individual development plans it had promised, displacing existing jobs and paying low wages. In addition too few trainees were going on to full-time jobs on completion of their training. In 1995 the Social Democratic government devised a recruitment subsidy for employers that took on unemployed workers (RAS). The proposal was criticised by almost all the other parties including the Left party. It was seen as expensive and misplaced. The money would have been better spent on the long-term unemployed, argued economists (*DN* 21/2/95). In 1997, this was belatedly recognized and RAS was replaced by a similar scheme directed at the long-term unemployed (*RD* 1997 No. 26 p. 17). The previous year, the government provided the finance for an additional 40 000 job creation placements within local government for long-term unemployed workers between the ages of 55 and 64 (*RD* 1996 No. 20 p. 3).

It was not just individual AMS programmes that were the subject of criticism during the 1990s. There were those who called for the abolition of AMS. In the early stages of mass unemployment fears were expressed about whether AMS could continue to perform an effective role. Even its Director-General predicted the collapse of *arbetslinje* if increased numbers simply resulted in people being slushed around a system of poor quality labour market schemes (Bernhardsson 1992). An expert group of researchers, appointed by the government to examine the effectiveness of labour market policy, stated that few adequate studies had been carried out and that the area was one seriously neglected by research (*RD* 1993 No. 21 p. 17). What work that had been done suggested that job creation schemes worked well, while pay subsidies and subsidies to industry and localities were fairly ineffective. For young people recruitment grants seemed to work better than job creation. The report concluded with the suggestion that labour market policy should be "comprehensive and directed towards *outsiders*" (that is the long-term unemployed and vulnerable groups) since this would give the best return and would not be inflationary.

Lars Calmfors, an economist, claimed that research, which showed that AMS measures were effective, was at best weak (Calmfors 1995). He too insisted that AMS measures were directed at well established *insiders* who represented the majority of voters rather than *outsiders* who faced the most difficult labour market situation. Calmfors argued that AMS should be abolished and replaced with independent, regionally organised bodies. A *Dagens Nyheter* editorial stated:

> The volume [of measures] is too high, not too low. It is a failure not a success. It is not efficient but desperate. In the absence of means that give results, billions are being spent to show good will. Symbols and potentiality have become more important than employment and cogency. (*DN* 11/2/95)

In the view of the editor, growth and jobs would be created by flexible pay, labour mobility and lower interest rates. This view was taken a step further by Anders Isaakson, a journalist, who criticised the whole concept of a right to employment (Isaksson 1994). He claimed that politicians, in order to get elected, promised what they could not deliver. Subsequently they finished up creating "opportunities" for the unemployed, who in return for high benefits, had to be forced onto various labour market schemes and submit themselves to the ineffective social engineering of counsellors, career advisors, therapists and rehabilitators. It would be better, in his view, to recognise that the epoch of the welfare state was over and establish a system in which the state provided a basic security and then allowed individuals to choose for themselves what they would do.

These criticisms led the General Director of AMS, to respond by arguing that AMS had not created the recession and mass unemployment which, in turn, had led the previous Centre-right coalition to create a large number of places on low quality schemes against AMS' advice (Bernhardsson 1995). Labour market policy had been forced by events to adopt a social role. He added:

> Let us assume that a researcher presents a study which shows that people admitted to hospital have a greater risk of dying than those who are not admitted. And that an even greater risk is run by those taken into intensive care. How many would draw the conclusion that the hospital should be closed down as soon as possible, beginning with the intensive care unit? (ibid.)

A further defence of AMS programmes came from a member of its own research section which claimed that "a person who participated in labour market measures has a 40 per cent better probability of finding employment after three years than a person who did not" (Harkman 1994 p. 10). Harkman also claimed that "the temporary employment scheme and labour market training were substantially more beneficial for finding employment for the participant than [are job creation schemes] and relief work" (ibid. p. 11). Harkman's conclusion was that "temporary interruptions of long periods of employment improve the probability of gaining employment" and that "those who have participated in ... [labour market measures] have thereby improved their position in comparison with those who have not" (ibid. p. 12).

The Social Democratic government accepted some of the criticism directed at AMS in its 1995 proposal called *A more effective labour market policy* where it was stated that:

> labour market measures ... should be directed in the first place to the long term unemployed ... and other vulnerable groups. The government, in its guidelines to AMS will stress this clearly. People who have been unemployed for over 6 months must be over-represented on the different measures. Further recruitment subsidies will only be used for this group. ALU and API must be reserved for the long term unemployed and for immigrants and refugees who lack experience

> of the Swedish labour market ... (Regeringens proposition 1994/95:218 p. 25).

The report of the Labour Market Committee appointed by the Centre-right government in January 1994 to examine the effectiveness of AMS was finally published in March 1996. It criticised the administration of AMS measures as being complicated and inflexible and as having unnecessarily detailed rules. It suggested that AMS should have a more limited set of aims: to keep vacancy times down, to reduce long-term unemployment and to combat long periods without regular work. The committee also recommended that AMS measures be more limited in their scope. It supported the idea of more individually-, goal-oriented action plans for the unemployed and was clearly sympathetic towards arguments which suggested that unemployment benefits were too high and the merry-go-round far too long. The risk of losing entitlement to *a-kassa* should, according to the report, be increased – presumably as an incentive to the unemployed to find work. As expected there was a big emphasis upon the need for more training in the form of apprenticeships for the young and competence development for those in employment (*RD* 1996 No. 8 p. 4).

Subsequently AMS measures came under further attack from government auditors who claimed that wage subsidies, job creation measures and public works programmes had a displacement effect in the short and the long term. In the case of measures for the young it was suggested that the displacement could be as high as 95 per cent (*RD* 1996 No. 34a p. 4). In a separate proposal to parliament, the auditors regretted that AMU, the organisation responsible for labour market training, had failed to evaluate its training programmes as required by law. Moreover, it was easier for unemployed academics to get onto training schemes (which even AMU admitted they did not need) than it was for groups in a vulnerable position such as those with disabilities and non-Nordic citizens. Even women were under-represented on training schemes (*RD* 1996 No. 34b p. 5e). AMU had been semi-privatised in 1993 and had to sell its training packages to AMS in competition with private providers. Its failure to do so almost led to bankruptcy in 1996. The Department of Employment and the leadership of AMU were both criticised by state auditors for mismanagement (*RD* 1997 No. 5 p. 4).

None of this surprised LO, whose spokespersons had been criticising 1990s' developments for some time. In place of a labour market policy which had been admired internationally, AMS had, in their view, become something to be ashamed of (Bäckström 1996). Backström argued that AMS had lost the supportive networks, created by SAF and LO, which had created its earlier success. Schemes were investigated after they had been introduced and had failed – rather than investigated prior to their introduction to test their likely success. AMU and Relief Work had improved people's employability, where more recent measures simply reduced the numbers of people in open unemployment. ALU and API had not provided coherent education or training. Instead they displaced real job opportunities, providing employers with free labour. As for the municipalisation of labour market schemes, Wennemo and Carlén claimed this had been a disaster. "Sweden is one labour market not 286", they wrote (Wennemo and Carlén 1998). "Volume measures" such as ALU and API, should be phased out. They were a product of a policy of mass unemployment and should be replaced by an economic policy aimed at increasing real employment not the control of inflation.

The early 1990s were difficult years for AMS. It was attacked for being over bureaucratic, inefficient, for displacing real jobs and for neglecting the hard-to-employ. There were calls for its abolition – in 1997 SAF joined the chorus – others wanted decentralisation and for more involvement by other bodies. Yet there remained a consensus that an active labour market policy was an important weapon in the fight against marginalisation. When I interviewed members of the Riksdag's labour market committee in 1995, no-one mentioned its importance in keeping a balance between inflation and unemployment, but the role of labour market measures in maintaining *arbetslinje* was something on which they could all agree. Nonetheless, AMS was being forced to adapt and change. For an organisation created to cater for up to 3 per cent of the workforce it had done a remarkable job in providing places for 7 per cent. But was the AMS of the late 1990s the same organisation which had inspired international recognition in Sweden's "golden era"?[6] It had survived, but in a way which neither employers' nor the employees' organisations entirely approved.

Active labour market policy and the EU

The Swedish government however felt sufficiently confident about the continued relevance of an active labour market policy to feel that it should be promoted within the EU (Regerings skrivelse 1996/97:80 p. 22). To this end the Social Democrats decided to propose a *sysselsättningsunion* – an employment union – to counter the emphasis upon monetary union (*RD* 1995 No. 37). Initial attempts by the government to do this were disappointing. However, the inclusion of a chapter on employment in the Amsterdam Treaty was widely regarded in Sweden as the happy outcome of their government's pressure and the influence of Allan Larsson. Larsson was Deputy-Director of DGV at the time but had been the General-Director of AMS in the late 1980s and subsequently became finance minister for a short time.

The meeting at Amsterdam resulted with an agreement on a $18 billion package to create 12 million new jobs (*DN* 2/10/97). The chapter on employment laid down objectives of promoting: a high level of employment and social protection, a co-ordinated strategy for employment, a skilled, trained and adaptable workforce, and labour markets responsive to economic change with the added requirement that the European Council would consider a joint annual report on progress from Member States (Duff 1997 pp. 59–60). In a commentary on the Treaty, Duff claimed that the origin of the chapter lay with a Swedish proposal in 1995. However, he also claimed that the commitment to "adaptable" work forces and "responsive" labour markets represented a "substantial drift to liberal opinion" (ibid. p. 65).

Swedish reactions to Amsterdam were not all favourable. SAF and Conservative interviewees took the view that it was a mistake for the EU to take on failed Swedish policies. Those on the left thought the Chapter was too vague and was in no way binding. This was a view subsequently endorsed even by AMS (*DN* 31/1/98). While some insisted that the annual review would force member states to act, others disagreed. Even ministers were uncertain as to the whether the targets set were concrete or illustrative (*DN* 2/11/97). Social Democrats like the MEP Soren Wibe thought little could be achieved by labour market measures alone. They needed to be supplemented by a Keynesian policy to stimulate economic growth (Schuck 1997). What was certainly true was that with France and the UK also wishing to show that the EU was doing something about unemployment, Sweden was in a good position to wield some influence.

Employment rights

The pattern which has emerged in this chapter so far, is for the Bourgeois government to worsen the employment benefits and services built up as part of the Swedish model in the name of economic efficiency and a flexible labour market only to be opposed by a united left opposition. On its return to government in 1994, the Social Democrats would then pursue similar policies opposed by the trade unions and the Left party. This pattern was repeated for employment rights.

In the corporatist 1970s the trade unions had brought about an important shift in the balance of power between employers and workers with the passing of two pieces of legislation in the last months of the 1973–76 Social Democratic administration. The Employment Protection Act of 1974 and the Co-determination Law which came into force in 1977. In the 1990s employers and the political right regarded this legislation as anachronistic and ripe for reform. They were seen as hindrances to the proper functioning of management. SAF demanded changes to the legislation mentioned above and for restrictions to be placed on the right to strike. A Committee set up to investigate employment rights proposed that employers should, in effect, be able to choose whom they should be able to make redundant. The three trade union federations – especially LO – wanted to retain the "last in, first out" (LIFO) principle since it gave them more power in negotiations with employers as to who should go and under what conditions. TCO produced a report which claimed that 80 per cent of employers were satisfied with the existing law and most of the rest could see some advantages in its retention (*DN* 30/3/93). In the event, the government produced its own set of watered down proposals which became law at the beginning of 1994 (*RD* 1993 No. 31 p. 4). LIFO was to be kept but employers could exempt two employees from the rule. The period during which new employees were on trial and could have their employment terminated was extended from six to nine months. Trade unions would no longer have a right to veto under the Co-determination Act and blockades against small firms were prohibited. It was claimed that these measures would enable companies to create more jobs – particularly for young people and the hard-to-employ. In December 1993 30 000 workers, bussed in by LO from all parts of Sweden, demonstrated against the new legislation in Stockholm (*DN* 16/12/93). The equivalent proportion of the workforce in Britain would have meant a demonstration of over 200 000. The rally was, of course, addressed by the leader of the Social Democrats.

On their return to office in 1994, the Social Democrats duly rescinded the previous government's legislation. But shortly after the new government set up a Commission to investigate employment rights with the aim of "modernising" them through an agreement between employer and employee representatives. It was hoped that proceeding by agreement rather than confrontation would produce a compromise in the Swedish tradition of the labour market parties. It was argued that existing legislation was rooted in the assumptions of the 1960s and that new legislation should concern itself with gender equality and the needs of the small business sector. By the time it was due to report however, the Commission had failed to agree a set of recommendations.

SAF continued to insist that secure jobs were "yesterday's model" and that Sweden needed a more flexible labour market (Tunhammar 1995). The Director-General of AMS also supported the demand for fewer rules and the revision of employment rights (*DN* 3/3/96). LO however continued to protest that there was no evidence that weaker employment rights led to more jobs being created. At first ministers said they would not introduce new employment measures unless there was an agreement. This was succeeded by a threat to introduce its own legislation if the labour market parties could not agree. The subsequent conflict was seen as a sort of civil war between LO and the Social Democratic party in which many party members would have their loyalties severely tested. LO started a "massive campaign" to influence public opinion (*DN* 24/8/96). It could not believe that the government was prepared to side with the employers. If legislation was threatened whenever there was no agreement, LO asked, what need did employers have to come to an agreement. LO started to make threats of its own, implying that Social Democratic members of the Riksdag with trade union connections might find it difficult to be re-selected at the next parliamentary election (*DN* 5/9/96). Employment rights were a central issue at LOs Congress in September 1996.

In its proposed legislation in November, a new form of employment was proposed whereby individuals could be taken on for discrete periods of between one month and 12 (up to 18 months for new firms) (*RD* 1996 No. 32 p. 7). At the end of this period their employment could be terminated. If they remained in their post, they would become permanent employees. Employers could have a maximum of five such employees. Local trade union branches could negotiate away their employment rights if they so wished. While TCO and SACO were not so critical, LO remained adamantly opposed to the changes supported by the Equal Opportunities Ombudsman who argued women employees would be particularly badly affected by them. When the proposals came to the Riksdag's Labour Market Committee, it was the Left party representative who presented LO's case (*RD* 1996 No. 38 p. 4). This time the demonstrations were not officially organised by LO nor were they as big as the one which objected to the Bourgeois government's legislation. The Prime Minister was booed in Skellefteå in September and a few thousand people marched in Stockholm in October and December. Not only was the latter addressed by Inger

Segelström, the leader of the Association of Social Democratic Women, but it was apparently attended by 60 Social Democratic members of the Riksdag (*DN* 27/11/96). The only concession made by the government, however, was to set up a *reference group* to oversee the effects of the new Law once it had been passed.

Although the government declared that it would enact no further measures on employment rights – even after the next election – pressure continued from within and without. The Association of Swedish Industry called for the scrapping of employment rights as did a number of economists, and the IMF and the OECD. All claimed that the Swedish economy, industry and employment would reap beneficial effects from a further erosion of employment rights. Organised labour had not prevented the passing of new legislation but it had – in its opposition to both governments – resisted the more draconian demands of neo-Liberal thinking.

Shorter working time

Mass unemployment is such an intractable problem that it attracts a variety of proposed solutions. With large numbers of people unemployed on the one hand and large numbers of employed people lacking leisure time and being under stress because of excessive work loads on the other, it is not surprising that some suggest that worksharing is the answer. This can take various forms – longer holidays, extended leave, less overtime, a shorter working day or week: the basic idea being that the less time worked by the employed creates jobs for the unemployed. For its advocates, worksharing is simple, for its opponents, simplistic. In Britain in the early 1980s, there was considerable debate about the idea but it came to nothing. There was support for work-sharing among some politicians, academics and various individuals but not in government, and only to a limited extent among trade unionists. If any country could make a success of work-sharing it would be Sweden. It's workers had already won generous rights to various kinds of leave – maternity, parental and educational. Swedes also have rights to long holidays. Swedes work hard but they enjoy their leisure. Moreover, Sweden has a tradition of taking rational ideas to their logical conclusion and willing the institutional means of implementing them.

Prior to the 1990s, many on the left, particularly women, had argued for a six-hour day. Such demands in the late 1980s were rejected on the grounds that there was a labour shortage. With the growth of unemployment similar ideas emerged. There were calls for work-sharing and a shorter working day but they lacked political clout. With the election of the Social Democrats a Commission was appointed to investigate working time, partly to oversee existing Swedish legislation on the subject and the implications of an EU directive and partly to find ways of "increasing flexibility, productivity and jobs" (*RD* 1994 No. 30 p. 17). Both the Left party and the Greens began to argue strongly for shorter working time – publicly and through motions in the Riksdag. The Left party argued that workers could work less without loss of pay – a prospect hardly likely to please employers. The Greens advocated an immediate 35-hour week (as opposed to the Swedish norm of 40 hours) with a subsequent reduction to 30. Nor were the right and centre parties hostile to such ideas. The Christian Democrats and the Liberal party both came up with proposals. Surveys of public opinion and even employers suggested that support for shorter working time was much wider than a small band of enthusiasts.

Among Social Democrats there were politicians and trade unionists for and against. The Association of Social Democratic Women had advocated shorter working time for many years. Early in 1996, TCO and one of its member unions SKTF (the Association of Municipal Service Workers) published a report on shorter working time which would "increase jobs, reduce unemployment and improve public finances" (Göransson and Mörtvik 1996). Using the economic forecasts of the National Institute for Economic Research, they claimed to show that a reduction in the working week of two hours over a five-year period (1996–2000) would increase employment by around 4 per cent; reduce unemployment by approximately 2 per cent; and improve the public finances (through higher taxes and contribution) without real pay being affected. The main disadvantage was that the purchasing power of households would be reduced and pay *rises* would be sacrificed. Although TCO took pains to say that this study did not necessarily represent it's own views, there is no doubt that TCO had a clear policy. In an interview conducted with one of its officials, it was said that:

> TCOs aim is that the working week should be reduced to 37.5 hours during the 1990s, 35 hours by the year 2000 and 30 early on in the century (Clasen, Gould and Vincent 1998 p. 81).

LO remained sceptical, as did the party leadership. At the Social Democratic Congress, in 1996, however, many delegates including the Women's Association and Metal Workers' Union supported the idea and it was agreed that if the labour market parties did not succeed in negotiating reductions in working time, the government would bring in legislation (*DN* 18/3/96).

When the Commission on working time finally reported in October 1996, its recommendations were hardly earth shattering. It stuck to the existing working week of 40 hours but recommended a degree of flexibility in its application. Over a period of ten weeks, the average number of hours worked should be 40. It also recommended that the previous overtime limit of 200 hours a year be halved (*RD* 1996 No. 28 p. 16). While no recommendation was made about shorter working time, it was suggested that the fifth week of holiday entitlement could be "saved up" to be used as leave at a later date. During the following year the consensus within the labour movement behind the demand for a shorter working week in exchange for lower wage demands built up. The Minister for Equality declared herself ready to introduce legislation if necessary. The special pre-election Congress in 1997 reaffirmed its commitment to a shorter working week by 1999 with the initial emphasis upon collective agreements.

The negotiating stance of the Metal and Paper workers' unions certainly included the suggestion that a shorter working week at the cost of extra pay be part of their wage agreements with employers. Moreover there was evidence that some employers were willing to consider such deals (*DN* 9/11/97). Conflict, however, arose as employers often expected more flexibility while the unions worried about their loss of control over the use of their members' time (*DN* 27/2/98).

Not a great deal had been achieved by September 1998. Few unions had made substantial agreements with the employers and the government did not raise the issue of legislation before the general election. Only time will tell whether this policy will actually be implemented. Nevertheless it was something of an achievement to get work sharing on the agenda of central government in the first place. This was certainly a victory for the left generally and for social democratic women in particular. Again it demonstrated the power of the labour movement to resist the prevailing neo-liberal tide and assert the right of the state to intervene in markets to achieve socially just and humane outcomes.

Conclusion

There were signs as the 1990s wore on that many people were becoming pessimistic about the possibility of returning to full employment and resigned to a future of mass unemployment as the price of running a competitive economy. Others refused to abandon the goal seeing it as the basis for a genuine welfare state. The Social Democratic government was criticised whenever it seemed to accept the neo-liberal rationale and the policies that went with it. Various sections of the labour movement and the Left party were vocal in their opposition. There were demonstrations and ministers were booed. Government policies were reversed as a result and initiatives were taken against the will of the leadership. Although the three Bourgeois parties went into the 1998 election promising to create 300 000 jobs – more than enough to return to full employment, they were not trusted in sufficient numbers. As there had been a leftward swing in the 1994 election in favour of the Social Democrats, so there was a leftward swing in the 1998 election – this time in favour of the Left party with its support for the public sector and shorter working time.

In Chapters 6 and 7 we saw how organisations representing the elderly and the women's movement gave voice to the interests of their members. In this chapter it was principally the labour movement which fought against attempts to reduce their members' benefits and job security. Against the Bourgeois government, the labour movement was united. Under the Social Democrats, many of those on the left fought the government. The split between the *modernisers* and the *traditionalists*, however, should not be seen as anything new. The history of the labour movement has always been characterised by differences between moderate and more extreme elements. What was important was that there was no successful attempt to emasculate the unions who continued to represent over 80 per cent of the workforce. The end result was a series of compromises between government, labour and business in which each gained something.

Lastly, the role of AMS, the Labour Market Board, deserves a mention. In spite of calls for its abolition, its role in preventing social exclusion and disaffection was widely recognised. As Socialstyrelsen acted as a defender of standards in health care and social welfare, so AMS played a useful part in ensuring that services for the unemployed remained high on the political agenda.

9
The Restrictive Line: Alcohol and Drugs

> *Interviewer*: I have been working in [the area of drugs and alcohol] since 1988 and looked at Sweden from a European perspective. What I have learnt is that we are so unique in so incredibly many areas ...
>
> *Mona Sahlin*. Why haven't we considered the uniqueness of the Swedish model at all levels until now?
>
> *Interviewer*: It is when you begin to compare us with other countries that the uniqueness stands out in all its glory.
>
> *Mona Sahlin*. We are so unique and successful in so many areas.
>
> (Thorgren 1994a p. 92).

Introduction

The interchange above is taken from the relatively liberal journal *Pockettidningen* in an issue devoted to alcohol and drug policy. The views expressed by the interviewer and the soon-to-be deputy prime minister, Mona Sahlin, were in the context of the potential threat to the Swedish *restrictive line* from future membership of the EU. Both parties to the interview were concerned about the way in which other European countries had, in their view, given up in the fight against alcohol and drug problems. Both were determined that Sweden should not follow the same route. It was while they were contemplating Swedish superiority in dealing with substance misuse that they began to wax lyrical about their country's uniqueness. It is an interesting passage, partly because it is an indication of the importance attached to alcohol and drug issues by Swedes, partly because it expresses the strong sense of superiority felt about Swedish institutions and partly because it explains why entry into Europe would have been a worrying step even for a pro-EU politician like Mona Sahlin.

The term *the restrictive line* is one used by Swedes to describe their policies for dealing with alcohol and drug problems. Restrictive here means the opposite of liberal. It is a very useful term since it can refer to legal restrictions, attempts to restrict the supply and demand for mind-altering substances and a sense of moral strictness or discipline. Sweden sees alcohol and drug problems as threats to public health which, if neglected, endanger the stability of society itself. The restrictive line is an important feature of Swedish social policy and, I would argue, of great cultural significance. Although "scientific" research supports the basic assumptions of the restrictive line, it owes much to the moral values and national identity of the Swedes and is a far cry from the liberal, pragmatic characteristics referred to by writers on Sweden in the 1960s and 1970s. The restrictive line represents an authoritarian and disciplined aspect of Swedish society, which most accounts of its welfare state neglect to mention or make light of.

While the main focus of this chapter will be on drug issues, it is almost impossible to understand Sweden's moral panic about drugs unless one knows something about the society's past and present relationship with alcohol. The first section will, therefore, deal with alcohol policy, the second on drug policy followed by an account of recent trends and indicators. The chapter will conclude with an attempt to explain Sweden's hard line.

Alcohol policy

The temperance tradition

The concern about alcohol relates back to the early years of industrialisation. The social dislocation caused by the industrial revolution led many to solve their social misery by resorting to alcohol. The severity of drink problems prompted an organised response in the form of a strong temperance movement that had strong links with two other *folkrörelser* (popular movements) – the labour movement and the free church[1] movement. Indeed, it was common to find that a member of one *folkrörelse* was a member of at least one of the other two (Lundqvist 1975). As recently as the 1950s the temperance movement could claim over 350 000 members – at least 10 per cent of the adult population (Höjer 1965 p. 52). While it was not unusual to find that employers supported temperance organisations in order to combat alcohol problems among their workers, trade unions and the Social Democratic party were even more concerned about the moral and physical health of the industrial working class. Manual workers could only improve their own living standards and their collective interests if their behaviour was disciplined. Values of conscientiousness and sobriety were promoted by employers and socialists alike.

So strong was the impact of temperance thinking that a referendum on prohibition in 1922 almost succeeded, with 49 per cent of the population in favour. What was adopted instead was a system of controls intended to keep alcohol consumption down. State wholesale and retail monopolies restricted the power of the alcohol industry to promote alcohol. Tight controls on licensing prevented the spread of pubs and cafés. High taxes on alcohol kept most people's consumption in check, as did ration books, which from 1913 to 1955 determined the differential monthly amount of alcohol adult men and women could consume. Controls on production, prices and the retail trade were one aspect of alcohol control. An important part too was played by local temperance committees (Gould 1988 p. 125). These committees were an essential feature of all municipalities and could influence whether a restaurant should be allowed to obtain or keep a licence to serve alcohol. They could also withdraw ration books. Their principal function was to discipline adults who, in the community's and their own view, drank too much. A scale of increasingly severe measures was established to deal with recalcitrant drinkers. First you were given a warning, then an *övervakare* (a lay probation officer) would be appointed to supervise your behaviour. If all else failed you would be taken into care for up to two years.

These temperance committees survived until 1981 when a new law on the care of adult misusers (LVM) established a more lenient regime. Temperance committees were abolished and their role transferred to Social Services Committees. Compulsory care was retained but an individual could only be taken into care in the first instance for two months and the circumstances under which a care order could be made were tightly regulated. The new LVM was intended to keep the numbers of alcoholics in compulsory care at a low level. The scope of compulsory care, however, was widened in 1981 to include drug misusers. In the second half of this chapter, we will see how the inclusion of drug misusers led, in effect, to a reversal of the liberal intentions of the original LVM.

The gradual "liberalisation" of the old temperance law was not without its critics. While there was cross party support for the new law, there were still many who favoured strong controls on alcohol. From time to time one would read in the Swedish press calls for a return to rationing. The policy rationale concerning the dangers of alcohol has taken many different forms over the decades. From the moral condemnation by religious and political groups, it progressed to the disease model favoured by Alcoholics Anonymous. Since the early 1970s, the *total consumption model* has been favoured. The assumption here was that only if total consumption by the whole population was kept low would the problems associated with alcohol – crime, domestic violence, alcohol-related illness and death – be kept to a minimum. To this end it was important to minimise the availability of alcohol. Underlying these rationales for a restrictive approach was a concern that Swedes had developed a particularly damaging drinking culture partly a result of being a spirit producing country. As recently as 1995, the National Institute for Public Health was able to claim that:

> The pattern of drinking in Sweden is not the same as in the wine-producing countries of central and southern Europe. The alcohol culture ... is characterised by a heavy concentration of drinking on weekends and festivals. To a greater extent than in other drinking cultures, people drink in order to become intoxicated. (National Institute for Public Health 1995 p. 5)

In the last twenty years, this pattern has begun to change. People are more likely to drink socially rather than in isolation. The consumption of wine and beer has increased at the expense of spirits. Moreover, many Swedes must drink very little since the average per capita consumption expressed in terms of litres of pure alcohol is very low in comparison with other developed countries.[2] In spite (or because) of the tough controls and the trend towards more social drinking, binge drinking still takes place on a worrying scale. On public holidays and when the school year finishes, many young people and even children procure alcohol illegally (the age limit for the purchase of alcohol is 20) and get drunk. Newspapers the day after these occasions report the difficulties faced by the police in dealing with the problem (for example *DN* 2/5/96).

The restrictive line on alcohol faced a number of difficulties in the 1990s. On the one hand social drinking of beer and wine was becoming the norm. Many Swedes were becoming tired of the paternalism of strict controls. On the other hand old habits were not disappearing. Binge drinking was still popular, and the home distilling of spirits remained substantial. Moreover, the social stresses and strains (unemployment, competitiveness at work, poverty) which led to alcohol abuse were on the increase.

The liberalisation of alcohol policy in the 1990s

The liberalisation of alcohol policy was partly the result of domestic pressures and partly to do with the EU. Public opinion polls indicated that most Swedes were tired of some aspects of the restrictive line. Alcohol could only be purchased in state-run liquor stores – *Systembolaget* – (which opened on weekdays only between 9.30 a.m. and 6.00 p.m. with late night opening until 7.00 p.m. on Thursdays!). When Systembolaget failed to cope with the demands for new-year celebrations at the end of 1991 the press gave voice to public frustration. The tabloid, liberal newspaper *Expressen* was particularly critical in one editorial:

> By bringing up generation after generation in the belief that queues [at Systembolaget] are an absolute necessity for the survival of Swedish culture – through talking about alcohol as "forbidden fruit" – the state monopoly contributes to the *infantilism* [my italics] amongst Swedes and their drinking habits. (*Expressen* 1992)

In 1992, Systembolaget began to experiment with self-service arrangements. There was even some discussion of the possibility of Saturday opening. According to Ugland, social groups which in the past supported the restrictive line had "lost much of their stronghold in the Nordic societies" (Ugland 1997 p. 14). Among the political parties, the Conservatives were the most keen on reform, the Social Democrats and Liberals were divided, while the Centre, Left and Christian Democratic parties preferred the restrictive line. The new Bourgeois government set up a parliamentary commission in December 1991 to evaluate alcohol policy and come up with a strategy for the future, particularly in the light of EU membership. One of its principal recommendations was that municipalities should take over responsibility from the state's county administration for the licensing of premises to serve alcohol (*RD* 1993 No. 16 p. 11). This change has made it easier to obtain a licence and has led to a substantial increase in the number granted. There was, however, considerable variation among local authorities no doubt because of their different political composition (*DN* 28/4/97). Other recommendations which were subsequently adopted made it possible for very light (almost non-alcoholic) beer to be served without the need for a licence; for hotel rooms to have mini-bars; for wine and beer to be served in theatre and concert intervals; and for restaurants to be able to serve alcohol without showing that they served a certain amount of food (*RD* 1995 No. 1b p. 13).

While, publicly, politicians claimed that the restrictive line would not be sacrificed in EU negotiations, it has been argued that little effort was made to preserve the old system (Surell 1997 p. 42). The outcome of negotiations was that four of Sweden's monopolies were abolished – import, export, production and wholesale (*RD* 1994 No. 36 p. 12). Only the retail monopoly, Systembolaget, was allowed to continue. When a grocer from the south of Sweden was prosecuted for selling alcohol in his store, he appealed to the European Court of Justice. The Court accepted that Systembolaget did not discriminate between different suppliers or put imported goods at a disadvantage and that it had an important public health role to play (Ugland 1997 p. 13). However, a number of policy actors interviewed by the author in 1998[3] seemed to think that even Systembolaget would eventually have to go. As a weak substitute for the four monopolies lost, a new administrative board – *Alkoholverket* – was recommended during the last month of the Bourgeois government (*RD* 1994 No. 28 p. 21). Alkoholverket was set up in 1995 to supervise the new privatised system and was empowered to grant licenses to importers and wholesalers.

Sweden was also forced to raise substantially the travel allowances for alcohol being brought into the country to 1 litre of spirits, three litres of strong wine, five litres of wine and 15 litres of strong beer. It is likely that these will be raised still further when the present agreement comes to an end in 2000. The effect of the increased travel allowances, coupled with the effect of the single market and the loss of border controls, has already been dramatic. The combined effect of cheap imports and increased smuggling led to a drop in legitimate domestic sales making it difficult to maintain high price levels. Research carried out in 1997 by the brewing industry, Systembolaget and the National Institute for Public Health showed that 13.5 per cent of all alcohol consumed was either smuggled in or illegally produced (*DN* 12/11/97). The figure for spirits was even greater, 34 per cent. Even this was likely to have been an underestimate since people were not always willing to admit to illegal activity nor was the survey likely to have reached people with serious drink problems. A spokesperson for the Public Health Institute actually believed that alcohol smuggling had become more profitable than drug smuggling with the result that criminal networks were also beginning to become involved in illicit home distilleries. The initial harmonisation of alcohol taxation on joining the EU had resulted in higher taxes being levied on the weakest beer (folköl) and lower ones on strong beer and spirits (*RD* 1994 No. 21 p. 19). Continuing high levels of smuggling, purchases from other countries – Denmark in particular – and home-brewing was expected to lead to even lower taxes being levied in the future.

In the middle of the 1990s, the authorities accepted that their strategy of high prices and limited availability was doomed and planned to place more emphasis on education and information. The Public Health Institute published a *National Action Plan* to counteract what it saw as the dangers ahead (Holmberg 1995). These included detailed estimates of what would happen to total consumption if prices were reduced to (i) Danish levels and (ii) still further to German levels. In parallel, estimates were made on the assumption that (a) Systembolaget would retain its monopoly, (b) wine and strong beer would be on sale in supermarkets and (c) spirits also would be on sale in supermarkets. In the worse case scenario (ii and c above), it was estimated that alcohol consumption would double to be among the highest in Europe. It was also calculated that this would result in 4000 additional alcohol-related deaths and 22 000 cases of assault. To prevent these research estimates coming to fruition it was suggested three objectives be pursued:

- the promotion of moderate drinking habits to minimise the risk of social and medical harm from alcohol and the reduction of drunkenness
- measures to defer the start of drinking and to limit alcohol and drunkenness amongst young persons
- abstention when consumption is especially hazardous

(Holmberg 1995 p. 19)

Combined, these amounted to a policy of *harm reduction*. Indeed, in a parallel publication, the chapter on preventive work begins with the statement, "The ultimate aim of Swedish alcohol policy is to reduce the harmful effects of alcohol" (National Institute of Public Health 1995 p. 18). It is important to note that in the field of illegal drugs such a policy has long been dismissed as an example of a *liberal* line.

Within the EU, the Government intended – in co-operation with the Finns – to press for EU wide research into the damaging effects of alcohol. While this might seem a sensible strategy, given that Cram

(1997) has argued that many social policy initiatives taken within the EU start with a research programme, the chances of a Euro-wide restrictive line on alcohol emerging is most unlikely. As Ugland argued, Sweden had been forced to accept a different institutional definition for the role of alcohol in society (Ugland 1997). In the EU, alcohol is a matter of commerce and agriculture first and a public health issue second. In Sweden, it has been the other way round.

Yet for all the changes, there remained an institutional resistance to change. By the end of the 1990s, proposals to open Systembolaget on Saturdays and introduce more self-service stores were still being discussed.[4]

Drug policy

The pursuit of a drug-free society

If harm reduction is now the official policy of the Swedish government as far as alcohol is concerned, it most certainly is not in the field of illegal drugs. Teaching drug users how to do least damage to themselves is regarded as dangerous, liberal thinking which ultimately leads to decriminalisation and legalisation. For restrictivists, the only acceptable goal for an individual is abstinence. During the 1980s, harm reduction policies became very popular in countries like Britain and the Netherlands. In Sweden, however, a different kind of transformation took place.

At the beginning of the decade, there was a genuine debate between the liberal and restrictive camps. The liberals accused the restrictivists of being repressive and the restrictivists in turn accused the liberals of neglecting the damage done to young people by drugs. The liberals had had their influence in the years leading up to the 1981 Social Services and LVM legislation. But the tide had already begun to turn even before the new laws came into force. The National Association for a Drug-free Society (RNS) was formed in 1969 as a campaigning organisation alongside the Hassela Group, a set of institutions which "cared for" young drug misusers in a tough-minded, disciplined way.[5] Both had been founded by hard line Marxists who saw drugs as a corrupting feature of an increasingly hedonistic capitalism, in much the same way as the early socialists saw alcohol. The task RNS set itself was to create a *drug-free* Sweden. Despite its left wing origins, the focus on a single issue ensured that recruits could be drawn from all walks of society, including enthusiastic conservatives. A Swedish colleague, involved with RNS in its early years, once told me that it set about achieving its goal of creating a strong organisation by adopting the techniques and philosophy of Sweden's other *folkrörelser.*

During the 1980s, the message of RNS was to become the dominating ideology in the field of drugs. So universally were its "truths" held that it became difficult for politicians, the press and even the media to criticise them. *Drogliberal* became a term of abuse. This ideology was best expressed by the RNS guru, Nils Bejerot,[6] a physician. It was based upon three important but related assumptions about the spread of drug misuse, the addictive nature of drugs and how drug problems should be tackled (Bejerot and Hartelius 1984). The epidemic model assumed that drug use spread like a disease: a new drug was used first in fashionable circles, permeated to criminals, prostitutes and the mentally unbalanced and finished up being used by those leading established ways of life.

The concept of addiction regarded drugs as having addictive properties which controlled and dominated people's lives. It followed that the best way of tackling drug problems was to prevent people; particularly the young, from using drugs in the first place. Bejerot argued that providing people with good education, secure jobs and decent housing was not enough (primary prevention); nor was it sufficient for the police to focus on suppliers since the minute you locked one away, another one would take their place (tertiary prevention). The only credible policy was to concentrate on the consumer (secondary prevention). Without consumption, without demand, there was no market. Only if politicians, the police, teachers and social workers made their disapproval of drugs absolutely clear through the pursuit of a drug-free society, could the problem be tackled. This is exactly what happened towards the end of the 1980s.

There were three major policy decisions made in 1988 and 1989 which demonstrate the powerful impact made by RNS on public thinking: the reform of LVM, the criminalisation of drug use and the refusal to adopt syringe exchange schemes (SES) (Gould 1989, and 1994a). Liberal thinking argued that people with serious alcohol and drug problems would only change through their own volition. That was why they had argued for the abolition of compulsory care in the years leading up to LVM. Restrictivists argued that those dependent on drugs, by definition, lacked the ability to exercise free choice and that society, therefore, had a duty to coerce them, if necessary, into treatment. The Social Affairs Minister, Gertrud Sigurdsen and the Prime Minister Ingvar Carlsson both supported the principles of the restrictive line and introduced legislation in 1989 to lengthen the maximum period of compulsory care for adults to six months. The measure was supported by all but a handful of MPs. Cross-party support was also given to a bill criminalising drug use. Most countries have criminalised the production, sale and possession of illegal drugs but in many it is not considered right to punish individuals for harm they do to themselves. The Social Democrats – unlike RNS and the Bourgeois parties – were not, however, prepared to go as far as making personal use an imprisonable offence. Drug users were to be fined only.

The other policy decision arose from a report by the medical section of Socialstyrelsen. This had examined the available international evidence on the provision of syringes to intravenous drug users to prevent the spread of HIV and evaluated a lone SES operating in Malmöhus county. It produced a report recommending the adoption of a nationwide syringe exchange experiment. However, whereas in countries like the Netherlands and Britain, it had been accepted that the spread of HIV and AIDS was greater than the threat from drug use, in Sweden it was argued that the threats were equally great. It was said that to give out needles to drug users to indulge in an activity which had been declared illegal would be to send conflicting messages. Wherever medical proponents of SES argued their case they were faced by vociferous RNS supporters. The proposal which went to the Riksdag in 1989 said that three counties could take part in an experimental project which would be closely monitored by Socialstyrelsen. In the event, only one county came forward and offered to participate: Malmöhus.[7] Only some parts of the medical profession, the medical section of Socialstyrelsen and most Liberal Party members of the Riksdag, argued in favour of the original proposal. Their opponents consisted of all of the other parties, the Ministry of Health and Social Affairs, the Government, the police, social workers and – most virulently of all – the social services section of Socialstyrelsen. The advocates of a drug-free society had won the debate in the 1980s. How did they fare in the 1990s?

Prison for drug users: the restrictive 1990s

When Bengt Westerberg, the Bourgeois government's Minister for Health and Social Affairs made a speech to RNS two months after the September election in 1991, the account in *Narkotikafrågan*, RNS' own journal declared, "The new minister sounds like a book by Nils Bejerot" (Olsson 1991 p. 36). Westerberg said:

> The government considers that the present law concerning the punishment for drug offences does not go far enough. The 1988 law

> that criminalised all use of drugs was like "hitting air". Since the punishment is fines only, the police have no right to demand urine tests :*[urine tests can only be required where the offence committed is an imprisonable one – author]* and cannot therefore prove that someone has misused drugs. We consider that consumption should be regarded as similar to all other ways of handling drugs. Consumption is the motor of the whole drug carousel. (ibid.)

The Ministry of Justice produced a report which recommended that the use of drugs be made an imprisonable offence (Ds 1992:19).[8] The report also suggested that "blood, urine and breath tests" become a matter for routine for probationers, prisoners and those on parole. While concerns were expressed about the reliability of testing procedures and the question of individual integrity, it was felt that the drug problem was too important for these issues to carry much weight. The report also suggested that a distinction be made between hard and soft drugs when it came to consider whether drugs were intended for possession or sale.

Many respondents to the report were positive about these recommendations. Socialstyrelsen and Kriminalvårdstyrelsen (the administrative board dealing with prisons and probation), for example, accepted its main provisions. Socialstyrelsen added the proviso that prison should be the punishment for established, rather than occasional, users (Socialstyrelsen 1992). Kriminalvårdstyrelsen felt that more comprehensive urine testing should enable the goal of drug-free prisons to be reached. This would mean increased resources as each test cost SEK 300 (£30).[9] Both administrative boards objected however to the distinction made in the report between hard and soft drugs. This, they claimed was tantamount to heresy. Restrictivists had long since held that no such distinction should be made. Cannabis was not a soft drug but an extremely harmful one. Socialstyrelsen reminded the producers of the report that the distinction was "associated with the legalisation line put forward by the authorities and organisations in, for example, the Netherlands, Denmark and England" (Socialstyrelsen 1992) and Kriminalvårdstyrelsen said that the distinction was made in "other European countries" not Sweden (Kriminalvårdstyrelsen 1992).

The, relatively, liberal association, RFHL, criticised the provisions in the report for making it possible for care-oriented sentences to be passed on misusers at a time when resources for care were being cut:

> A gigantic social disarmament has just begun. Half of our treatment homes stand empty, community care has been hit by massive cuts,

> preventive measures have a low priority, a redistribution from voluntary to compulsory care has taken place.
>
> (RFHL 1992)

In RFHL's view, society already had sufficient compulsory means at its disposal to be able to deal with drug misuse. Criminalisation would deter misusers from seeking help. Stockholm University's Institute for Social Research also criticised the report (Institutet för Socialforskning 1992). The criminalisation of drug use, it claimed, violated a principle of Swedish law that self-inflicted action should not be a criminal offence. Moreover, governments, it said, had previously been committed to another principal – that there should be a general protection against forced body examinations. The adoption of increasingly harsh measures was the inevitable result of the unrealistic goal of a drug-free society.

The final Government proposition was approved by the Riksdag and had the overwhelming support of the representatives of the political parties that formed the coalition – the Conservative, Liberal, Centre and Christian Democratic parties. New Democracy, the maverick, anti-immigration party, vigorously supported the government line. Unlike the measures taken in 1988 and 1989, referred to above however, the majority of Social Democrats and the Left party members of the Riksdag voted against (Riksdagsbiblioteket 1993).[10] The government's Conservative spokesperson emphasised the *caring* aspect of imprisonment and compulsory testing!

> To place demands is, in this respect, to care. Our policy means that we care about people who are likely to end up in social misery.
>
> (Riksdagens snabbprotokoll, 1992/93:83, p.41)

Spokespersons for the parties of the left insisted that the proposals represented too great an emphasis on force and punishment and neglected the need for more expenditure on social provision. Even on the left, however, the spectre of a "stream of narcotics" was raised and Sweden's superiority over other European countries in dealing with drug problems highlighted.

Drug testing

The unrealistic aim of a drug-free society necessitated more and more extreme measures. Throughout the 1990s drug testing in the workplace became more frequent, more acceptable but also, at times, controversial.

Newspapers began to report drug-testing stories in the early 1990s. Drug tests did not have a basis in law and were governed by no guidelines. A labour court judgement in 1991 seemed to give the green light to employers to test their employees if they so wished, but there were still no guidelines or regulations. Employers in both the private and the public sectors tested new employees and subsequently introduced random testing. In Huddinge[11] hospital, 400 tests were carried out in 1992 but by 1997 the figure had reached 40 000 (*DN* 8/8/97). One in three large firms were regularly testing their workforce by 1997. Unions and union organisations often complained that such tests were demeaning. Research showed that between 30 per cent and 40 per cent of the results were faulty and trade unions took action on behalf of those wrongly accused (*DN* 23/2/93; 15/4/96). LO even called for an investigation by government but nothing seemed to be able to stop the spiralling of workplace testing.

The desire to test spread even to schools. In 1997, a school in Borlänge, wanted to test pupils without having to contact parents first. Seeking permission, it was argued, would take time and time could lead to negative test results (*DN* 26/9/97). It, therefore, proposed that parents agree to such testing in principle in advance and sign a document giving the school the right to test their sons and daughters if they wanted to. The rector was unable to understand why such a proposal should be criticised.

> Such tests are not new. They have been used before. Why shouldn't one do it if the guardian and the pupil are in agreement? We don't force anyone to be tested. (ibid.)

"The only culture police in the Western world"

The legislation on drug use also led to increased police surveillance at rave parties. Rave culture, with its implicit endorsement of drug use, was always going to come into conflict with those responsible for policing the drug trade. In Sweden, the fear generated by the restrictive line, and the criminalisation of drug use would seem to have exacerbated that conflict. Soon after the law on use was passed the Chief of Police warned that:

> We will strike early against these [rave] parties. They won't get the chance to turn the tables on us. We will harass them again, and again and again. (*DN*. 13/4/93)

A freelance journalist writing a book on techno-culture described dance culture as "glorifying drugs", saying that, "It had spread *from Britain to the rest of Europe* [my italics] and had established a stronghold in Sweden in the early 90s" (Larsson 1996). As early as 1993, arrests were being made of young people attending rave parties. Hundreds of youngsters would gather to find out the secret location of the rave and the job of the police was to discover the secret before it was too late. When the police attended raves, arrests were inevitably made. A large rave in Stockholm's Docklands outlasted police supervision because of problems concerning overtime pay (*DN* 26/2/96). As a result a new form of policing was devised. A special *Rave Commission* was set up consisting of young police officers who were given special training by staff at the Maria Ungdomsklinik – a clinic for young misusers in Stockholm whose personnel were committed restrictivists (*DN* 3/7/97). The head of the clinic confirmed Bejerot's worst fear when he said:

> This is a new group of people for us. They are Swedish middle class youngsters who are socially well-established, they have coped with school and have socially well-adapted parents (ibid.).

Stockholm police even paid for members of the Rave Commission to visit a large rave festival described as a "drug dealer's paradise" in Berlin to familiarise them with the coming threat (*DN* 14/7/97).

The newspaper *Arbetaren* commissioned the journalist Magnus Linton to investigate the actions of the Rave Commission and the effect it was having on young people (Linton 1998). Linton described the 18-strong team of police officers as "the only culture police in the Western world". Critics of the police, according to Linton, alleged that:

> integrity-transgressing controls and systematic supervision of every rave happening has a devastating effect on the positive values within the culture and in effect is a sharp oppression of young people who have chosen an alternative life style. (ibid. p. 305)

Linton clearly felt that the law on drug use had made such close supervision possible. Parents would phone and ask the police what they were doing about rave parties. The Rave Commission would attend and on the basis of "behavioural characteristics" would question, arrest and demand urine tests of certain dancers. The police claimed that 90 per cent of those arrested proved positive. Linton insisted that the harassment and injustice involved in getting such results was counterproductive.

Young people became paranoid about their behaviour in case they should be arrested. The police reported individuals apprehended to Social Services and their parents "without waiting for the test results" (ibid. p. 307). Linton quoted young people as saying that they were learning from the Internet about the more liberal attitudes which prevailed in other countries. This led them to think of Swedish policy as laughable. One young user complained that narcotics were no longer being defined in terms of their "addictive" potential but whether or not they induced "euphoria".[2] Not in terms of the damage they did but whether they caused happiness. The police officer interviewed by Linton could not see the difference. He claimed he had a basic knowledge of drugs and knew the devastation they caused. It was the mission of the rave police to rid society of its number one problem. "If we can eliminate drugs, all other problems will solve themselves", he said (ibid. p. 309). It was this evangelistic fervour that led one critical social worker to describe the police as being like "indoctrinated soldiers" (ibid. p. 310).

The EU and drug policy

The perceived threat to Swedish society was not only from domestic drug users and liberals but from the surrounding countries of Europe. Sweden became a member of the EU for economic reasons but had no desire to be infected either by foreign drug cultures, drug treatment practices or liberal ideas. EU countries, Russia and the Baltic states were regarded suspiciously as the sources of the drugs that came into Sweden. Moreover, the drug problems of countries like the UK, Switzerland and the Netherlands were seen as a terrible indictment of liberal experiments. In the run-up to the referendum on EU membership, a significant part of the debate concerned fears about the implications for Sweden's restrictive line on drugs. Would the single market and the Schengen agreement result in more drugs flooding into the country? Would attempts be made to harmonise drug policies? Would the legalisers of the European Parliament (EP) succeed in their aims? These fears were frequently expressed in newspapers, official reports and campaigning journals.

Soon after Sweden became a member of the EU, a series of articles was published by *Dagens Nyheter* – Sweden's broadsheet equivalent of the *Guardian* – under the headline *Europe on its knees in the face of heroin* (*DN* 23/4/95). It emphasised European drug problems while simultaneously rubbishing harm reduction and de-criminalisation policies as attempts to protect society from the consequences of crime while ignoring the needs of addicts. Official reports and journal articles depicted a country under threat. One showed a deserted part of the Swedish coast under the title "We will never surrender"; another an island occupied by an idyllic Swedish cottage being invaded by a rat with syringes in its pocket. The editor of *Narkotikafrågan* wrote three books on the depths of depravity into which Germany, the Netherlands and the UK had sunk. In the British volume, John Marks – an advocate of prescribing controlled drugs to those dependent on them – is referred to as "Dr Drug, the charismatic psychiatrist". The advertising blurb on the cover said that the books "should be obligatory reading for Swedish MEPs" (Olsson 1996).

RNS members kept a watching eye over local authorities, politicians and administrators to ensure they did not stray from the path of righteousness. Anita Gradin, Sweden's EU Commissioner, was constantly being exalted to take a more proactive line on drugs. Calls were made for the resignations of EU officials like Emma Bonino who were advocates of legalisation (Cederschiöld 1996). RNS had also been instrumental in setting up EURAD (Europe Against Drugs), ECAD (European Cities Against Drugs) and in promoting parental groups in other countries with titles like "Parents Against Drugs". Swedish officials sitting on various European and international committees dealing with drug issues advanced only one set of arguments – the restrictive line. In interviews I conducted with Swedish MEPs in 1998 – covering a range of social policy issues – drugs was the only issue on which they were all united (Gould 1999b). These interviews, quite by chance, coincided with the first major illustration of concerted Swedish pressure – the presentation of the D'Ancona report to the European parliament.

The report by the Committee on Civil Liberties and Internal Affairs, chaired by the Dutch MEP Hedy D'Ancona, was a brave attempt to liberalise and harmonise drug policy throughout the EU. In January 1998 a report was submitted with 13 recommendations. The first suggested that the divergent approaches of member states to drug problems was impeding co-operation between them. Other recommendations called for a greater degree of pragmatism, local harm reduction experiments, more local autonomy, hard drugs to be supplied on prescription as a form of treatment and the promotion of:

> reform of the UN conventions of 1961, 1971 and 1988 such that the contracting parties are authorised to *decriminalise the consumption* of

> illegal drugs, to regulate the trade in cannabis and its derivatives and to permit the medical prescribing of methadone and heroin. (European Parliament 1997)

The report might have stood a chance of approval by the EP were it not for two factors. The first was an explicit instruction from the British Government to Labour MEPs not to subscribe to any document recommending any form of decriminalisation. The second factor was the hostility to the report shared by *all* Swedish MEPs. The bulk of amendments came from Swedish MEPs on the left and the right of the political spectrum (European Parliament 1998a). They wanted it to be made clear that "drug laws fall within the jurisdiction of member states". They wanted member states to stick to the international conventions which they had ratified and for all signatories to be evaluated in terms of the extent to which they honoured the conventions. They were hostile to any idea of local autonomy and any "form of legalisation". Finally, one amendment called explicitly for support for the aim of a *drug-free society*.

RNS also sent two of its members to join the ECAD group to lobby against the Report (Nordin and Cnattingius 1998). They claimed that their intensive lobbying alongside the work of Swedish MEPs had "turned opinion and stopped the proposal". In the final version of the Report, published in May 1998, harm reduction was hardly mentioned, decriminalisation had been removed and the aim of a drug-free society had been inserted (European Parliament 1998b). This, however, was not enough for RNS. The organisation wrote to all the members of D'Ancona's Committee asking them to reject the new set of proposals (Johansson 1998a). In the version which went to the vote in October, the "liberals" regained a little ground. The aim of a drug-free society was replaced by the recommendation that the goal of treatment should be a "drug-free life" (Johansson 1998b). Abstinence had won over harm reduction.

Trends and indicators

The fear and anxiety generated in Sweden about alcohol and drugs would seem to be disproportionate. There is every reason to believe that the problems are less severe than in many other European countries. Nonetheless, some indicators suggest that the situation deteriorated during the 1990s; that the emphasis on penal measures became more marked; and that financial difficulties made the maintenance of the restrictive line more difficult.

Use and misuse

Statistics in the field of substance misuse are notoriously difficult to rely on and to interpret. The apprehension of people for drug influenced behaviour can depend as much on police behaviour and policy as the incidence of drug use; illegal production, dealing and smuggling can only be roughly estimated; and self report statistics rely heavily upon the honesty and memories of the participants. However, it would be remiss not to refer to some of the trends that have taken place in the 1990s in the light of the policy issues already discussed.

Although a degree of liberalisation took place within the field of alcohol policy, there was little obvious change in people's drinking habits or behaviour. Annual alcohol consumption expressed in litres of alcohol per capita has remained steady in Sweden since 1980s at just over six litres. The big change was in the kind of alcohol drunk with Swedes more likely to drink beer and wine and less likely to drink spirits. Sweden lay 30th in a list of 39 countries in terms of alcohol consumption with countries like France and Portugal consuming over 10 litres per capita. (Drogutvecklingen i Sverige 1999 p. 262). Official figures however did not include illegally produced spirits and smuggling both of which were thought to have increased in the 1990s.

Figures on offences for drunkenness were substantially reduced between 1975 and 1998 with the biggest change in the behaviour of adults over the age of 20 (ibid. p. 249). More worrying was the behaviour of schoolchildren. Self report studies showed an increase in the percentage of 16 year olds who had drunk illegal sprits in the previous year from just over 30 per cent in 1991 to 40 per cent in 1998 and a rise in reported drunkenness from 36 per cent to 40 per cent (ibid. pp. 221–2). Moreover, the differences between the sexes was marginal in both these sets of figures. Research in Stockholm suggested that the main factors behind figures like these were fears about the future, boredom with school and truancy (Matsson and Romelsjö 1998).

There was also an increase in drug use among the young in the 1990s. Annual self report surveys carried out among grade nine school students and young people undergoing military service training show that there was a decline in reported use in the 1980s but that it has almost returned to 1982 levels in the last decade (see Table 9.1).

Restrictivists had argued, in the late 1980s, that their approach was effective because the figures for self reported use were coming down. That trend has been reversed in the 1990s. Moreover, a survey of "heavy drug users" known to the authorities showed that there had been an increase from 12 000 in 1979 to 17 000 in 1992 (Olsson,

Table 9.1: Percentage of young people who have used drugs at some time

	Grade 9		Conscripts	
	Male	Female	Male	Female
1982	8	8	16.3	
1989	3	3	5.8 (1988)	
1996	8	7	14.3	
1998	9	6	16.4	

Source: Alkohol- och narkotikautvecklingen i Sverige 1997 pp. 246, 248; Drogutvecklingen i Sverige 1999.

Byqvist and Gomér 1994). This figure was likely to have risen further in the 1990s. Whatever the reasons behind these trends, it could hardly be claimed that the restrictive line itself was working. Alec Carlberg, the secretary of RFHL, once argued that Sweden's success in keeping substance misuse problems down in the past was probably due to its comprehensive welfare state, its low level of unemployment and its generous provision of services for misusers (Thorgren 1994b). In the 1990s, there was a deterioration in all three. Without them, the restrictive line would seem to be little more than rhetoric. Indeed, the liberal camp in Sweden argued that drug and alcohol problems among the young increased in the 1990s, largely due to the rise in youth unemployment. Carlberg, together with Lenke and Sunesson, claimed that the rise in use showed that the emphasis upon control rather than welfare had been counterproductive and that resources wasted on punitive measures would have been better spent restoring the country's social infrastructure (Carlberg, Lenke and Sunesson 1997).

Penal measures

There were 6400 people found guilty of drug offences in 1986 (*Kriminalstatistik* 1998). This figure rose steadily to 7600 in 1991 and to 11 400 in 1997. Over 85 per cent were men. In 1997, nearly 30 per cent of those found guilty (3200) received custodial sentences, with 2000 receiving sentences of six months and less and 270 receiving sentences of more than two years. Such figures are not very high in comparison with Britain but they included the offence described above as *drug use*. As mentioned above, this was regarded as a minor offence when it was introduced in 1988 and was punishable by a fine. In 1993 it became an imprisonable offence. Table 9.2 shows that in the following year there was a sudden upsurge in those found guilty of drug use. Between 1994 and 1997, the numbers grew three-fold and by 1997, drug use

Table 9.2: Persons found guilty of using drugs

1988	1989	1990	1991	1992	1993	1994	1995	1996	1997
14	113	98	105	72	139	1 111	2 184	3 227	3 719

Source: Kriminalstatistik 1995; BRÅ-rapport 1999:2.

accounted for one third of all those guilty of drug offences. Most of the sentences consisted of fines only but in both 1996 and 1997, about 50 people went to prison for drug use (BRÅ-rapport 1999:2).

A study of the operation of the law making drug use an imprisonable offence showed that it was used by the police with great enthusiasm (Dahlberg and Lorentzon 1999). As a result of being able to carry out urine and blood tests on suspected users police were able to report them to social services. Research suggested that very little happened subsequently in terms of positive measures. Social workers could not make people accept care or treatment simply because they were under the influence of a drug, nor were users willing to avail themselves of help. Moreover, while the police were out catching users, the number of dealers and smugglers charged with offences declined considerably (Hasselgren 1999 p. 5). Perhaps this was part of the grand strategy of harassing the consumer.

Another indicator that drugs became more widely used in the 1990s was the number of seizures by customs and the police. These rose from around 7000 in the early 1980s to 11 000 in 1995/96 (Alkohol- och narkotikautvecklingen i Sverige 1997 p. 255). Only 8 per cent of these were for heroin and cocaine, the rest were for cannabis (33 per cent), amphetamine (39 per cent) and depressants etc. (15 per cent).

Treatment and rehabilitation services for substance misusers

The emphasis upon penal measures, particularly the enforcement of the drug use law, led many in the field of substance misuse to fear that the balance between different aspects of Swedish policy had shifted. Previously, equal importance had been attached to prevention care and penal measures. It was now thought that penal measures had come to dominate (Barfoed 1999). The concern about alcohol and drug problems in the 1980s had led to an increase in treatment and rehabilitation services. Most municipalities and counties developed local treatment units to deal with problems of misuse and there was an expansion of both compulsory and voluntary provision within institutions.

During the 1990s, the numbers of misusers in compulsory and voluntary care were lower on the 31 December 1997 than in 1989. The percentage decline in *all* admissions from 1991 to 1997 was greater than those where only drugs were involved. This suggests that the decline in cases where only alcohol was misused was much greater than those involving drugs (see Table 9.3).

The decline in compulsory placements was of course accompanied by cuts to the number of homes. In 1993 there were 40 homes for compulsory care. By 1998 this had been reduced to 15. The number of places available fell from 1300 to 350 over the same period (Insatser för vuxna missbrukare 1993; and correspondence with officials in Socialstyrelsen).

The high point for those in compulsory care occurred in 1991 with a figure of 753. Thereafter financial considerations took precedence over ideological concerns (*RD* 1998 No. 36b p. 13). The rhetoric remained the same but during a decade when successive governments were finding it difficult to save money, compulsory care could be cut without affecting the welfare of the general public. This is not surprising as it was estimated by the Swedish Audit Commission (RRV) as far back as 1993 that the costs of care for a seasoned misuser could be as high as SEK 2–3 million (£2–300 000) (*DN* 29/1/93). Nor was this costly provision successful. Research carried out by Anders Bergmark of Stockholm's Socialhögskolan suggested that most misusers returned to their old habits after a period of care and that those not receiving care had the same recovery rates (25 per cent) as those who did (*DN* 13/6/96, Larsson 1999 p. 39).

Whether or not total expenditure and provision for misusers was reduced in the 1990s seems to be a matter for debate. Liberal and restrictive activists spent much of the 1990s complaining about cuts to services. Even the Director of CAN (Swedish Council for Information on Alcohol and Other Drugs) Björn Hibell claimed that, "Resources for preventive measures, care and treatment have been weakened" (Hibell 1999

Table 9.3: Numbers of adult misusers in compulsory and voluntary care on 31 December 1989–97

Year	Compulsory	Voluntary	Total
1989	748	4 291	5 039
1991	753	4 168	4 921
1997	304	2 996	3 571

Sources: Insatser för vuxna missbrukare 1997.

p. 2). Others felt that more resources were going to the penal aspects of drug policy at the cost of the social (Barfoed 1999). However, Socialstyrelsen claimed that it had carried out a thorough investigation into provision and that it had found no evidence for a general reduction after 1994 – suggesting that if it occurred at all it was in the early 1990s. Institutional care, the board argued, had been replaced by alternatives.

> Interviews with officers in charge of substance abuser care in six municipalities have revealed strong disapproval of LVM care. The cost of this care is out of all proportion to its quality and effects. The value of LVM is frequently called into question ... The diminution of LVM care in recent years has been counterbalanced by an augmentation of both outpatient and voluntary institutional care. (Socialstyrelsen Följer upp och Utvärderar 1998:3)

This view was supported by others who suggested that the rhetoric about savings never became a reality (Bergmark and Oscarsson 1998). They claimed that the duration of care had been greatly reduced, thus enabling the system to cope with greater numbers. Bergmark and Oscarsson also showed how the real costs of care had remained stable from 1993 to 1996.

While compulsory care provision might have been reduced and its effectiveness brought into question, there has been no suggestion that LVM be scrapped. Socialstyrelsen remained of the view that "*the Swedish model* in the sense of high utilisation of institutional care for heavy abusers, still holds good" (Socialstyrelsen Följer upp och Utvärderar 1998:3 p. vi). Tham put it slightly differently when he said that, "The belief in treatment is ... closely linked to the social engineering approach associated with the welfare state model" (Tham 1998 p. 409). Like other aspects of alcohol and drug policy, it was evidence of a "weak liberal tradition" in which "it sometimes seems difficult to argue in terms of civil liberties" (ibid. p. 410).

A culture of sobriety

Van Solinge, a Dutch researcher, in his study of the *Swedish drug control system*, painted a gloomy picture of drug use in Sweden (Van Solinge 1997). He clearly felt that problems were going to get worse and that the restrictive line was inadequate to deal with them. He also concluded that its failure was bringing about a change in attitude and policy. He had visited areas of poverty, many of which were isolated suburbs in which most of the inhabitants were estranged, unemployed members of ethnic minorities. Drug misuse in such areas would, he suggested, fester and a politics of repression and control would only exacerbate matters. He claimed this view was shared by an increasing number of people in Sweden. Certainly, by the end of the 1990s, prominent members of the liberal camp were more optimistic that a policy shift was on the cards.

Just because a policy does not work, however, does not mean that it will be abandoned, even in a society which has been described as both rational and pragmatic. As Garland pointed out in his discussion of prisons, it is known that they do not work in the sense of keeping crime down, but that they act as a cultural marker of society's disapproval of certain kinds of behaviour (Garland 1985). Research in Sweden has consistently shown that compulsory care of people with alcohol or drug problems is pretty ineffective, but it is difficult to imagine that any government might abolish it completely. Nor is the ineffectiveness of the restrictive line likely to lead to its abandonment. The fact is that Swedish social policy was fixated by alcohol in the past and is fixated by drugs now. The latter fixation can with justification be described as an example of *moral panic*.

A moral panic is usually held to involve an overreaction to social issues by the media and the public, a widespread consensus among powerful social élites and an urgent demand for political action (Cohen 1972; Hall *et al.* 1978; MacRobbie and Thornton 1995 Watney 1989). These elements existed in Sweden, in the 1990s, in relation to drug issues to a marked degree. The ideology of the restrictive line led to an exaggeration of what drugs did, their addictive potential and the problems they created. The consensus about drugs in Sweden embraced all political parties; the penal and social professions; most academics and researchers; as well as the media. Those who questioned the efficacy of the restrictive line were deemed to be drug liberals who, by definition, had nothing useful to contribute to discussions about drug policy. The advocates of the restrictive line with their unrealistic aim of a drug-free society called for increasingly invasive forms of social control. Describing a phenomenon as a moral panic, however, does not get us very far. We have to ask why Swedes should experience a moral panic about certain issues and not others.

A society's fixation or moral panic can tell us something significant about the values and culture which permeate its institutions. Its fears are an expression of its vulnerability. Whatever challenges fundamental boundaries of acceptable behaviour is a threat to the social order (Douglas 1966). As we saw in Chapter 2, Sweden's reputation and image as a society in the twentieth century has rested upon its rational approach to social economic and political issues. The pursuit of a perfect society has been based upon rational means. Its economy, welfare state and political institutions have all reflected a commitment to rationality. This commitment has enabled the country to exploit the forces of capitalist production and the bureaucratic apparatus of the state. It drew on Protestant values of self control and sobriety. Daun has shown how self-control is a characteristic of the Swedish mentality (Daun 1996). While the values of sobriety and self control were universally valued by capitalism, in Sweden they were particularly so. That in turn explains why their opposites were so disapproved of and feared – drunkenness and a lack of inhibition.

Affluence, travel and the experience of other cultures has made the threat of alcohol seem less severe. Today it is drugs that are seen to threaten prized values and behavioural patterns. If the young become dependent on mind altering substances and endorse hedonistic values, what will become of Sweden's distinctiveness as a society? The forces of globalisation have not only brought economic competition – a serious enough threat in itself – but they have brought immigrants, their cultures, their alien values and their strange drug habits. New technologies, which the Swedes successfully embrace more than most, have also brought new means of elation, solace and inebriation. How can the Swedish character and Swedish institutions survive when the very essence of what the country stands for is challenged by a new generation of chemical threats? This link with nationalist sentiments is not frivolous. Tham's analysis of newspaper and media articles clearly demonstrated the perception of drugs as a threat to national institutions and identity (Tham 1991). His findings have been confirmed by subsequent studies (Gould 1996b; Gould, Shaw and Ahrendt 1996).[13] Sweden's moral panic is an exaggerated response to the threat of drugs. It is a defence of rational values which has itself become exaggerated and irrational.

Conclusion

Alcohol and drug policies are important aspects of public health policy. The temperance movement may have declined in significance and influence, but it has been succeeded by a new *folkrörelse* committed to the idea of a drug-free society. Sweden came close to prohibiting alcohol in 1922 but adopted a restrictive policy instead. This is now being eroded by membership of the EU. Its modern equivalent, the restrictive line on drugs, has taken the aim of a drug-free society to its logical extreme by criminalising drug use and legitimating increasingly invasive forms of control. The end result is a policy which demonises drug users, liberal academics and policymakers, and those forces within the EU that are trying to accommodate new drug cultures and behaviours in ways which do least damage to the integrity of its drug-using citizens.

10
Apollo versus Dionysus

> What hopes must awaken in us when all the most certain signs augur . . . the gradual awakening of the Dionysian spirit in our contemporary world.
>
> (Nietzsche 1993 pp. 26 and 94)

> Not only secretiveness makes the Swedes silent: its a whole system of anxieties, a perception of the world as extremely dangerous, treacherous. The source of the treachery is, one must surmise, themselves as much as the Other.
>
> (Sontag cited in Daun 1996 p. 83)

Introduction

Sweden began the 1990s in a bad way. It was finding it increasingly difficult to maintain its welfare state and its commitment to full employment in the face of an increasingly globalised economy. Other countries had adopted policies of deregulation and privatisation during the 1980s. They had become more competitive. They had cut their public and social expenditure and slimmed down their provision of state welfare. Faced with this alternative scenario, two Swedish governments had to make difficult decisions about whether and how they were going to change the Swedish model. The previous chapters have concentrated on the detail of these changes. In this chapter, the significant characteristics of these changes will be related to the themes set out in Chapters 1 and 2 where the international forces of postmodernity were contrasted with those of Swedish modernity. It is suggested that although change has taken place, mainly because of external pressures, political, institutional and cultural resistance to change has been strong. The cultural analysis is taken a step further by arguing that it is useful to think of modernist Sweden as an *Apollonian* society functioning in a postmodern *Dionysian* world.

The Swedish welfare state

This study opened with the question "What has happened to the Swedish welfare state?" In Mishra's view, the persistence of high unemployment throughout the 1980s disqualified a country from the continued use of the term welfare state (Mishra 1993). The European welfare state, he argued, had been predicated upon the Keynesian policy of full employment. Without full employment, it was difficult for governments to maintain high levels of welfare expenditure. They began to adopt a much more stringent approach to claimants and eligibility, the quality of services declined and provision was shared between the state and other actors. Moreover social divisions widened and the solidarity maintained by welfare expenditure was replaced by a two thirds/one third society.

All this happened in Sweden during the 1990s. Unemployment drove some people to the margins. Those on social assistance fared badly in comparison with other groups. The poor, young people, the long-term unemployed and lone mothers became worse off in the 1990s. Many of the poor belonged to non-Nordic ethnic minorities. They had not established a strong foothold in the labour market nor rights to the more "respectable" welfare benefits. Such people – officially and unofficially – were, by the end of the 1990s, seen as a cost rather than a benefit to the economy. They had become more segregated from the rest of the population. More resentment was felt towards them by Swedes who had been hit by the recession and who saw ethnic minorities as either "on benefits" or "taking their jobs". In its more extreme forms this racism had manifested itself in violent attacks, murder and the rise of neo-nazism. During the 1990s, the gap between immigrants and the rest of the population in terms of political participation also worsened considerably. A report from the Democracy Commission claimed that:

> The marginalisation of immigrants is the most dramatic change in terms of political equality in our time (*RD* 1999 No. 39 pp. 18–19).

Others had been driven to the margins by public policy initiatives. The behaviour of drug users had been criminalised; surveillance had increased; and their services had been reduced. Whereas countries like the Netherlands had taken a pragmatic view of drug use and had tried to normalise the behaviour and integrate the individual, Swedish policy had been to increasingly alienate and marginalise. The same may happen to prostitutes with the passing of the sex trade legislation. In spite of the rhetoric of feminist solidarity, it was difficult to avoid the suspicion that yet another form of behaviour associated with poor foreigners was about to be demonised. Solidarity still existed but those on the margin – the socially-excluded – had increased.

In spite of all this it would be difficult to deny that Sweden, at the end of the 1990s, remained a fine example of a welfare state. The Swedish welfare state continued to compare well with other welfare systems. Public and social expenditure remained high as, of course, did taxation and contribution levels. Although the percentage of employees in the private welfare sector doubled between 1991 and 1997, at 8.5 per cent of the total of those employed in health care, welfare and education, it was still low (cited in SOU 2000:3 p. 181). The state remained the major player in the provision of public and social services and a great deal was done for the welfare of the mass of the population. Most of the elderly enjoyed and will continue to enjoy, relatively high state pensions. Employed people received social insurance benefits which were earnings-related. Health services and childcare continued to be of a high quality. Women could still claim to live in one of the most gender equal societies in the world. Nor had the welfare state been inimical to emerging social groups demanding recognition. The Greens had achieved parliamentary representation; people with disabilities had been empowered with new legislation and the right to personal assistants; while gay men and lesbians benefited from anti-discrimination legislation and the legal recognition of their partnerships.

There had then been change, even deterioration, but what was remarkable to an outsider was the resilience of the system. Earnings-related social insurance benefits had been reduced from 90 per cent of income to 75 per cent but, despite pressure from some quarters to reduce them further, they were raised to 80 per cent. Cuts had been made to services but the government was anxious to show that they would be restored as soon as was prudently possible. Full employment had not been abandoned as an aim of economic policy and unemployment was being reduced significantly. Moreover, employment rights were still jealously guarded and the redistribution of work had been forced onto the political agenda by an alliance between the women's movement, the Left and Green parties. The new pension system remained one which would guarantee a good quality of life to most pensioners. Taxation was still not only the highest in the world but promising to cut taxation was not an election winner. Membership of the EU had been feared by large numbers of people because it was felt that it would lead to lower standards in employment, gender equality and welfare. In the end, however, the principal victim was the alcohol control system which many Swedes had already come to regard as out dated. Moreover, the political consensus behind a drug-free society remained strong.

Why, given the outside pressures from the world economy, and international institutions like the IMF, OECD and the EU itself, and internal pressures from the political right and business interests, had the welfare system changed relatively little? I would like to suggest that we can analyse the resistance to changing the welfare system by looking at it in political terms, in institutional terms and in terms of culture.

Political resistance

Sweden's system of proportional representation (PR) did not result in majority governments in the 1990s. The Centre-right government was a minority four party coalition. The clear-cut neo-liberal intentions of the Conservatives were lost in a constant stream of negotiations with their partners. Proposals to reduce public and social expenditure were watered down by a long budgetary process which allowed inter- and intra-party interests in the Riksdag to make amendments which often resulted in little change. Moreover, the three-year mandate was clearly insufficient to allow a reforming government to make much headway before having to think in terms of the next election. To some extent these limitations were recognized and reforms brought in. The Social Democratic government benefited from both a slim line budgetary system and a four-year parliament. Ironically, it was therefore able to do more to reduce public expenditure than its predecessor.

While the Swedish PR system limits the possibility of majority government, it does not predetermine how the Swedish electorate will vote. Had Swedes really wanted a system change in 1991 more could have voted for the Conservative party. Swedes have steadfastly refused to give the Conservatives more than 23 per cent of the votes. Between elections, public opinion polls indicated 30 per cent support but this never became a reality. In Britain the landed interest had always been associated with the Conservatives and a large section of the working class had traditionally given them its support. Neither situation existed in Sweden. There, the landed interest had developed its own (the

Agrarian, now Centre) party, which had been happy on many occasions to co-operate with the Social Democrats. Nor has Sweden a strong tradition of working class conservatism even though class voting patterns have, in recent decades, become more volatile.

The flirtation with neo-liberalism was short lived and led to a rejection of the centre-right parties in the 1994 election. While the Social Democrats received a healthy 45 per cent of the votes, they still required the support of one of the smaller parties and subsequently settled for the Centre party. If the Conservative aims of 91 had been moderated by their coalition partners so the Social Democrats were at times limited by the Centre party. They could have chosen to co-operate with the Left party but clearly felt that the country at that time would not have been best served by undiluted socialist politics. This changed in 1998, when the electorate showed its displeasure with the Social Democrats, not by shifting its allegiance to the centre and the right but to the left. It was clear to Göran Persson that many of his party's traditional supporters had deserted to the Left party. Co-operation in these circumstances dictated that an attempt should be made to govern with the latter's support. The electorate had declared itself to be no more happy with the financial prudence of the Social Democrats than it had been with the neo-liberal intentions of the Bourgeois bloc.

Both governments in the 1990s had to proceed by consensus and co-operation. The two spectacular examples of this were the agreement reached with the Social Democrats during the economic crisis of 1992 and the cross-party negotiations which led to the new pensions legislation of 1997. There was also a consensus on the issue of gender equality. The Centre-right set up Commissions to investigate women's relative lack of power and the violence they experienced. Given that the latter was a subject which has been almost taboo for many years, this was commendable. Subsequently it was the Social Democrats who passed legislation, which had cross-party support, to further protect women from male aggression.

The Centre-right government was, of course, not helped by the role played by the Liberal leader, Bengt Westerberg, who became the Minister for Health and Social Affairs. Westerberg was reluctant to dismantle the welfare state and even showed himself to be an expansionist on the issue of disability. Given his status as Carl Bildt's partner for the neo-liberal manifesto of 1991, his defence of welfare was difficult for his Conservative colleagues to criticise. Westerberg would not have been out of place as a minister in a Social Democratic government. Indeed, while in office, he even co-authored a book defending the welfare state with Sture Nordh, the Chairperson of SKTF (the municipal service workers' union) (Nordh and Westerberg 1993).

The Social Democratic government itself might have made more savings and cut more services than its predecessor, but it did so reluctantly, out of economic necessity. While the traditionalists criticised the modernisers for betraying the labour movement, government ministers were not acting as neo-liberal converts. Their attitude was not so different to those of Social Democratic leaders prior to Olof Palme. As Bergström says:

> Talk of a retreat from the Swedish model is ahistorical. The struggle for equality and efficiency has been expressed differently from one period to another. (Bergström and Vredin 1997 p. 245)

The current leadership has also been concerned with efficiency as well as equality. They knew that changes were necessary if Sweden was to be able to compete in the international economy. Their analysis *might* have been faulty and some of the measures they took *might* have been ineffective, but they did not act as committed neo-liberal ideologues. They continued to share the aims and aspirations of their traditionalist critics. Their recognition of the need for cuts, savings and efficiencies was not allowed to get out of hand however. There were other factors acting to prevent them from being carried away.

Institutional resistance

Considerable emphasis has been placed in recent years on the importance of institutions in social policy analysis. While there are different schools of thought within institutionalism, what they stress in common is "the role of institutions in articulating individual and pressure group preferences" (Immergut 1992 p. 20). Immergut said of Sweden:

> Proper representation for policy issues is a matter of consensual agreements between interest groups whose large memberships and democratic procedures ensure their responsiveness to the public. (ibid. p. xii)

Administrative boards

Rothstein has argued that the responsiveness of many Swedish political institutions has to do with the aims and aspirations of the early Social

Democrats. In particular, Gustav Möller, Minister for Social Affairs for many years in the 1930s and 1940s, is credited with ensuring that old and new institutional forms could not easily be obstructed by established civil service bureaucracies (Rothstein 1985). Sweden's administrative boards date back to the nineteenth century and have the task of administering the policies framed for government by civil servants. When the Social Democrats came to power in the 1930s they ensured that the boards were run by those whose interests were directly affected by them. AMS has traditionally been dominated by trade union representatives; educationists sit on educational boards; local authorities, social workers and the medical profession are represented on Socialstyrelsen. It was partly for this reason that SAF decided in the early 1990s to withdraw its support for such corporatist institutions. In its view, they were packed with Social Democratic sympathisers.

We can see that both AMS and Socialstyrelsen played important roles in policy development in the 1990s. AMS came under threat but survived. Whatever criticisms people had of AMS, there was agreement that the Active Labour Market Policy preserved the "working line" – the belief that it was better for the unemployed to engage in some useful work related activity rather than simply receive cash benefits. AMS was vigorous in its own defence arguing that could not be expected to solve the problem of mass unemployment. Nor could it do a proper job if governments were only prepared to finance poor quality projects. The belief in the efficacy of AMS was evidenced by the Social Democratic government's proposal that the EU should adopt an approach similar to that of Swedish labour market policy. Socialstyrelsen was even more proactive with its criticism of counties and municipalities for their failings. Its supervisory role ensured that considerable publicity was given to failings in the field of health care, the care of the elderly, the disabled and those living on social assistance. The research carried out and the guidelines issued in a number of controversial policy areas meant that neither central nor local government could escape the neglect of their social policy responsibilities.

Popular movements

In spite of Assar Lindbeck's warnings about the way in which state financed interest groups could have a disproportionate impact on public expenditure, little was done to reduce either their influence or their state financing. Sweden boasts a wide range of national and local associations for all sorts of activities and interests. According to Petersen, "Well over half the adult population are members of one or several associations" (Peterson 1999 p. 46). Many of these are grouped in what are called *folkrörelser* – or popular movements – "large, well-organised federations" (Wijkström 1999). They see themselves as having shared interests and ideals and co-operate with each other to exert their influence upon local and national politicians. The *folkrörelse* tradition goes back to the years of industrialisation when the labour, free church and temperance movements emerged. Organisational skills and democratic principles were imparted in a "study circle society built upon the ideal of conscientious workers who knew their obligations and demanded their rights" (cited in Wijkström 1999 p. 21). But they have adapted to voice the views of citizens in a society where the forces of commercialism and the mass media can so easily dominate issues of public importance (Johansson 1978). Olof Palme stressed the importance of *folkrörelser* when he addressed a temperance meeting in 1975:

> If our striving for participation and community is to be made a reality, if we want to build a more human, gentle and caring society, we need popular movements. We need them in all their variety. Such a society has the best opportunity to engage people for common purposes. It is a *folkrörelse* society (cited in Johansson 1978 pp. 7–8).

Their significance is also illustrated by the fact that there is a government minister for *folkrörelser*.

In contrast to other countries, a greater proportion of voluntary workers in Sweden are also members of their organisations (Wijkström 1999 p. 15). Whenever they feel threatened, *folkrörelser* have the resources to make their voices heard. In this study's specialist chapters, the impact of popular movements was only too evident.[1] The pensioners' movement was vociferous in attacking poorer services and lower pensions for their members. The women's movement was not content to settle for Sweden having the reputation of being the world leader in gender equality. They were highly critical of the significant inequalities that remained within the system. The labour movement organised its members to demonstrate and attack the Social Democratic government's attempts to reduce unemployment benefits and employment rights and was largely successful in doing so. Membership of trade unions remained high throughout the 1990s largely because no government was prepared to abolish their link with earnings-related unemployment benefit. Trade unions are still a strong and vital part of the Swedish policy making process. As for the temperance movement, it may lack the power it once had but it remains a force to be reckoned with. Its contemporary equivalent – the anti-drug movement – campaigns strongly for values of sobriety, not only within Sweden but also within the EU.

Consultation, corporatism, compromise and consensus

Not only does the state routinely finance, encourage and consult interest groups, but the system of involving them in the policy making process is an important institutional feature of Swedish politics. Commissions to investigate social issues are set up as a matter of course. They are not left to the whim of individual governments. Earlier chapters often referred to such commissions. They produced proposals on pensions, employment measures, on gender issues, on EMU. Commission membership is broadly based and not exclusive. Parliamentary commissions have a membership made up of all political parties. When the Social Democrats tried to appoint a male academic to chair the commission on women's power, women's groups successfully lobbied to have him replaced by a woman. Once established, a commission is expected to seek evidence and views from a broad cross-section of Swedish society. Moreover, once it has produced a report, its proposals are sent out on remiss to many relevant organisations. These are usually published and taken into consideration by government before any new legislation or change in policy is introduced.

Swedish modernist, corporatism provided the basis for economic growth and a comprehensive system of social security. The spirit of compromise and consensus which inspired them continues to thrive. Even if the political system may have even become more pluralist, what is important is that government and private enterprise are constrained by other strong countervailing forces. The New Right weakened such forces in countries like Britain to the detriment of its welfare state. In Sweden, the institutions which sustain the welfare state have not been weakened or abandoned. They operate vociferously in its defence. That does not mean they always win but it has meant that much of the welfare state has survived. The old corporatism proceeded by compromise and consensus and the avoidance of unnecessary and damaging conflict. Not only do these qualities continue to operate within the political system and between trade unions and employers, but also between the polity and civil society. Swedish society in the middle of the twentieth century was characterised by three "historical compromises". In the 1990s the same institutional principles have characterised a rational approach to social policy.

Research

This brings us to one more important institutional feature of the Swedish policymaking process – the importance attached to scientific research. Commissions are expected to carry out their own research or, as in the case of the Commission on women's power, to make use of existing research. Governments have continued to finance independent social research in universities and other research bodies, much of which is either critical of central and local government policies. Although the organisation of official statistics has been reformed – much has been devolved from the Central Bureau to Administrative Boards – the range of consistent and high quality material published by state organisations enables policymakers and the public at large to continue to engage in informed debate.

Social science research continues to enjoy high status in a society which values science and technology and has always devoted considerable resources to research and development. Marquis Childs was impressed by the number of Swedish households with telephones in the 1930s. Today, Sweden boasts the highest per capita use of mobile phones and personal computers. Sweden is technologically advanced and its social sciences continue to be positivistic. Although there are those who indulge in discourse analysis and postmodern navel-gazing, social research tends to be heavily statistical. This has the advantage of carrying a lot of weight in terms of research into inequalities and inefficiencies. The quantitative artillery aimed at the effects of government policies and economic change helps to maintain the fortress of the welfare state.

Cultural resistance

Institutionalism may be a preferable approach to policy analysis than an individualistic counting of heads. However, it is not enough in itself. We have to ask what sustains institutions. Part of the answer is culture – society's system of norms and values. It was fashionable in the 1960s and 1970s among conflict theorists to deride cultural analysis and reduce it to a matter of dominant class interests and ideology. One of the beneficial outcomes of postmodern thinking has been a renewed emphasis upon culture as a source of identity and as a potent social force. Having said that, most studies of contemporary culture continue to avoid discussions of national culture. While one can understand social scientists wanting to avoid the over-simplification, static analysis and reification of national culture, that should not mean its almost complete avoidance.

In Sweden the work of Åke Daun has provided impressive support for the idea of national culture and character. He has suggested that one of the reasons for Swedes not being keen to admit to having a national identity in the postwar years was that in the age of modernity "the idea of Sweden as a modern country, and one distinguished by justice and rationality" seemed to suggest that "Swedes . . . did not have any special culture" (Daun 1996 p. 2). They thought of themselves as having reached the advanced stage of not having a national identity in contrast to more primitive societies that clung to "picturesque customs and irrational beliefs" (ibid.). His book was based upon a wide range of ethnographic studies and attitude surveys, carried out by himself and other researchers, Swedes and non-Swedes. Time and again he referred to a range of interrelated characteristics: the strong emotional objection to confrontation and heated argument;[2] controlled behaviour; and feelings; a preference for the softly-spoken; orderliness and punctuality; seriousness and rationality; limited opportunities for the loosening of norms and the expression of feelings. These characteristics are exactly what one would expect to find in a rational orderly society. To accept the findings of Daun, as I do, is not to endorse the simplistic and stereotypical. On the contrary, Daun himself admits and discusses the rich variation in the Swedish mentality. No-one is suggesting there are no irrational Swedes or Swedes who do not express their feelings spontaneously. In Sweden as in all societies, there is a wide range of behaviours, values and feelings, from the rational to the irrational; from the clean to the dirty; from the fun-loving to the puritan; from the inhibited to the passionate.

What marks one society from another, however, is the tendency for a set of norms, a median, a pattern to emerge over time. It is the mix and balance that is important. Nor does Daun suggest that the Swedish mentality is immutable:

> The belief in rationality will presumably be increasingly challenged, spreading confusion as a result. More and more people have difficulties believing in the "grand modernisation project" – that is, building up a modern, humane welfare state, with its quality of life and intrinsic rationality. (ibid. p. 212)

Perhaps more Swedes than previously question the value of state welfare, but an awful lot continue to prefer it. Attitudes towards alcohol may be changing but sobriety has been adopted and adapted by the anti-drugs movement. Hedonism and commercialism exist in Sweden but orderliness and moderation are more prevalent qualities. "Though much is taken, much abides." If there is such a thing as a society in the first place then one must accept that some things are relatively enduring – social structures, institutions and culture.

What I want to suggest is that an important reason for the survival of the Swedish welfare state is not just political and institutional but cultural.[3] There are those – like Esping-Andersen and Korpi – who prefer to emphasise the role of the labour movement in the creation and maintenance of a universalistic set of social policies. Rothstein, another example, was very critical of Yvonne Hirdman's thesis that early welfarism was influenced by the social engineering ideas of the Myrdals (Hirdman 1989). He claimed that Hirdman had focused too much on the Myrdals' ideas and not enough on Möller's practice (Rothstein 1998 p. 173). If this is so then many other Swedish academics, apart from Hirdman, share his sin (including Olsson 1990 p. 21, Holgersson 1994 p. 117 and Petersson 1999 pp. 53–4). I would suggest that it is a mistake only to dwell on the political aspect of institutions. One has only to take Rothstein's example of the administrative boards to demonstrate the point. While Möller might well have had a brief historical significance, the boards themselves go back to the nineteenth century.

As institutions, they pre-date the Social Democrats long reign from 1932. Moreover the boards are made up representatives of a range of organisations with differing political preferences and social attitudes. To discuss the Swedish welfare state with reference only to Social Democratic values is rather narrow and reductionist. The irony is that Rothstein admits in his *Just Institutions Matter* that Swedes are no more egalitarian or leftist than the English or the Germans (Rothstein 1998 p. 132). Swedes have been electing Social Democratic governments all these years, not because they are Social Democrats themselves but because when they look at what the different political parties have to offer, the Social Democrats have come closest in spirit to what they perceive as their own values and interests. Svallfors, who Rothstein often quotes with approval, expressed it well when he said simply that Swedes recognized a greater public interest. They strove for integration and wanted to avoid marginalisation. Swedes approve of a strong state which seeks to regulate and control unpredictable social forces – whether it be the privately owned economy, unemployment, coping with old age or being under the influence of mind altering substances.

While not dismissive of matters of individual liberty and choice there is a greater tendency to trust the state than in Anglo-Saxon countries. As Tham put it, "The liberal ideas which developed in Europe [in the nineteenth century] probably exerted less influence in Sweden" (Tham 1998 p. 410). It is a country with a "weak liberal tradition" (ibid.).

Through the welfare state, among other institutions, Sweden has sought to create a rational, stable society in which the vast majority of its people can lead rational, orderly, enjoyable and healthy lives. As I intimated in the opening chapter, this Apollonian vision was bound to come into conflict with the Dionysian forces of a postmodern world.

The Apollonian society

Bryman, in a review of the sociological literature, has summarised the distinction between the Apollonian and the Dionysian as follows (Bryman 1978):[4]

Apollonian	*Dionysian*
Order and form	Disorder and chaos
Control	Excess, ecstasy
Self restraint	Impulsiveness
Temperance	Spontaneity
Predictability	Unpredictability
Reason and rationalism	Instinctiveness and irrationality

The Apollonian/Dionysian conflict is a universal one; it exists within us as individuals; and within and between societies and cultures. How much constraint, how much freedom from constraint do we want to experience; how much should society allow? Without constraint there can be no order, without freedom there can be no individuality and creativity. Too much moderation makes us dull, too much excess leads to destruction. Nietzsche used the dichotomy to discuss aspects of ancient Greek tragedy. Although he defined them as opposite tendencies, he, initially, also saw them as complementary. Good drama, he thought, could not exist without both elements.

> These two very different tendencies walk side by side usually in violent opposition to one another, inciting one another to ever more powerful births, perpetuating the struggle of the opposition only apparently bridged by the word "art"; until, finally, by an effort of the Hellenic "will", the two seemed coupled, and in this

> coupling they seem at last to beget the work of art that is as Dionysian as it is Apollonian. (Nietzsche 1993 p. 14)

Apollo could not live without Dionysus! The "Titanic" and the "barbaric" were, in the end, just as necessary as the Apollonian (Ibid. p. 26).

Ruth Benedict, the American anthropologist, used the dichotomy to describe the different cultures of American Indian tribes. Most of them were Dionysian.

> American Indians as a whole . . . valued all violent experience, all means by which human beings may break through the usual sensory routine, and to all such experiences they attributed the highest value. (Benedict 1961 p. 58)

In contrast, the culture of the Pueblos of New Mexico was Apollonian.

> Whether by the use of drugs, of alcohol, of fasting, of torture, or of the dance, no experiences are sought or tolerated among the Pueblos that are outside the sensory routine. The Pueblos will have nothing to do with disruptive individual experiences of this type. The love of moderation to which their civilisation is committed has no place for them. Therefore they have no shamas (ibid. p. 68)

Ritual dance for many Indians was wild, abandoned and ecstatic but for the Pueblo Zunis it was "a monotonous compulsion of natural forces by reiteration" (ibid. p. 66).

Within capitalism the Apollonian/Dionysian conflict has taken place over time. It was there in the early stages of capitalism. Protestantism can be seen as an Apollonian reaction against the Dionysian excesses of medieval Catholicism. Weber saw the Protestant ethic as closely linked with the development of capitalism, with an emphasis upon production, saving and investment. (Weber 1930) The Protestant ethic was about work and the avoidance of hedonism. However, Campbell has reminded us, that alongside the Protestant ethic, there existed a romantic ethic which celebrated consumption and pleasure (Campbell 1987). Early capitalist societies created new forms of leisure and fashion. Capitalism never was simply about production, it was inevitably about consumption from its very inception. The process of individuation which resulted in the individualism of free enterprise capitalism and the Protestant's individual relationship with God also produced the acquisitive consumer concerned with conspicuous consumption and fashion statements. The asceticism and austerity we associate with the religious ethic of early capitalism was a response to the indulgence and frivolity with which it co-existed. The two exist beside each other in dynamic conflict, but at any one time one will tend to dominate. We can distinguish between periods of time where there are greater attempts to control indulgence and excess and other times when there is a greater degree of licence.

Apollonian modernity is associated with production, rationality, security and control and Dionysian postmodernity with consumption, the unpredictable and liberty. Under conditions of modernity it was still fashionable on the left to criticise capitalism for promoting materialistic values. Capitalism, it was argued, created false needs in order to make a profit. Austerity was good, consumption a moral evil. Yet under conditions of postmodernity, even the post-Fordist left conceded that consumerism could be celebrated (Mort 1989). What had been previously condemned for built-in obsolescence could now be seen as a justifiable expression of individual preference, fashionable taste and even political expression. Competition and choice, which previously had been slogans of the right, were now appropriated by the left. People should be free to choose their own lifestyles, their sexual orientation and, in the view of some, their drugs.

It is hardly surprising that Nietzsche and Foucault became the inspiration of many postmodern writers. Nietzsche came to reject the Apollonian while Foucault was the personification of the Dionysian. Nietzsche criticised ascetic priests for their Apollonian morality of resentment. They were men of negation. They sought to control what was instinctive and spontaneous and replace it with worthless compassion. Instead of good being defined as what was noble, it became identified with "the miserable, the poor, the powerless and the low" (Nietzsche 1996 p. 19). In Nietzsche's day the priestly caste of old became those philosophers and political thinkers who concerned themselves with "the welfare of the greatest number" (ibid. p. 38). It was a short step from here to Foucault's disciplinary archipelago with its priestly army of experts, psychologists, criminologists, social workers all set on exerting their control over the industrial masses (Foucault 1991). Modernity in this context was not about humanity, progress and liberation, but discipline, repression and control. Apollonian logic and rationality was put to the service of state bureaucracies.

In the last 20 years we have lived through a more Dionysian age. Capitalism was freed of the shackles of state control and regulation; hitherto repressed social groups have demanded recognition and celebrated their identity and diversity; artists and intellectuals threw away the constraints of rigid genres and forms of expression; and social scientists abandoned the restricting canons of scientific truth. In its *extreme* form, liberation became licence and consumption excessive. As we sought more pleasure, ate more food, drank more alcohol, we became more obese, bloated and inebriated. Drug-taking and drug problems were widespread. Censorship of sex was made redundant; pornography and the sex trade flourished. Environmental pollution threatened the entire planet, HIV and AIDS threatened the human species. Excess became a way of life.

I have deliberately used exaggerated language to emphasise the adverse effects of recent social and economic change in an attempt to suggest the fear and anxiety many would have felt faced with such a scenario. It is a perspective of the postmodern world shared by Baudrillard, with his repugnance for global obscenity, violence and obesity. His was not simply outrage about manifestations of individual behaviour but at the obscenity of a whole culture, the violence of nuclear destruction and the obesity of information technology. "The saturation of systems brings them to their point of inertia", he cried in *Fatal strategies* (Baudrillard 1990 p. 25)

Apollonian excess – irrational rationality

I would suggest that we can understand why many Swedes have tried to defend their welfare state and their restrictive line on drugs if we see the world in Apollonian and Dionysian terms. Swedes abhor Dionysian excess. Moderation and restraint characterise the culture. The Swedes are proud of their single word *lagom*, meaning "just right", "not too much, not too little". They had created an Apollonian society in which technocrats ensured that people's lives were planned almost to perfection. State economic policy regulated private enterprise, AMS regulated fluctuations in the labour market, housing experts planned new suburbs which considered all of the needs of their inhabitants, social insurance schemes ensured that most people had benefits close in value to their incomes when they faced sickness, unemployment and old age. Newspapers were subsidised to allow a wide range of political views to find expression. Even participation was planned. Dissenting groups were given state funds to channel their protests in a constructive way.

Whatever could threaten the system was guarded against. Everything was orderly, clinical and clean. Swedish homes, offices and factories were neat and tidy. When you went into someone's home, you removed your shoes. When you went to a swimming bath, you took a shower first. Outside dirt should not pollute the clean inside (Douglas 1966).

In the 1980s and 1990s, the outside world could only appear threatening to those living in a pristine laboratory. It seemed dirty, chaotic and diseased. Order was threatened by disorder. The economy was being threatened by the chaotic competitiveness of the free market. National sovereignty was being eroded, national boundaries were being weakened. Sweden had become multi-cultural with a wide range of ethnic minorities from southern Europe, the Middle East and Africa. Alien norms and values were destroying the People's – clean and tidy – Home. The country was in danger of being polluted by the international trades in sex and drugs. Drugs in particular took on a symbolic significance in this context. They were, by and large, foreign substances which first crossed the country's borders and then threatened the bodily boundaries of the young. They induced excitability and euphoria – extremes of feeling and behaviour. They epitomised excess. They were seen as addictive and controlled those who took them. Addiction was a disease and a disease that could become an epidemic. Drugs were more than just another social problem, they were a threat to a way of life. They symbolised a hostile, Dionysian world. Small wonder then that Swedes should wish to defend both their welfare state and the aim of a drug-free society.

In so far as Swedish values, institutions and culture have been protected, one might argue that the country's defensive strategy has been, relatively, effective. From a Social Democratic point a view, it is encouraging that the neo-liberal hegemony has had a limited impact upon the Swedish welfare state. Understanding why the system has shown such persistence, however, should not blind us to its difficulties and failings. The belief that the Swedes have in their system has more than a trace of national superiority. There is too often a tendency to exaggerate Swedish merits and foreign faults. "How unique we are", it was said when looking at other countries. "That's mainly an immigrant problem", it was said of domestic violence. "Whoever would have thought it could happen in Sweden", it was asked when Palme was assassinated, when unemployment rose, when motorcycle gangs fought each other, when immigrants were shot, when neo-nazis planted car bombs. A degree of delusion has been going on for some time.

Moreover, the belief in the superiority of the system and the desire for Apollonian perfection has led to a tendency to go to policy extremes. All welfare had to be provided by the state. Public buildings, facilities and equipment had to match the best quality the private sector had to offer; social insurance benefits approached 100 per cent of earnings; planners tried to provide for all needs; all children of ethnic minorities had to have tuition in their home language. Unemployment could not just be low, it was brought down to less than 2 per cent. It was not enough to fight drug problems, Sweden had to become a drug-free society. After being criticised for neglecting the issue of violence against women, the new Swedish legislation tried to cover areas other countries had neglected and in particular, made the buying of a prostitute's services an imprisonable offence. Few other countries have felt this necessary and few feminists have made such a demand. It is another example of the need to be best in the class, to go further than everybody else, to lead the world. Swedes have a tendency to take their Apollonian logic to extremes and like most extremism, it contains an element of intolerance.

Conclusion

Economic and technological forces may have precipitated structural change in many societies but they have not had the same effect universally. In Sweden a combination of political, institutional and cultural resistance, combined with a sense of national superiority, have ensured the preservation of many Swedish policies and values. But belief in modernist rationality should not blind Swedes to their shortcomings. What is needed for the twenty first-century, in my view, is a revival of a more pragmatic identity. *Cosmopolitan* Swedes need to confront the reactionary idealism of the *locals* and come to a more realistic assessment about what is to be preserved of the old and what rejected. More humility is needed. Faults must be recognized and admitted. Perfection cannot be attained. Imperfection must be accepted and tolerated. A pragmatic strategy on state welfare, on drugs and other moral issues might ultimately be the best safeguard of an Apollonian society.

The logic of my own argument would suggest that the forces that defend Swedish welfare will continue to exert a strong influence in the field of social policy. I hope that the Swedish example will act as a brake on the willingness of other EU governments to abandon the ideals of the welfare state. To the extent that Sweden remains a laboratory for the rest of us, I hope we will continue to benefit from its experiments – so long as we can distinguish between those which work and those which do not.

Notes

1. Postmodern world . . .

1. Alongside Sweden's material and welfare achievements, the wartime co-operation with the Nazis would have to be included, the adverse treatment of Jews, the compulsory sterilisation programme, the high numbers of people placed in compulsory mental institutions and, more recently, the restrictive line on drugs.
2. Foucault actually lived in Sweden from 1955 to 1958, while teaching at Uppsala University. *Histoire de la Folie* was begun there (Macey 1993 p. 73). He does not refer at length to this experience in his writings (which is at the very least interesting if not Freudian) and was disillusioned to find a more disciplined and intolerant society than the country's liberal and humane reputation had led him to expect. It was made clear to him that the rambling ideas of his proposed PhD thesis would not be acceptable to the positivistic approach to the social sciences prevailing at Uppsala. His riotous, hedonistic social life was frowned upon. Moreover, given the title of his first book *Surveillir et punir* it is impossible to believe that a French intellectual was not profoundly affected by a country where alcohol rationing had only just ceased and where alcoholics could be taken into compulsory care. Surveillance had a long history in Swedish welfare policy (Gould 1988, Holgersson 1981).
3. It is one thing to be sceptical about the humane, progressive claims of modernity, it is another to be cynical to the point of denying many of its beneficial outcomes. In my view many of those who take their inspiration from Foucault and Nietzsche verge upon the cynical.
4. Decriminalisation of cannabis is *de jure* the official policy of the Netherlands. In Britain there is a large degree of *de facto* decriminalisation practised by different police forces.
5. Joakim Palme, of Stockholm University's Institute for Social Research (SOFI) has been asked by the government to write an evaluation of the Swedish welfare state in the 1990s. A preliminary report appeared in 2000 (SOU 2000: 3). The final version is likely to be published early in 2001.
6. Ginsburg cites Baldwin (1990) as someone who has stressed the importance of the agrarian and middle classes in shaping Sweden's welfare system. One of my initial attempts to understand Swedish welfare also emphasised the role of what I called the salaried middle class (Gould 1982).
7. I am thinking in particular of Peter Baldwin's *The politics of social solidarity* (Baldwin 1990).

2. Modern society

1. I have yet to visit a Swedish home – flat, house, publicly- or privately-owned, working or middle class – that doesn't have a feeling of light, space, order and cleanliness. In flats it is still common to find communal launderettes and even cellars.
2. I have adopted Rothstein's translation of "Att lägga livet till rätta" (Rothstein 1998 p. 172).
3. The Commission on sterilisation reported in 1999 and recommended that those who had been sterilised unnecessarily be compensated. The government proposed a figure of SEK 175 000 (around £13 500) for each victim (*RD* 1999 No. 11 p. 18).
4. The Riksdag publishes a useful booklet explaining the rules about flag size and where and at precisely what times of day it can be raised and lowered.

3. The "People's Home"

1. This is no more than a sketch since the reader can find many excellent accounts of the pre-1990s welfare state in other sources. Perhaps the best of these is to be found in Sven Olsson's *Social policy and the welfare state in Sweden* (1990).
2. Among 24 developed countries Sweden ranked seventh in terms of GDP per capita in 1950, eighth in 1960, seventh in 1970, twelfth in 1980 and ninth in 1985 (Ersson 1991 p. 202).
3. Approximately £17 000 at the time.

4. Political and economic change

1. The post and telephone services were given more independence and a degree of deregulation and competition took place (private communication with Conservative member of the Riksdag).
2. It would paint a more accurate picture if one said that the really affluent countries by this criteria were the USA, Luxembourg, Denmark and Norway; followed by a group consisting of Austria, Belgium, Canada, Iceland, Japan and Switzerland. Sweden belonged to a third tranche with about ten other countries including France, Germany, and the Netherlands. It is difficult to believe, but Finland, Ireland and the UK were slightly ahead of Sweden.
3. *Dagens Nyheter* claimed there had been 120 changes to taxes in three years with rises three times greater than reductions (*DN* 7/8/97).
4. According to two articles in *Dagens Nyheter*, this thesis is advanced by Bo Malmberg and Thomas Lindh of Uppsala University (*DN* 1/11/95) and Göran Schubert an ex-civil servant in the Finance Ministry and now with Nordbanken (*DN* 13/6/98).

5. Social insecurity

1. Former leader of the Swedish Pensioners' Interests Party.
2. More accurately 23 county councils and 3 large communes not included in counties – Gothenburg, Malmö and Gotland.
3. One ought to say in passing that the latter allowances are an important way of preventing social exclusion and of maintaining the importance of trade unions and the unemployment funds they administer.
4. A view shared by the Dutch researcher Van Solinge who was concerned that the suburban ghettos he visited in Stockholm and Gothenburg could become breeding grounds for drug and crime problems (Van Solinge 1997).

6. Grey policies

1. When one considers the abrupt, ill-planned, ill-thought out way in which the Conservative government in Britain unilaterally made major changes to the British pension system, there is something very impressive about the way in which Swedish democracy works.
2. The percentage for 1992 was 1.3, for 1995 and 1998, 1.6. These figures are derived from Socialstyrelsen and SCB statistics on the numbers of SA recipients in different age groups and SCB yearbook statistics on population.
3. The link with political parties is not a direct one. Both organisations claim to be independent. However, RPO has traditionally recruited from blue collar workers and RPF from white collar workers.

7. The state of women

1. Segelström was the chairperson of the women's section of the Social Democratic party. The context for this quotation was a public opinion poll which showed 76 per cent of the population in favour of the law criminalising punters. Clearly for such a result many men must have been in favour.
2. Interviews took place in September 1999 in Stockholm. They included representatives of the women's sections of all the parliamentary parties, two umbrella organisations – SAMS and Sveriges Qvinnoråd, and two organisations for battered women ROKS (National Organisation of Battered Women's Shelters) and SKR (Swedish Association of Women's Shelters).
3. After the 1998 election Mona Sahlin was appointed to a ministerial post within a new Department for Commercial Affairs.
4. The pay of full-time women workers in 1998 as a percentage of men's is particulary high for industrial manual workers (91 per cent)and those working for the municipalities (90 per cent). Those working for central government (85 per cent), the counties (71 per cent) and as white collar workers for industry (77 per cent) fared worse (*RD* 1999 No. 34 p. 5).
5. "Piga" in Swedish means maidservant.
6. The actual word was nollvision which translated literally as nil vision would not make much sense. I think zero tolerance suggests the intended sentiment.

7. Another – Sven-Axel Månnsson, a prostitution researcher from Gothenburg University – resigned in protest at what he assumed was going to be the Commission's recommendation, namely to punish both parties.
8. When a Swedish woman MEP proposed that the Member States also act against pornography and prostitution, the European Parliament's committee on women rejected it as being moralistic and having little to do with violence against women. The Dutch chair of the committee had previously criticised Anita Gradin for her "Swedish and narrow-minded view of prostitution" (*DN* 26/9/97). This is interesting in the light of the section on drug policy in Chapter 8, where Sweden and the Netherlands were again at loggerheads.
9. The truth was that many liberally minded members of the European Parliament could not take Swedish policy seriously for the same reason that many of them literally burst out laughing when a Left party MEP told them about the sex buying legislation (*DN* 26/9/97).
10. Over half (11 out of 20 ministers) at the time of writing.

8. Responses to unemployment

1. SCB website 18/4/00 – www.scb.se/snabb/akuswe.asp
2. This is the nearest equivalent in English of the Swedish phrase which translates literally as *to stand at the labour market's disposal.*
3. Strictly speaking AMS is subsumed under Arbetsmarknadverket (AMV) which also has responsibility among other things for the Employment Services.
4. Similar programmes were introduced by British governments when faced with an explosion in unemployment. *Ungdomspraktik* resembled the British Job Creation and Youth Training Schemes; ALU, the Community Programme; and API, Work Experience placements.
5. A Commission appointed to investigate the effectiveness of *Samhall*, Sweden's organisation for providing disabled people with sheltered employment, found it to have enjoyed little success in placing its workers in the mainstream labour market. Only 3 per cent per annum found work on the outside. The Commission called for a strengthening of Samhall's rehabilitation activities (*RD* 1997 No. 22 p. 14).
6. More and more school students were encouraged to stay on for a third year in the Gymnasium and both adult and higher education received funds with the aim of keeping unemployment figures down.

9. The restrictive line

1. The term "free church" is used in Sweden to denote sects such as the Methodists and Baptists, which in Britain would be described as nonconformist.
2. In 1995, Swedes consumed a per capita average of 5.3 litres of alcohol and was ranked 31 out of 38 developed countries. The French, Germans, Danes, Spaniards and Portuguese consumed over 10 litres. Interestingly, Britain consumed only 7.3 (Alkohol och narkotikautvecklingen i Sverige 1997 p. 243).

3. See Gould 2000 for a fuller account of the interviews.
4. It was decided at the end of 1999 to allow Saturday opening of Systembolaget in selected areas on an experimental basis. Opening times during the week were to be extended to 8.00 in the evening. At the same time, the purchase and possession of illegal spirits became an imprisonable offence.
5. Other organisations form part of the anti-drug *folkrörelse*, notably FMN or *Parents Against Drugs*.
6. Bejerot had researched the outcome of "liberal" prescribing of controlled drugs by other doctors in the 1960s and concluded that it had been a disastrous failure. A subsequent examination of his findings by two criminologists, showed his analysis to be extremely faulty (Lenke and Olsson 1996). The point is that this period of drug policy entered into the folklore of RNS as an example of what happened when you allowed liberal values to dominate. Bejerot died in 1988.
7. The syringe exchange scheme in Malmöhus county has been allowed to continue throughout the 1990s, but its evaluation apparently has so far "failed" to throw light on whether or not such schemes reduce HIV infection or whether they inadvertently encourage drug use. This is odd as between 1989 and 1993 no intravenous drug-user in the county had been infected with HIV largely due to SES (*DN* 14/5/93).
8. For a more detailed account of the policy process on this issue, see Gould 1994b.
9. Even prior to the report 70 000 urine tests were being carried out each year. The cost would have been in the region of SEK 20 million.
10. No attempt was made to reverse the law when the Social Democrats returned to office in 1994.
11. One of Stockholm's large teaching hospitals.
12. Since some mushrooms can be a source of such euphoria and since mushroom picking is a revered, traditional aspect of Swedish culture, this could present the authorities with some unforeseen problems.
13. The link between hostile attitudes to drugs, immigrants and nationalist sentiments has been further demonstrated in Gould 1998.

10. Apollo versus Dionysus

1. I selected the four specialist areas (the elderly, women, employment and drugs) for a variety of reasons already mentioned in Chapter 1. Moreover, I was already aware of the *folkrörelse* tradition and its contemporary relevance. Indeed, my interviewees in September 1998 would often refer to their organisation as being part of a wider *folkrörelse*. But it was only when I reached the end of the second draft of this book that it suddenly occurred to me that Chapters 5–8 each contained excellent illustrations of this institution. I felt rather like the man who discovered that he had been speaking prose all his life.
2. Which would not surprise anyone familiar with the dignified boredom of the Riksdag in comparison with the schoolboy antics of the British House of Commons.

3. This is supported in a study of all the Nordic welfare states where it is argued that "The Nordic model is so firmly rooted in the institutions and in the culture and everyday life of people that (party) politics do not affect it." (Heikkilä *et al.* 1999 p. 272)
4. I have omitted two distinctions listed by Bryman – *individuation/communion with others* and *constraint and hierarchy/freedom and equality*. Although they could be applied usefully to Sweden, to include them would involve considerable discussion which would, I think, confuse the essence of the argument.

Bibliography

DN: Dagens Nyheter (dd/mm/yy)

13/9/91 "Prostitutionen minskar"
16/10/91 "Pensionärer kräver hjälp"
30/3/92 "Allt fler prostituerade"
18/10/92 "Flyktingpolitik döms ut"
29/1/93 "Knarkvård för tre miljarder"
23/2/93 "Knarktest inget att lita på"
30/3/93 "Åtta av tio personalchefer nöjda med LAS"
13/4/93 "Polisens metoder ifrågasatta"
14/5/93 "HIV-smittan hejdad"
12/10/93 "Männen måste ge sig ifrån makten"
20/10/93 "Fortsatt splittring om pension"
7/12/93 "För dyra sjukhem"
16/12/93 "Protest samlade massorna"
24/2/94 "Ekonomer ense om försämring"
26/2/94 "Här fanns jobben som försvann"
27/3/94 "Invandrare ofta fattigare"
11/4/94 "Nytt system ger mer pension"
3/5/94 "Mjuk start för nya pensioner"
14/5/94 "Ny uppgörelse om delpension"
22/7/94 "100 000 i länet mår dåligt"
8/9/94 "Äldrevården sämre och dyrare"
16/9/94 "AMS får samköra dataregister"
21/9/94 "Oron för arbetslöshet avgjorde valet"
6/12/94 "Skärpta krav för arbetslösa"
14/12/94 "Kommuner bryter mot lagen"
11/2/95 "Det finns ingen arbetsminister"
21/2/95 "Felriktat anställningsstöd"
8/3/95 "Besparingen som försvann"
23/4/95 "Europa på knä för heroinet"
14/6/95 "40% av vården bort"
10/8/95 "Över en miljon svenskar pensionssparar"
6/10/95 "Handikappade får dåligt stöd"
1/11/95 "Fyrtiotalister ger oss goda år"
7/1/96 "Handikappade kvinnor missgynnas"
15/1/96 "Socialbidrag extremt olika"
17/2/96 "Inga löften till mammor"
20/2/96 "Dåligt med hjälp till äldre invandrare"
26/2/96 "Rejvfesten fick fortsätta ostörd"
3/3/96 "Arbetsrätten kan luckras upp"
9/3/96 "Flera kommuner bryter mot lagen"
18/3/96 "Nu står vi eniga vägen"

13/4/96 "Fler kvinnor ska till toppen"
15/4/96 "Drogtest allt vanligare"
2/5/96 "Valborg firades med gängslagsmål"
10/5/96 "Allt fler nära bidragsnorm"
11/5/96 "Äldre tar strid om makten"
5/6/96 "Arbetslösheten städas inte bort"
6/6/96 "Här vajar svenska flaggan till vänster i dag"
13/6/96 "Många narkomaner återfaller"
10/8/96 "Äldre kan få lägre socialbidrag"
24/8/96 "LO berett starta massiv kampanj"
5/9/96 "Ovärdigt en arbetarregering"
27/9/96 "Gamla gardet på marsch"
5/10/96 "Avgift för hemhjälp varierar"
6/10/96 "Räkna ut ditt bidrag"
17/10/96 "Sverige stänger gränserna"
18/10/96 "Regeringens politik buades ut"
19/10/96 "Persson hårt ansatt"
24/10/96 "Storm mot Winberg"
1/11/96 "Kronan hade inte skuggan av en chans"
3/11/96 "De spelade bort sexton miljarder"
6/11/96 "Allt svårare överklaga"
9/11/96 "Nyanlända fattigast"
27/11/96 "5000 marscherade mot regeringen"
28/12/96 "4 av 10 tror inte pensionen räcker"
30/12/96 "Privatläkare tvingas slut"
10/1/97 "Skärpt ton om pensioner"
20/1/97 "Hälsa på väg att bli klassfråga"
27/1/97 "Bottenplats för Botkyrka"
4/4/97 "Kränkande socialtjänst"
28/4/97 "Kortidsjobben allt fler"
28/4/97 "Lättare få alkoholtillstånd"
5/5/97 "Svenska läkare arbetar minst"
15/5/97 "EMU kan hota välfärd"
17/5/97 "En av fyra törs inte byta jobb"
15/6/97 "Svårt slå vakt om hög skatt"
16/6/97 "Unik utväg för utsatta kvinnor"
3/7/97 "Samarbete mot missbruk"
14/7/97 "Knarkhandlarnas paradis"
6/8/97 "Snabb ökning av kortidsjobben"
7/8/97 "120 förändrade skatter på tre år"
8/8/97 "Drogtest på jobbet ökar"
2/9/97 "Barnfamiljer 90-talets förlorare"
4/9/97 "Barn i Sverige har det bra"
14/9/97 "Köpa sex blir kriminaliserat"
26/9/97 "De gröna oense om bordeller"
26/9/97 "Skola kräver drogtest"
27/9/97 "Svårt testa arbetslust"
2/10/97 "EU satsar på jobben"
28/10/97 "Den osäkra assistansen"

28/10/97 "M vill satsa på äldreomsorg"
31/10/97 "Osäker tid för barnen"
2/11/97 "Spricka om EU-mål inom regeringen"
9/11/97 "Arbetsgivare tar upp förkortad arbetstid"
12/11/97 "Olaglig sprit allt vanligare"
30/11/97 "Barnomsorg tvingas banta"
2/12/97 "Lättare för invandrare få jobb"
10/12/97 "Svenskarna avskyr EU mest"
13/12/97 "De nya socialbidragen"
19/12/97 "Krafttag mot kvinnovåldet"
16/1/98 "Personalbrist ger fler liggsår"
31/1/98 "Ny EU grundlag döms ut"
24/2/98 "Barnfamilj på rätt ort gör klippet"
27/2/98 "Striden gäller makten över arbetstiderna"
11/3/98 "Pigdebatten väcker heta känslor"
16/3/98 "Fp vill skärpa straff för brott mot kvinnor"
28/3/98 "Många oroliga för att inte orka"
3/4/98 "Solna ska bli ett föredöme"
25/4/98 "Varför inte nollvision om kvinnomisshandel"
30/5/98 "Arbetskraften måste bli rörligare"
13/6/98 "För få i yrkesaktiv ålder"
28/7/98 "Fler vill betala mer i skatt"
2/8/98 "Bötfall kommuner som struntat i LSS"
2/8/98 "Sexhandeln blir brutalare"
3/8/98 "Politiker försvarar kriminalisering"
22/9/98 "Valresultat"
11/11/98 "Primärvården sviker de äldre"
28/12/98 "Psykiskt sjuka utan stöd"
13/3/99 "Missnöjet med vården ökar"
22/5/99 "Svenska 'miralklet' har en baksida"
19/6/99 "Kortidsjobb allt vanligare"
11/8/99 "Okända öden i välfärdstaten"
12/11/99 "Privata alternativ ökar starkt"

RD: Riksdag och Departement

1993 (number)

13 Arbetslöshetsersättningen sänks.
14 Enhetliga socialbidrag i hela landet.
16 Kommunerna tar över sprittillstånden.
17 100 000 handikappade får det bättre med ny lag.
21 Bra arbetsmarknadspolitik ersattes med inflationsbekämpning.
22 Sänkt ersättning till arbetslösa.
25 Kraftigt höjda dagisavgifter om vårdnadsbidraget införs.
28 Alla barn får rätt till dagis och fritidsplats.
30 Ädelreformen dyr för sjuka åldringar.
31a Ändrad turordning när många sägs upp ska hjälpa små företag.
31b Ädelreformen har brister men fungerar i stort sett bra.
32 Alla måste betala in till a-kassan.

1994

01a Lättare för privatlaäkare att etablera sig.
01b Pensionärerna har fått det bättre.
01c Ja till vårdnadsbidrag och till lats på dagis.
05 Löneskillnader mellan könen måste redovisas och åtgärdas.
14 Pensionsförslagets finansiering oroar remissinstanser.
15 Ungdomar – ekonomiska förlorare.
18 Centrum för kvinnor som utsatts för våld.
21 EU ger billigare sprit men dyrare folköl.
22 Sämre villkor för arbetslösa.
28 Alkoholverket ny myndighet.
29 Röstandelar och riksdagsmandat.
30 Kortare arbetstid ska utredas igen.
36 Vin och sprit-monopolet upphävs – Systemet blir kvar.

1995

01a Stopp för läkaretablering.
01b Kommunen kontrollerar krogens kvalitet.
11 Kriminellt att sälja och köpa sex.
24 Ny arbetslöshetsförsäkring ska tåla ekonomiska svängningar.
25 Kvinnomisshandlare ska få svårare att klara sig från straff.
29 Framgång för EU-motståndare men soffliggarna var flest.
34 Återhämntning fortare än väntat.
36 Lumt intresse för jämställdhet inom staten.
37 Sverige vill sätta Europa i arbete.
38 Skatteomläggningen nödvändig reform men fel tid.

1996

01 Arbetlöshet gör invandringen dyr.
08 Arbetsförmedlingen bör förmedla jobb.
13a Utgiftstak ska skapa budgetdisciplin.
13b Lågutbildade kvinnor är arbetsmarknadens förlorare.
14 Få kvinnor i toppen.
20 Halverad arbetslöshet allt svårare att nå.
23 Delade meningar om kvinnofridsbrott.
32 Fackklubbarna kan avtala bort anställningskyddet.
33 Hotande sjukvårdskris.
34a AMS-åtgärder tränger undan vanliga jobb.
34b Svaga grupper missgynnas i AMU-utbildning.
36 Gamla med vårdbehov ska ha rätt att flytta
38 Nya arbetsrätten ger inga jobb.

1997

05 Staten har misskött AMU.
07 En socialhjälpsnorm för hela landet.
09 Inget behov en stärkt likalönelag.
14 Budgeten ska gå ihop under nästa år.
18 Brist på omtanke i äldrevården.

19 Svårare få ersättning när kas och a-kassan slås ihop.
20 Fler handikappade ska åka kollektivt.
22 Samhallanställda ska ut på arbetsmarknaden.
25 Steriliseringenspolitiken granskas.
26 IT-utbildning för 10,000 personner.
34 Ångest vanlig folksjukdom.
37a Äldrevård i förfall.
37b Svårt anställa kvinnlig VD.

1998

01 Premiereserven blir 2.5 pro cent.
06 Kvinnofrid ska stoppa kvinnomisshandlare.
11 Primär vården klarade besparingar bra.
13a För stora överskott.
13b Skattesänkningar får vänta – vården går före.
14 Äldrevården ska bli bättre.
15a Arbetsgivare måste anmäla sextrakasserier.
15b Nya pensionen 15 pro cent lägre.
19 Förbjudet att köpa sex.
22 Ny lag ska skydda handikappade i arbetslivet.
36a Sjuka får välja behandling.
36b Tvångsvård för miljoner.

1999

07a Alla har fått det sämre utom pensionärerna.
07b Arbetslösheten slår hårt i betong förorterna.
11 Tvångssteriliserade kan få 175,000 kronor.
34 Sverige är mest jämställt.
39 Den politiska jämlikheten har avstannat.

Other published sources

ACMD (1982) *Treatment and rehabilitation*, HMSO, London.

Agell, S., A. Björklund and A. Harkman (1995) "Unemployment insurance, labour market programmes and repeated unemployment in Sweden", *Swedish Economic Policy Review*, Vol. 2 No. 1.

Alkohol-och Narkotikautvecklingen i Sverige (1997) Rapport Nr 5, Folkhälso-institutet/Centralförbundet för alkohol-och narkotikaupplysning, Stockholm.

Ambjörnsson, R. (1989) "The conscientious worker: ideas and ideals in a Swedish working class culture", *History of European ideas*, Vol. 10 No. 1, pp. 59–67.

Anderberg, P. and B. Jönsson (1997) "USA överlägset Sverige". *Dagens Nyheter*, 9 August.

Andersen, J.G., P.A., Pettersen, S. Svallfors and H. Uusitalo (1999) "The legitimacy of the Nordic welfare states" in M., Kautto, B., Heikkilä, Hvinden, S. Marklund, and N. Ploug *Nordic welfare policy: changing welfare states*, Routledge, London.

Andersen, P. (1999) *Hej då, Sverige*! Moderna Tider, May.

Arbetsmarknadsdata (1999) Arbetsmarknadsstyrelesen, Gnesta, February.

Arvidsson, C. (1995) "Det får inte sparas mer", *Dagens Nyheter*, 9 January.

Arvidsson, L., K. Pettersson and S. Svensk (1994) "Bra för kvinnorna", *Dagens Nyheter*, 11 April.

Auer, P. and C. Riegler (1994) "Sweden: the end of full employment" *Employment Observatory*, No. 46, Berlin.

Bäckström, A. (1996) "En politik att skämmas för", *Dagens Nyheter*, 3 October.

Baldwin, P. (1990) *The poltics of social solidarity: class bases of the European welfare state*, Cambridge University Press, Cambridge.

Bard, A. (1999) "Min kropp är min", *GT-Expressen*, 3 February.

Barfoed, E. (1999) "En narkotikapolitik i obalans", *Alkohol och Narkotika*, No. 2 pp. 12–13.

Baudrillard, J. (1990) *Fatal strategies*, Pluto Press, London.

Beck, U., Giddens, A. and S. Lash (1994) *Reflexive Modernization*, Polity Press, Cambridge.

Begler, A-M. (1995) "Flytingars socialbidrag permanentas", *Dagens Nyheter*, 20 September.

Begler, A-M. (1997) "Bidragssänkingen räcker inte", *Dagens Nyheter*, 1 April.

Begler, A-M. (1996) "Socialbidraget ingen mammapeng", *Dagens Nyheter*, 17 June.

Begler, A-M. and J. Andersson (1998) "Anmälda misshandelsfall ökar dramatiskt", *Dagens Nyheter*, 15 September.

Bejerot, N. and J. Hartelius (1984) *Missbruk och motåtgärder*, Ordfront, Stockholm.

Benedict, R. (1961) *Patterns of culture*, Routledge, London.

Bergh, J. (1997) "Bara rika får vård", *Dagens Nyheter*, 2 July.

Berglind, H. (1994) "Förtidspensioneringen och utslagning på arbetsmarknaden", in *Förtidspension – en arbetsmarknadspolitisk ventil*? SOU 1994:148, Socialdepartement, Stockholm.

Bergmark, A. and L. Oscarsson (1998) "Hur styrs missbrukarvården?" *Socionomen*, No. 4 pp. 47–53.

Bergqvist, C. and A-C. Jungar (2000) "The Swedish gender model and the EU: adaptation or diffusion?" in L. Hantrais (ed.) *Gendered policies in Europe: reconciling employment and family life*, Macmillan, London.

Bergström, V. (1993) "Varför överge den svenska modellen", *Tiden*, No. 4.

Bergström, V. and A. Vredin (1997) "Den svenska modellen är död, leve den svenska modellen!" in V. Bergström (ed.) *Arbetsmarknad och tillväxt*, Ekerlids Förlag, Stockholm.

Bernhardsson, G. (1992) "Arbetslinjens kollaps", *Dagens Nyheter*, 30 January.

Bernhardsson, G. (1995) "Ambitionen har fått sänkas", *Dagens Nyheter*, 13 September.

Bildt, C. (1998) "Program formas för ny regering", *Dagens Nyheter, 31 January*.

Billig, M. (1995) *Banal nationalism*, Sage, London.

Blake, M. (1997) *Grey power? political mobilisation among pensioners in Sweden*, Faculty of Social Sciences, Stockholm University, Stockholm.

Blomberg, R. (1993) "Risk för fel ingrepp", *Dagens Nyheter*, 12 January.

Boethius, M-P. (1994) "En genant valrörelse" *Dagens Nyheter*, 17 September.

Boethius, M-P. (1995) "Sällan skådad orgie i sexism" *Dagens Nyheter*, 23 September.
Boethius, M-P. (1997) "Utred mediernas skuld", *Dagens Nyheter*, 27 September.
BRÅ-rapport 1999:2 *Narkotika statistik*, Brottsförebygganderådet, Stockholm.
Bratt, P. (1997) "Marknadens väg till makten", *Dagens Nyheter*, 4 May.
Brink, J. (1999) "Därför säger RFSU nej till torsklagen", *Arbetaren*, No. 7 pp. 8–11.
Brunnberg, K. (1991) "Election year 1991", *Current Sweden*, No. 385.
Brunsdon, E. and M. May (1995) "Swedish health care in transition", in E. Brunsdon and M. May (eds) *Swedish welfare: policy and provision*, Social Policy Assocation, London.
Bryman, A. (1978) *Apollo and Dionysius in social thought*, Department of Social Sciences, Loughborough University, Loughborough.
Bunton, R. (1998) "Post-Betty Fordism and neo-liberal drug policies", in J. Carter (ed.) *Postmodernity and the fragmentation of welfare*, Routledge, London.
Calmfors, L. (1995) "Lägg ner AMS", *Dagens Nyheter*, 19 July.
Calmfors, L. and J. Herin (1993) "En ny arbetslöshetsförsäkring" in *Ersättning vid arbetslöshet*, SOU 1993:52, Stockholm.
Campbell, C. (1987) *The romantic ethic and the spirit of modern consumerism*, Blackwell, Oxford.
Carlberg, A., L. Lenke and S. Sunesson (1997) "Narkotikamissbruket ökar kraftigt", *Dagens Nyheter*, 24 March.
Carlén, S. (1999) "Avskaffa könsdiskriminering i arbetskadeförsäkring", *Morgonbris*, No. 3–4 pp 22–3.
Carlson, A.C. (1978) *The roles of Alva and Gunnar Myrdal in the development of a social democratic response to Europe's "population crisis" 1929–1938*, Mimeographed copy of a PhD thesis, University Microfilms International, Michigan and London.
Cederschiöld, C. (1996) *Press release*, Stockholm City Hall, 8 December.
Cerny, P.G. (1990) *The changing architecture of politics*, Sage, London.
Chamberlayne, P., A., Cooper, R. Freeman and M. Rustin (1999) *Welfare and culture in Europe*, Jessica Kingsley Publishers, London.
Childs, M. (1936) *Sweden: the middle way*, Yale University Press, New Haven.
Clarke, J. (1998) "Coming to terms with culture", unpublished paper presented to the annual conference of the Social Policy Association 14–16 July, University of Lincolnshire and Humberside.
Clasen, J., A., Gould and J. Vincent (1998) *Voices within and without: responses to long term unemployment in Germany, Sweden and Britain*, Policy Press, Bristol.
Cohen, S. (1972) *Folk devils and moral panics: the creation of mods and* rockers, MacGibbon and Kee, London.
Cram, L. (1997) *Policy-making and the EU*, Routledge, London.
Daatland, S.O. (1997) "Welfare policies for older people in transition? Emerging trends and perspectives", *Scandinavian Journal of Social Welfare*, No. 6 pp. 153–61.
Dahlberg, K. and Lorentzon, P. (1999) "Tydlig signal men är den verkningsfull?" *Alkohol och Narkotika*, Stockholm pp 15–17.
Daun, Å. (1996) *Swedish mentality*, The Pennsylvania University Press, Pennsylvania.
Douglas, M. (1966) *Purity and Danger*, Penguin, Harmondsworth.

Drogutvecklingen i Sverige (1999) Folhälsoinstitutet/Centralförbundet för alkohol- och narkotikaupplysing, Stockholm.

Ds (1992:19) *Åtgärder mot bruk av narkotika samt ringa narkotikabrott*, Stockholm, Justitie Departementet.

Ds (1977:22) *Remissyttranden över betänkandet Sverige och EMU*, Finansdepartementet, Stockholm.

Ds (1994:108) *Arbetsmarknad och arbetsmarknadspolitik 1993*, Arbetsmarknadsdepartementet, Stockholm.

Ds (1995:12) *Kommunernas ansvar för ungdomar under 20 år*, Arbetsmarknadsdepartementet, Stockholm.

Duff, A. (1997) *The treaty of Amsterdam*, Sweet and Maxwell, London.

Edin, P-O. (1995) "EMU måste bli ett vänsterprojekt", *LO-Tidningen*, No. 33.

Edin, P-O. and D. Andersson (1997) "Förändra lönebildningen helt", *Dagens Nyheter*, 25 June.

Edin, P-O. and S. Carlsson (1993) "Wibble jagar spöken", *Dagens Nyheter*, 10 March.

Eduards, M. (1997a) "Interpreting women's organising" in G. Gustafsson, M. Eduards and M. Rönnblom (eds) (1997) *Towards a new democratic order? women's organising in Sweden in the 1990s*, Publica, Stockholm.

Eduards, M. (1997b) "The women's shelter movement" in G. Gustafsson, M. Eduards and M. Rönnblom (eds) (1997) *Towards a new democratic order? women's organising in Sweden in the 1990s*, Publica, Stockholm.

Ekberg, J. (1996) "Invandrarna i pensionsystemet", *Social Vetenskaplig Tidskrift*, Number 4.

Eklund, K. (1993) *Hur farligt är budgetunderskott?* SNS Förlag.

Ellingsaeter, A.L. (1998) "Dual breadwinner societies: provider models in the Scandinavian welfare states", *Acta Sociolgica*, No. 41 pp. 1–96.

Elman, R.A. (1996) *Sexual subordination and state intervention*, Berghan Books, Oxford.

Elman, R.A. and M. Eduards (1991) "Unprotected by the Swedish state: a survey of battered women and the assistance they receive", *Women's Studies International Forum*, Vol. 14 No. 5.

Elmér, Å., S. Blomberg, L. Harrysson and J. Petersson (1998) *Svensksocialpolitik*, Studentlitteratur, Lund.

Eribon, D. (1991) *Michel Foucault*, Harvard University Press, Cambridge, Mass.

Erlandsson, G., P-O. Edin and S. Carlsson (1997) "Konkurrensen hotar välfärden", *Dagens Nyheter*, 22 May.

Ersson, S. (1991) "Appendix: some facts about Swedish politics", *West European Politics*, Vol. 14 No. 3.

Esping-Andersen, G. (1985) *Politics against markets: the social democratic road to power*, Princeton University Press, Princeton, NJ.

Esping-Andersen, G. (1990) *The three worlds of welfare capitalism*, Polity Press, Cambridge.

European Parliament (1997) *Report containing a proposal on the harmonisation of the member state's laws on drugs A4-0359/97*, Strasbourg.

European Parliament (1998a) *Amendments to the D'Ancona Report*, Strasbourg.

European Parliament (1998b) *Second report containing a proposal on the harmonisation of the member state's laws on drugs A4-0211/98*, Strasbourg.

Eurostat (1997) *Labour force survey*, Luxembourg.

Eurostat (1997) *Eurostat yearbook*, Luxembourg.
Eurostat (1999) *Eurostat yearbook*, Luxembourg.
Eurostat (2000) *Internet data.*
Expressen (1992) "Det är något fel på Systemet", 4 January.
Expressen (1998) "Invasion av prostituerade", 2 April.
Fernow, N. (1992) "Swedish elder care in transition", *Current Sweden*, No. 392, Swedish Institute, Stockholm.
Fleisher, W. (1956) *Sweden: the welfare state*, Greenwood Press, Connecticut.
Foucault, M. (1991) *Discipline and punish: the birth of the prison*, Penguin, London.
Fraser, N. (1995) "Recognition and redistribution: dilemmas of social justice in a 'post-socialist' age", *New Left Review*, No. 212 pp. 68–93.
Frykman, J. (1996) "On the move: the struggle for the body in Sweden" in C.N. Serematakis *The senses still: perception and memory as material culture in modernity*, University of Chicago Press, Chicago.
Furniss, N. and T. Tilton (1977) *The case for the welfare state*, Indiana University Press, Bloomington.
Gahrton, P. (1997) *Vill Sverige bli län i EU-stat?* Gröna Böcker, Lund.
Garland, D. (1985) *Punishment and Welfare: a history of penal strategies*, Gower, Aldershot.
Gaunt, D. (1996) "Etnicitet, åldrande och hälsa", *Social Vetenskaplig Tidskrift*, Number 7–8.
Ginsburg, N. (1993) "Sweden: the social-democratic case" in A. Cochrane and J. Clarke *Comparing welfare states: Britain in international context*, Sage Publications, London.
Ginsburg, N. (2001) "Sweden: the social-democratic case" in A. Cochrane and J. Clarke *Comparing welfare states: Britain in international context*, Sage Publications, London.
Göransson, B. and R. Mörtvik (1996) *Kortare arbetstid*, TCO, Stockholm.
Gould, A. (1982) "The salaried middle class and the welfare state in Sweden and Japan", *Policy and Politics*, Vol. 10 No. 4 pp. 417–38.
Gould, A. (1988) *Conflict and control in welfare policy*, Longman, Harlow.
Gould, A. (1989) "Cleaning the People's Home: recent developments in Sweden's addiction policy", *British Journal of Addiction*, Vol. 84 No. 7, pp. 731–41.
Gould, A. (1990) "Alcohol and drug policies in Sweden and the UK: a study of two counties" in N. Manning and C. Ungerson (eds) *Social policy review 1989–90*, Social Policy Association, London.
Gould, A. (1993a) *Capitalist welfare systems*, Longman, Harlow.
Gould, A. (1993b) "Opposition to syringe exchange schemes in the UK and Sweden", *Journal of European Social Policy*, Vol. 3 No. 2, pp. 107–18.
Gould, A. (1993c) "The end of the middle way?" in C. Jones, (ed.) *New perpectives on the welfare state in Europe*, Routledge, London.
Gould, A. (1994a) "Sweden's syringe exchange debate: moral panic in a rational society", *Journal of Social Policy*, Vol. 23 No. 2, pp. 195–217.
Gould, A. (1994b) "Pollution rituals in Sweden: the pursuit of a drug free society", *Scandinavian Journal of Social Welfare*, Vol. 3 No. 2 pp. 85–93.

Gould, A. (1995) "The Swedish system in turmoil: debate, conflict and change" in E. Brunsdon, and M. May, *Swedish welfare: policy and provision*, Social Policy Association, London.

Gould, A. (1996a) "Sweden: the last bastion of social democracy" in V. George, and P. Taylor-Gooby, *European welfare policy: squaring the welfare circle*, St. Martin's Press, New York.

Gould, A. (1996b) "Drug issues and the Swedish press", *International Journal of Drug Policy*, Vol. 7 No. 2 pp. 91–103.

Gould, A. (1998) "Nationalism, immigrants and attitudes towards drugs", *International Journal of Drug Policy*, Vol. 9 pp. 133–9.

Gould, A. (1999a) "The erosion of the welfare state: Swedish social policy and the EU", *Journal of European Social Policy*, Vol. 9 No. 2.

Gould, A. (1999b) "A drug-free Europe? Sweden on the offensive", *Druglink*, Vol. 14 No. 2 pp. 12–14.

Gould, A. (2000) "Swedish social policy and the EU social dimension" in L. Miles, (ed.) *Sweden and the EU evaluated*, Continuum, London.

Gould, A. (2001) "The criminalisation of buying sex: the politics of prostitution in Sweden", *Journal of Social Policy*, Vol. 30 No. 3.

Gould, A., A. Shaw and D. Ahrendt (1996) "Illegal drug: liberal and restrictive attitudes" in R. Jowell, J. Curtice, A. Park, L. Brook, and K. Thomson, *British Social Attitudes: the 13th report*, Dartmouth, Aldershot.

Greve, J. (1978) *Royal Commission on the Distribution of Income and Wealth, background paper number 6: Low incomes in Sweden*, HMSO, London.

Grunewald (1997) "Sabotage mot handikappreform", *Dagens Nyheter*, 4 April.

Guardian (1999) "Car bombs explode Sweden's self-image", 3 July.

Gustafsson, G. (1997a) "A cultural perspective on women, politics and democracy" in G. Gustafsson, M. Eduards and M. Rönnblom, (eds) *Towards a new democratic order? women's organising in Sweden in the 1990s*, Publica, Stockholm.

Gustafsson, G. (1997b) "Ringing the changes for an unknown future" in G. Gustafsson, M. Eduards and M. Rönnblom, (eds) *Towards a new democratic order? women's organising in Sweden in the 1990s*, Publica, Stockholm.

Hall, S. C. Critcher, T. Jefferson, J. Clarke and B. Roberts (1978) *Policing the crisis: mugging, the state and law and order*, Macmillan, London.

Harkman, A. (1994) *Unemployment, labour market measures and their influence on the probability of gaining employment*, Arbetsmarknadsstyrelsen, Solna.

Harvey, D. (1989) *The condition of postmodernity*, Blackwell, Oxford.

Hasselgren, S. (1999) "Det hänger på balansen", *Alkohol och Narkotika*, No. 2 p. 5.

Heclo, H. and M. Madsen (1986) *Policy and politics in Sweden*, Temple University Press, Philadelphia.

Hedborg, A. and I. Thalén (1993) "Vi har tagit intryck av kritiken", *Dagens Nyheter*, 15 January.

Hedborg, A. and R. Meidner (1984) *Folkhemsmodellen*, Rabén and Sjögren, Borås.

Heikkilä, B. Hvinden, M. Kautto, S. Marklund and N. Ploug (1999) "Conclusion: The Nordic model stands stable but on shaky ground" in M. Kautto, B. Hvinden, Heikkilä, S. Marklund and N. Ploug, *Nordic welfare policy: changing welfare states*, Routledge, London.

Hewitt, M. (1992) *Welfare, ideology and need: developing perspectives on the welfare state*, Harvester Wheatsheaf, Hemel Hempstead.

Hibell, B. (1999) "Det kan kosta att spara", *Alkohol och Narkotika*, No. 2. p. 2.

Hillyard, P. and S. Watson (1996) "Postmodern social policy: a contradiction in terms?" *Journal of Social policy*, Vol. 25 No. 3 pp. 321–46.

Hirdman, Y. (1989) *Att lägga livet till rätta: studier i svensk folkhemspolitik*, Carlssons, Stockholm.

Hirdman, Y. (1993) "Husmor I det lilla livet" in *Välfärdens brytpunkt*, Akademeja, Stockholm.

Hobson, B., S. Johansson, L. Olah and C. Sutton (1995) "Gender and the Swedish welfare state" in E. Brunsdon and M. May, *Swedish welfare: policy and provision*, Social Policy Association, London.

Hobson, B. and M. Takahashi (1997) "The parent–worker model: lone mothers in Sweden" in J. Lewis, (ed.) *Lone mothers in European welfare regimes*, Jessica Kingsley Publishers, London.

Höjer, J.A. (1944) "Reformkrav och framtidsyver inom hälso- och sjukvård" in *Ett genombrott*, Tidens Förlag, Stockholm.

Höjer, K.J. (1965) *Svensk nykterhetspolitik och nykterhetsvård*, Norstedts, Stockholm.

Holgersson, L. (1981) *Socialvård, Tiden*, Stockholm.

Holgersson, L. (1994) "Building a people's home for settled conscientious Swedes", *Scandinavian Journal of Social Welfare*, Vol. 3 No. 3 pp. 113–20.

Holmberg, B. (1995) *National plan of action*, National Institute for Public Health, Stockholm.

Horgby, B. (1986) *Den disciplinerade arbetaren*, Almqvist and Wiksell, Stockholm.

Huntford, R. (1971) *The new totalitarians*, Allen Lane, London.

Hydén, L-C., P. Westermark and S-Å. Stenberg (1995) *Att besluta om socialbidrag*, Socialstyrelsen, Stockholm.

Immergut, E.M. (1992) *Health politics: interests and institutions in Western Europe*, Cambridge University Press, Cambridge.

Inghe, G. and M-B. Inghe (1970) *Den ofärdiga välfärden*, Tidens Förlag, Stockholm.

Insatser för vuxna missbrukare (1993) Statistiska Centralbyrån, Stockholm.

Insatser för vuxna missbrukare (1997) Socialstyrelsen, Stockholm.

Institutet för Social Forskning (1992). *Remissyttrande över Ds 1992:19*, Stockholm.

Invandrarprojektet 1998:1 *Levnadsförhållanden hos fyra invandrargrupper födda i Chile, Iran, Polen och Turkiet*, Socialstyrelsen, Stockholm.

Isaksson, A. (1994) "Avskaffa rätten till arbete", *Dagens Nyheter*, 6 September.

Jenkins, D. (1968) *Sweden: the progress machine*, Robert Hale, London.

Johansson, A. (1992) "Färre åtgärder på sjukhus", *Dagens Nyheter*, 9 July.

Johansson, A. (1993) "Allt fler barn kastas ut", *Dagens Nyheter*, 7 July.

Johansson, A. (1994) "Kaotiskt val i flera landsting", *Dagens Nyheter*, 25 March.

Johansson, I. (1978) "Behöver vi folkrörelserna?" in H. Alsén, (ed.), *Behöver vi folkrörelserna*? Tidens Förlag, Stockholm.

Johansson, L. (1997) "Äldreomsorgen före och efter ädelreformen", *Socialmedicinsk Tidskrift*, No. 6–7 pp. 277–83.

Johansson, P. (1998a) "Brev till EU-parliamentariker", *Narkotikafrågan*, No. 3.

Johansson, P. (1998b) "EU stöder FNs konventioner", *Narkotikafrågan*, No. 5–6.

Johnson, N. (1987) The welfare state in transition, Harvester, Hemel Hempstead.

Jonsson, B. (1995) "Nej till nya nedskärningar", *Dagens Nyheter* 16 January.

Jonsson, O. and B. Kuritzén (1998) "Överklassen får särbehandling", *Dagens Nyheter* 31 July.

Kautto, M., B. Hvinden, Heikkilä, S. Marklund and N. Ploug (1999) *Nordic welfare policy: changing welfare states*, Routledge, London.

Kjellander, C-G. (1991) "Vårdbidrag höjs med 30 pro cent", *Dagens Nyheter*, 17 December.

Klingensjö, L. (1994) *Jobbet i stället för bidrag*, Svenska Kommunförbundet, Stockholm.

Korpi, W. (1983) *The democratic class struggle*, Routledge and Kegan Paul, London.

Korpi, W. (1989) "Power, politics and state autonomy in the development of social citizenship", *American Sociological Review*, Vol. 54 pp. 309–28.

Korpi, W. (1995) *Arbetslöshet och arbetslöshetsförsäkring i Sverige*, EFA, Arbetsmarknadsdepartementet, Stockholm.

Kriminalstatistik 1995 (1997) Brottsförebygganderådet, Stockholm.

Kriminalvårdstyrelsen (1992) *Remissyttrande över Ds 1992:19*, Norrköping.

Larsson S. and K. Sjöström (1979) "The welfare state myth in class society" in J. Fry. *The limits of the welfare state*, Saxon House.

Larsson, A. (1992) "Ni skapar en djup kris", *Dagens Nyheter*, 10 March.

Larsson, G. (1996) "Handikappanpassa genom tvång", *Dagens Nyheter*, 4 March.

Larsson, R. (1999) "Grunden för Hasselas pedagogik står fast", *Alkohol och Narkotika*, No. 40 pp. 39–40.

Larsson, S. (1996) "Allt mer liberal attityd till droger", *Dagens Nyheter*, 12 February.

Lash, S. and J. Urry (1987) *The end of organised capitalism*, Polity Press, Cambridge.

Lehto, J., N. Moss and T. Rostgaard (1999) "Universal public social care and health services" in M. Kautto, B. Hvinden, Heikkilä, S. Marklund and N. Ploug *Nordic welfare policy: changing welfare states*, Routledge, London.

Lenke, L. and B. Olsson (1996) "Legal drugs – the Swedish legalising experiment of 1965–67 in retrospect". Paper presented at the *Conference on Drug Use and Drug Policy*, Amsterdam, 26–8 September.

Leonard, P. (1997) *Postmodern welfare*, Sage, London.

Lindbeck, A. (1997) *The Swedish experement*, SNS Förlag, Stockholm.

Lindén, E. (1998) "Gender perspektiv ska höja kvalitet i försäkring", *Social försäkring*, No. 4 pp. 19–21.

Linnell, S. (1998) "Fattigdom ökar – och rikedom", *Pockettidningen R*, No. 1.

Linton, M. (1998) "The rave commission – the only culture police in the world", *International Journal of Drug Policy*, Vol. 9 No. 5 pp. 305–310.

Lundberg, P. and J. Zetterburg (1997) "Sänk arbetsgivaravgifterna", *Dagens Nyheter*, 19 August.

Lundqvist, S. (1975) "Popular movements and reforms 1900–1920" in S. Koblik, *Sweden's development from poverty to affluence 1750–1970*, University of Minnesota Press, Minneapolis.

Macey, D. (1993) *The lives of Michel Foucault*, Hutchinson, London.

MacRobbie, R. and S. Thornton (1995) "Re-thinking moral panic for multi-mediated social worlds", *British Journal of Sociology*, Vol. 46 No. 4.

Mattson, U. and A. Romelsjö (1998) "Tidig alkoholdebut och ökat berusningsdrickande", *Alkohol och Narkotika*, No. 3 pp. 35–7.

Ministry of Finance (1999) *Sweden's economy*, April, Stockholm.

Ministry of Health and Social Affairs (1981) *Social Services Act*, Stockholm.

Ministry of Labour (1998) *Power, economy, gender*, Stockholm.

Mishra, R. (1993) "Social policy in a postmodern world" in C. Jones (ed.) *New perspectives on the welfare state in Europe*, Routledge, London.

Morris, R. (ed.) (1988) *Testing the limits of social welfare*, Brandeis University Press, Boston.

Mort, F. (1989) "The politics of consumption" in S. Hall and M. Jacques *New times: the changing face of politics in the 1990s*, Lawrence and Wishart, London.

Murray, R. (1989) "Fordism and post-Fordism" in S. Hall and M. Jacques *New times: the changing face of politics in the 1980s*, Lawrence and Wishart, London.

Myrdal, A. (1944) "Internationell och svensk socialpolitik" in P. Nyström and H. Thylin (eds) *Ett genombrott: den svenska socialpolitiken*, Tidens Förlag, Stockholm.

Myrdal, A. (1968) *Nation and family: the Swedish experiment in democratic family and population policy*, MIT Press, Massachusetts.

National Institute for Public Health (1995) *Swedish alcohol policy*, Stockholm.

Nietzsche, F. (1993) *The birth of tragedy*, translated by Shaun Whiteside, Penguin, London.

Nietzsche, F. (1996) *On the genealogy of morals*, translated by Douglas Smith, Oxford University Press, Oxford.

Nordh, S. and B. Westerberg (1993) *Välfärdsstatens vägval och villkor*, Brombergs, Stockholm.

Nordin, G. and K. Cnattingius (1998) "Så stoppades EU-förslaget", *Narkotikafrågan*, No. 2.

Novak, A. (1998) "Kvinnor med handikapp dubbelt diskriminerade", *Pockettidningen R*, No. 2 pp. 4–7.

OECD (1997) *Sweden: economic survey*, Paris.

OECD (2000) *Economic surveys: Russian Federation*, Paris.

Ohlsson, P.T. (1993) *Gudarnas ö:om det extremt svenska*, Brombergs, Stockholm.

Olsson, O., S. Byqvist and G. Gomér (1994) "The prevalence of heavy narcotic abuse in Sweden in 1992", *Scandinavian Journal of Social Welfare*, Vol. 3 No. 2 pp. 81–4.

Olsson, P. (1991) "Bravo Westerberg!" *Narkotikafrågan*, No. 5–6 p. 36.

Olsson, P. (1996) *Smack city: Storbritannien och narkotikan*, Sober förlag and RNS, Stockholm.

Olsson, S. (1990) *Social policy and the welfare state in Sweden*, Arkiv, Lund.

Oscarsson, S. (1998) "Vilseledande om framtidens pensioner", *Riksdag och Departement*, No. 18.

Palme, J. and S-Å. Stenberg (1998) *Arbetslöshet och välfärd*, Norstedts Tryckeri, Stockholm.

Palme. J. and I. Wennemo (1998) *Swedish social security in the 1990s: reform and retrenchment*, Socialdepartement, Stockholm.

Penna, S. and M. O'Brien (1996) "Postmodernism and social policy: a small step forwards?" *Journal of Social Policy*, Vol. 25 Pt 1 pp. 39–62.

Pension reform in Sweden (1998) Ministry of Health and Social Affairs, Stockholm.

Persson, G. (1998) "Vi skapar 100,000 nya företag", *Dagens Nyheter*, 22 February.

Persson, I. (1990) "The third dimension: equal status between Swedish women and men" in I. Persson (ed.) *Generating equality in the welfare state*, Norwegian University Press, Oslo.

Peterson, M. (1999) "The traumatic dismantling of welfare: the Swedish model in global culture" in P. Chamberlayne, A. Cooper, R. Freeman and M. Rustin (eds) *Welfare and culture in Europe: towards a new paradigm in social policy*, Jessica Kingsley Publishers, London.

Pettersson, U. (1995) "Social services and community care in Sweden", in E. Brunsdon and M. May *Swedish welfare: policy and provision*, Social Policy Association, London.

Pierson, C. (1991) *Beyond the welfare state*, Polity Press, Cambridge.

Pierson, C. (1998) *Beyond the welfare state*, Polity Press, Cambridge.

Pontusson, J. (1992) "At the end of the third road: Swedish social democracy in crisis", *Politics and Society*, Vol. 20 No. 3, pp. 305–32.

Pred, A. (1995) *Recognising European identities*, Routledge, London.

Raaum, N.C. (1995) "The political representation of women: a bird's eye view" in L. Karvonen and P. Selle (eds) *Women in Nordic politics: closing the gap*, Ashgate, Aldershot.

Randqvist, M. (1995) "Regerings konferensen 1996", *LO-Tidningen*, No. 33.

Regerings proposition 1994/95: 218 *Ett effecktivare arbetsmarknadspolitik*, Stockholm.

Regerings skrivelse 1996/97: 80 *Berättelse om verksamheten i Europeiska unionen*, Riksdagen, Stockholm.

RFHL (1992) *Remissyttrande över Ds 1992:19*, Stockholm.

Rhodes, M. (1996) "Globalisation and Western European welfare states", *Journal of European Social policy*, Vol. 6 No. 1 pp. 305–28.

Riksdagens snabbprotokoll 1992/93:83. Riksdagen, Stockholm 25 March.

Riksdagsbiblioteket 1992/93: 83 *Voteringslist*, Riksdagen, Stockholm 25 March.

Rojas, M., B. Carlson and P. Bevelander (1997) "Så skapas en etnisk underkalass", *Dagens Nyheter*, 20 April.

Rosenthal, A.H. (1967) *The social programmes of Sweden*, University of Minnesota Press, Minneapolis.

Rothstein, B. (1985) "Managing the welfare state: lessons from Gustav Möller", *Scandinavian Political Studies*, Vol. 8 No. 3.

Rothstein, B. (1998) *Just institutions matter: the moral and political logic of the universal welfare state*, Cambridge University Press, Cambridge.

Ruth, A. (1984) "The second new nation: the mythology of modern Sweden", *Nordic Voices*, No. 2 Spring.

Sahlin, M. (1997) *Med mina ord*, Rabén Prisma, Stockholm.

Sainsbury, D. (1993) "Dual welfare and sex segregation of access to social benefits", *Journal of Social Policy*, Vol. 22 No. 1.

Salonen, T. and S. Sunesson (1996) "Obekväma siffror förtigs", *Dagens Nyheter*, 7 June.

Schuck, J. (1996) "Pensionär 90-talets vinnare", *Dagens Nyheter*, 5 October.

Schuck, J. (1997) "Wibe sätter jobben främst", *Dagens Nyheter*, 11 October.

Schymann, G. (1995) "EU hänvisar kvinnor till 'atypiska' arbeten", *Vi Mänskor* No. 3.

Scott, K. (1999) "Svårt för invandrare att få jobb", *Socialforskning*, No. 3 pp. 14–15.

Segelström, I. (1999) "Svenska män är bäst i världen på jämställdhet", *Morgonbris*, No. 6.
Sillén, B. (1990) "86 pro cent vill ha systemskifte", *Dagens Nyheter*, 14 December.
Smith, A.D. and M. Zaremba (1997) "Outcasts from Nordic super-race", *Observer*, 24 August.
Socialstyrelsen (1992) *Remissyttrande över Ds 1992:19*, Stockholm.
Socialstyrelsen 1994:10 *Social rapport 1994*, Stockholm.
Socialstyrelsen 1996:8 *Socialbidrag 1995*, Stockholm.
Socialstyrelsen 1997:14 *Social rapport 1997*, Stockholm.
Socialstyrelsen 1998:9 *Äldreuppdraget: årsrapport 1998*, Stockholm.
Socialstyrelsen Följer upp och Utvärderar 1998:3 *Balans i missbrukarvården*, Socialstyreslen, Stockholm.
Socialtjänsten 1999:5 *Socialbidrag 1998*, Socialstyrelsen, Stockholm.
Södersten, B. (1990) "The Swedish tax reform", *Current Sweden*, No. 375, The Swedish Institute, Stockholm.
Södersten, B. (1992) "Orgie i verklighetsflykt", *Dagens Nyheter*, 20 December.
Socialstyrelsen-rapport 1999:9 *Social och ekonomisk föränkring bland invandrare från Chile, Iran, Polen och Turkiet*, Socialstyrelsen, Stockholm.
SOU 1987:19 *Commission on women's representation*, Stockholm.
SOU 1993:16 *Nya villkor för ekonomi och politik*, Stockholm.
SOU 1993:117 *EG kvinnorna och välfärden*, Stockholm.
SOU 1995:15 *Könshandeln*, Stockholm.
SOU 1995:7 *Obligatoriska arbetsplatskontakter för arbetslösa*, Stockholm.
SOU 1996:51 *Grundläggande drag i en ny arbetslöshetsförsäkring*, Stockholm.
SOU 1996:150 *En allmän och sammanhållen arbetslöshetsförsäkring*, Stockholm.
SOU 1997:139 *Hemmet, barnen och makten*, Stockholm.
SOU 1998:6 *Ty makten är din*, Stockholm.
SOU 1999:97 *Ökade socialbidrag*, Stockholm.
SOU 1999:97 *Socialtjänst i utveckling*, Stockholm.
SOU 2000:3 *Välfärd vid vägskäl: utvecklingen under 1990-talet*, Stockholm.
Squires, P. (1990) *Anti social theory: welfare, ideology and the disciplinary welfare state*, Harvester Wheatsheaf, London.
Ståhl, I., K. Wickman and C. Arvidsson (1993) *Suedosclerosis*, Timbro, Stockholm.
Ståhlberg, A-C. (1991) "Lessons from the Swedish pension system" in T. Wilson and D. Wilson (eds) *The state and social welfare*, Longman, London.
Ståhlberg, A-C. (1995) "The Swedish pension system: past, present and future" in E. Brunsdon and M. May *Swedish welfare: policy and provision*, Social Policy Association, London.
Ståhlberg, A-C. (1997) "Sweden: on the way from standard to basic security" in Clasen, J. *Social Insurance in Europe*, Policy Press, Bristol.
Statistical abstract of Sweden (1985) Central Bureau of Statistics, Stockholm.
Statistical abstract of Sweden (1986) Central Bureau of Statistics, Stockholm.
Statistical yearbook of Sweden (1994) Central Bureau of Statistics, Stockholm.
Statistical yearbook of Sweden (1995) Central Bureau of Statistics, Stockholm.
Statistical yearbook of Sweden (1998) Central Bureau of Statistics, Stockholm.
Statistical yearbook of Sweden (1999) Central Bureau of Statistics, Stockholm.
Statistical yearbook of Sweden (2000) Central Bureau of Statistics, Stockholm.
Stephens, J.D. (1979) *The transition from capitalism to socialism*, Macmillan – now Palgrave, Basingstoke.

Surell, V. (1997) "Skyll inte på EU!" *Socialpolitik*, No. 1.

Svallfors, S. (1996) *Välfärdsstatens moralisk ekonomi*, Boréa, Umeå.

Svensson, H. and J-Å. Brorsson (1997) "Sweden: sickness and work injury insurance", *International Social Security Review*, Vol. 50 No. 1.

Swedish Institute (1992) "Child care in Sweden", *Fact sheets on Sweden*, Stockholm.

Szebehely, M. (1999) "Omsorgsarbetets olika former", *Sociologisk forskning*, No. 1 pp. 7–32.

Tännsjö, T. (1997) "Hedervärd tvångsterilisering", *Dagens Nyheter*, 29 August.

Taylor-Gooby, P. (1994) "Postmodernism and social policy: a great leap backwards", *Journal of Social Policy*, Vol. 23 No. 3 pp. 385–404.

Taylor-Gooby, P. (1997) "In defence of second best theory: state, class and capital in social policy", *Journal of Social Policy*, Vol. 26 Pt 2 pp. 171–92.

Tham, H. (1991) "Narkotikakontroll som nationellt projekt", *Nordisk Alkoholtidskrift* Vol. 9 No. 2 pp. 86–97.

Tham, H. (1998) "Swedish drug policy: a successful model?" *European Journal on Criminal Policy and Research*, No. 6 pp. 395–414.

The Swedish budget: budget statement and summary (1998) Finansdepartement, Stockholm

The Swedish budget: budget statement and summary (1999) Finansdepartement, Stockholm

Thorén, A. (1997) "Sista chansen för pensionärspartiet", *Dagens Nyheter*, 9 November.

Thorgren, G. (1994a) "Vi ska inte ge upp", *Pockettidningen*, Vol. 24 No. 2 pp. 89–95.

Thorgren, G. (1994b) "Europa har förlorat kampen mot narkotikan", *Pockettidning*, Vol. 24 No. 1 pp. 14–22.

Thorslund, M. and M. Parker (1995) "Strategies for an ageing population: expanding the priorities discussion", *Ageing and Society*, No. 15, pp. 199–217.

Thorslund, M., Å. Bergmark and M. Parker (1997) "Difficult decisions on care and services for elderly people: the dilemma of setting priorities in the welfare state", *Scandinavian Journal of Social Welfare*, No. 6 pp. 197–206.

Tilton, T. (1979) "A Swedish road to socialism: Ernst Wigforss and the ideological foundations of Swedish social democracy", *American Political Science Review*, Vol. 73 pp. 505–20.

Titmuss, R. (1970) *The gift relationship*, Allen and Unwin, London.

Tomasson, R. (1970) *Prototype of modern society*, Random House, New York.

Tunhammar, G. (1995) "Fast jobb gårdagens modell", *Dagens Nyheter*, 1 November.

Ugland, T. (1997) "Europeanisation of the Nordic alcohol monopoly systems", *Nordisk Alkohol och Narkotikatidskrift*, Vol. 14.

Välfärdsfakta (1997) Socialdepartementet, Stockholm.

Välfärdsfakta (1998) Socialdepartementet, Stockholm.

Välfärdsfakta (2000) Socialdepartementet, Stockholm.

Van Solinge, P.B. (1997) *The Swedish drug control system*, Uitgeverij Jan Mets, Centre for Drug Research, University of Amsterdam.

Vår trygghet (1988) Folksam, Stockholm.

Vår trygghet (1991) Folksam, Stockholm.

Vår trygghet (1993) Folksam, Stockholm.

Vår trygghet (1994) Folksam, Stockholm.

Vår trygghet (1996) Folksam, Stockholm.
Vår trygghet (1997) Folksam, Stockholm.
Vår trygghet (1998) Folksam, Stockholm.
Verney, D. (1972) "The foundations of modern Sweden: the rise and fall of Swedish liberalism", *Political Studies*, Vol. 20.
Vinterhead, K. (1997) "Kyrkan stödde steriliseringar", *Dagens Nyheter*, 5 September.
Vogel, J. (1998) "Pensionärer 90-talets vinnare", *Dagens Nyheter*, 3 January.
von Sydow, E. (1998) "Katolikerna tappar mark i EU", *Riksdag och Departement*, No. 23.
Wallström, M. (1996) "Skär ner äldrevårdens skull", *Dagens Nyheter*, 26 October.
Wallström, M. (1997) "Extrapengarna måste gå till vården", *Dagens Nyheter*, 9 April.
Wallström, M. (1998) "Nu får äldrevården mer personal", *Dagens Nyheter*, 26 March.
Watney, S. (1989) *Policing desire: pornography, AIDS and the media*, University of Minnesota Press, Minneapolis.
Weber, M. (1930) *The Protestant ethic and the spirit of capitalism*, Unwin University Books, London.
Wennemo, I. and S. Carlén (1998) "Sluta dölja arbetslösheten", *Dagens Nyheter*, 12 January.
Wijkström, F. (1999) "Svensk organisationsliv" in U. Bystedt and J. Gadd (eds) *Folkrörelse och föreningsguiden*, Utbildningsförlag Brevskolan, Stockholm.
Wilensky, H.L. (1975) *The welfare state and equality*, University of California Press, Berkeley.
Wilson, D. (1979) *The welfare state in Sweden*, Heinemann.
Zaremba, M. (1997a) "Delusions of racial purity", *Guardian*, 3 September.
Zaremba, M. (1997b) "Ett offer för rekordåren", *Dagens Nyheter*, 27 September.
Zaremba, M. (1999) *Den rena och den andra: om tvångsteriliseringar, rashygien och arvsynd*, Bokförlaget DN, Stockholm.

Index